C00 17676754
EDINBURGH CITY LIB

D0229353

BERLIN

1945

THE FINAL RECKONING

BERLIN

1945

THE FINAL RECKONING

Karl Bahm

LEO COOPER

This edition first published in 2001 by
Pen & Sword Books Ltd
47 Church Street
Barnsley
South Yorkshire
S70 2AS

ISBN 0-85052-833-X

Editorial and design by
Amber Books Ltd
Bradley's Close
74-77 White Lion Street
London N1 9PF

Project Editor: Charles Catton
Editor: Vanessa Unwin
Designer: Brian Rust
Picture Research: Lisa Wren

Printed and bound in Italy - Nuova GEP, Cremona

Picture Credits
AKG London: 11 (t), 19, 38-39, 40, 48, 59 (b), 63 (b), 66, 67, 68 (t), 71, 76, 78, 79, 81 (t), 88-89, 93 (b), 94, 96 (t), 100, 102 (t), 103, 121 (b), 127, 131, 132, 135 (b), 136 (both), 137, 140, 141, 142, 143 (b), 144, 147 (b), 150, 154 (b), 155, 156, 158-159, 160 (both), 161, 163, 165 (t), 166 (b), 167, 168 (b), 169 (both). **Society for Co-operation in Russian & Soviet Studies (SCRSS):** 8 (t), 20-21, 23 (t), 28, 29 (t), 41, 42 (both), 52 (t), 63 (t), 84, 104-105, 107, 115 (t), 125 (t), 134, 143 (t), 153 (b), 154 (t), 171. **Süddeutscher Verlag:** 14 (b), 17 (both), 22, 23 (b), 24, 27, 30, 31 (b), 32, 33, 34 (both), 37, 44 (b), 46, 47, 49, 50, 52 (b), 53, 55, 64 (t), 69, 72, 73 (both), 74 (both), 77, 85 (b), 87, 90, 92, 93 (t), 96 (b), 98, 110, 111 (both), 114, 120, 124, 126 (both), 145 (t), 146, 148, 149 (t), 151, 162 (t), 165 (b), 166 (t). **TRH Pictures:** 9 (b), 12 (b), 14 (t), 16, 25 (t) (USNA), 25 (b), 36 (both) (USNA), 44 (t), 45, 51, 59 (t), 62, 70, 81 (b), 82, 101, 121 (t), 122 (both), 123, 125 (b), 129 (both), 133 (both), 138-139, 147 (t), 149 (b), 157, 164, 168 (t), 170 (both). **Ukrainian Central State Archive of Cine-photo Documents:** 6-7, 9, 10, 11 (b), 12 (t), 13, 15, 18 (both), 29 (b), 31 (t), 35, 43, 56-57, 58, 60 (both), 61, 64 (b), 65, 68 (b), 75, 80, 83, 85 (t), 86, 91, 95, 97, 102 (b), 106 (both), 108 (both), 109, 112, 113, 115 (b), 116, 117, 118-119, 128, 130, 135 (t), 145 (b), 153 (t), 162 (b).

Maps by Patrick Mulrey

Contents

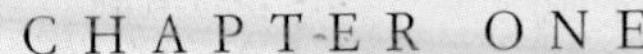

CHAPTER ONE

Introduction:
The War Comes to Germany

After the glory years of 1939–42, the tide of the war turned against Germany at Stalingrad, and by 1944 it became clear that soon, for the first time since the Napoleonic era, foreign troops would tread on German soil on their march towards the capital of Hitler's Third Reich: Berlin.

By the beginning of 1945, Nazi Germany's 'Thousand-Year Reich' was rushing towards its apocalyptic end, exactly 12 years after it began. On 30 January 1933, Adolf Hitler had been appointed Chancellor of the troubled Weimar Republic by President Paul von Hindenburg. After rapidly subordinating all political and military authority – as well as the social and cultural fabric of the country – to the dictates of his party, the *Nationalsozialistische Deutsche Arbeiterpartei* (NSDAP, the National Socialist German Worker's Party) Hitler began preparing for a war, the likes of which the world had never seen.

The war was formally unleashed on 1 September 1939, when one and a half million German troops invaded neighbouring Poland. Within days, the superbly trained and equipped Wehrmacht troops had vanquished the ill-equipped Polish Army. But, contrary to Hitler's expectations, the violation of Poland's sovereignty precipitated declarations of war on Germany from both France and Great Britain. After eight months of bluster and ultimatums – the so-called *Sitzkrieg* (sit-down war) or 'phoney war' in the West – the Germans finally launched a western

Left: The end of Germany's dreams of dominance: the corpses of three German soldiers killed in fighting for the city of Mogilev in Belorussia, liberated by the Red Army in June 1944, soon after the D-Day landings in Normandy.

offensive in May 1940. The *Sitzkrieg* became a *Blitzkrieg* as the French were defeated in just over a month, and were forced to sign a humiliating armistice in the very same spot in the forest of Compiègne, in the same train carriage, in which the German empire had been forced to sue for peace at the end of World War I. The newsreels of Hitler dancing his little jig of joy upon hearing of the French capitulation, and German troops marching down the Champs-Élysées, were seen all over the world. Great Britain, protected by the English Channel and the skill and bravery of the Royal Air Force, held out alone against Germany throughout the rest of 1940 and the first half of 1941. But although they had had to give up their plans for an invasion of Britain, the Germans were in undisturbed control of most of Western and Central Europe. With Austria, Poland, Czechoslovakia, Holland, Belgium, Luxembourg, Denmark, Norway, and France occupied or under the control of client states, and friendly regimes in Italy, Spain, and Hungary, Germany could now turn her attentions East.

On 22 June 1941, at 0330 hours, mechanised Wehrmacht divisions, supported by Luftwaffe fighter-bombers, poured across the Niemen River into Russia. The date had been carefully chosen for its historical significance. Exactly 129 years before, on 22 June 1812, an apparently invincible Napoleon Bonaparte had also crossed the Niemen to attack Russia. However, Hitler should have studied his history a little more closely; Napoleon was forced to begin his disastrous retreat only six months after invading, eventually losing 95 per cent of his troops to combat and the Russian winter. Although it would take longer, and cost even more lives, a similar fate would befall the German invaders.

Above: German confidence in the early days of Operation Barbarossa: With German troops closing on Moscow, the placard, dated 2 October 1941, reads 'The Russian must die that we may live.'

Despite its having started late – the original launch date was May – 'Operation Barbarossa' initially made fantastic progress, raising expectations of a repeat of the Blitzkrieg against Poland. Hitler's plan, which he had been formulating since shortly after the signing of the Russo–German Pact, called for 120 German divisions to annihilate Russia within five months, before the onset of the winter. Hitler wasn't the only one so confident of a German victory. In July, the American General Staff had issued 'confidential' memoranda to US journalists that the collapse of the Soviet Union could be expected within weeks.

But Russia, a vast country tremendously rich in natural resources, manpower, and a fierce patriotism, was far from finished. If unprepared for the precise moment of the German attack, the Red Army was neither as small, as ill-equipped, nor as lacking in fighting spirit as the Nazis' ideology proclaimed it to

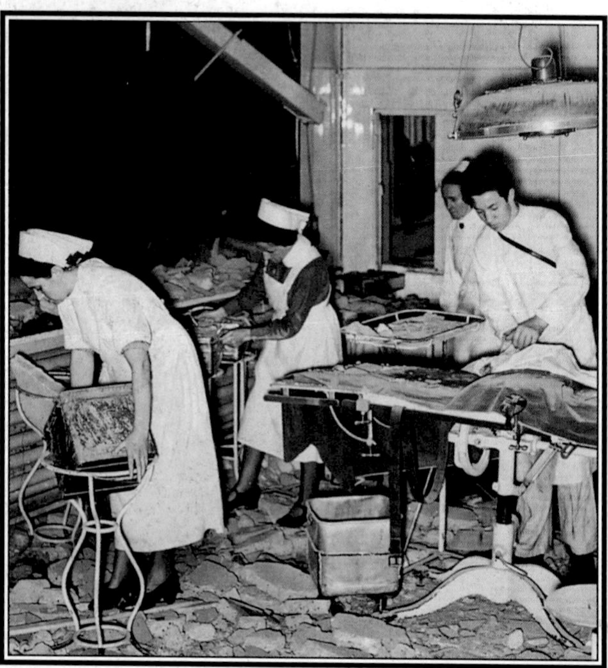

Left: The 'carpet bombing' which was inflicted on Germany by the Allies spared no sector of German society. Here staff clean up the operating room of Robert Koch hospital in Berlin after an air raid.

be. A month and a half into the campaign, on 11 August, the Chief of the German General Staff, Franz Halder, wrote in his diary:

'It is becoming ever clearer that we underestimated the strength of the Russian colossus not only in the economic and transportation sphere but above all in the military. At the beginning we reckoned with some 200 enemy divisions and we have already identified 360. When a dozen of them are destroyed the Russians throw in another dozen. On this broad expanse our front is too thin. It has no depth. As a result, the repeated enemy attacks often meet with some success.'

Not only had the Germans underestimated the sheer number of forces available to the Red Army, they had also underestimated how well equipped it was. Many of the Wehrmacht's best generals reported with astonishment and a large amount of fear on the appearance of the Russian T-34 tank, the existence of which German intelligence had not an inkling. So well constructed and armoured that German anti-tank shells bounced off it, the T-34 instilled in the German soldier what General Blumentritt later called 'tank terror'. These kinds of intelligence miscalculations would plague the Germans throughout the rest of the war.

But possibly the Germans' greatest miscalculation was their ideologically driven belief that Slavic soldiers would be no match for the 'Aryan' Germans and that the Soviet Union, once attacked, would disintegrate into chaos and revolution. 'We have only to kick in the door,' Hitler assured his generals, 'and the whole rotten structure will come crashing down.' Instead, the German invasion – launching what the Russians still call 'the Great Patriotic War' – loosed among the peoples of the Soviet Union a tremendous surge in patriotism, both Soviet patriotism and Russian, Ukrainian, Georgian and other national patriotisms. At this point, nearly a quarter century after the revolution, and just after the terrible purge years of 1934 and 1940, there could have been little naiveté about the nature of the Communist regime. Despite a tremendous amount of resentment and antipathy towards the Communist leaders, the peoples of the Soviet Union remained, for the most part, passionately committed to the sovereignty of the state, as well as to the individual nations of which it was made up. This was a fact which westerners have

Below: German soldiers swing a field gun into position during training exercises. The successful military adventures and massive build-up, boosting the economy, made the war effort popular amongst most Germans.

never properly understood, and the Germans were to pay dearly for their misunderstanding.

By the end of November, with the fearsome Russian winter at full howl, Germany's drive to Moscow had staggered and come to a frozen, weary halt on the outskirts of the city. The Wehrmacht's Third and Fourth Tank Groups had penetrated as far as Istra, fewer than 25km (15 miles) north of Moscow, while the Second Panzer Army and the Fourth Army were further away on the south and west. Throughout the first week of December the Germans made repeated efforts to regain the momentum and take Moscow. But their exhaustion and losses, their overstretched supply lines, the seemingly limitless Soviet manpower resources, and above all the vicious, numbing cold – which froze solid exposed flesh, turned oil to sticky sludge, and made metal parts as brittle as icicles – defeated every attempt. With the German units ordered to hold their positions at all costs, the Soviets now went on the offensive, led brilliantly by Marshal Georgi K. Zhukov, the man who would, in three and a half years, drive his armies into the Germans' own capital, Berlin.

Only a year later, the Germans suffered their worst defeat yet, at Stalingrad. After capturing most of the totally destroyed city in a series of campaigns in the autumn of 1942, they were cut off and finally forced in January 1943 to surrender, against Hitler's explicit orders. They had endured three months of exceptionally brutal street fighting. Of an original force of over 285,000 men, only 91,000 exhausted, hungry, and frozen men were left to surrender.

The German defeat at Stalingrad was a turning point of huge importance in the war. In practical terms, of course, it meant that the Soviets retained their access to the oil and food of southern Russia and the Caucasus. It also marked an end to the Germans' drive across Eastern Europe and the beginning of their long retreat back to Germany. But possibly even more important was the symbolic significance of the battle, for both Germany and the Soviet Union. For the Soviet people, it was a huge morale-booster at a time when Leningrad was still suffering under its two-and-a-half year siege. The American journalist Alexander Werth, who spent some of the war years in the Soviet Union, attended a victory party in Stalingrad held shortly after the Germans' surrender.

'Here was a big spread, and with plenty of vodka, and my neighbour was a red-nosed colonel who had already had a good number of drinks. "We've done them in," he cried, "half a million of them! Here, come on, drink to the heroes of Stalingrad – Do dna, bottoms up!" ... He beat his chest. "Look," he cried, pointing to his Red Star, "yesterday I received this from our great government! Zhukov – I worship Zhukov. He planned the whole thing, he and our Great Stalin. Halkin-Gol, where we routed the Japs – that was just a rehearsal. But Stalingrad, that was the real stuff! Hitler's best divisions were destroyed there. And who destroyed them? We Russian people did it!"'

For the Germans, obviously, the battle had the opposite effect. German historian Walter Goerlitz called Stalingrad 'a second Jena and ... certainly the greatest defeat that a German Army had ever undergone'. The Nazi state proclaimed four days of official national mourning, with all theatres, cinemas and cabarets closed. It was an appropriate response: it was in fact the beginning of the painful death of the

Left: 'General Winter' has been reputed to be the Russians' best defence against attack. But, despite an initial failure of preparation, the Red Army by 1942 was a superbly trained and equipped modern fighting force.

Above: Lieutenant-General Konstantin K. Rokossovskii commanded the Don River Front at Stalingrad, which played a key role in the entrapment and annihilation of the German Sixth Army.

Below: After their crushing victory at Stalingrad, the Red Army slowly but inexorably drove the Germans out of Soviet territory, by August 1944 reaching the banks of the Vistula in German-occupied Poland.

Third Reich. For the next 26 months the Germans would be fighting an entirely defensive war, ever closer to home. Even future German offensives – like Kharkov in 1943 and the Ardennes in 1944 and 1945 – would be essentially defensive manoeuvres.

Once the Third Reich's war effort started to unravel, trouble came in spades. During the summer of 1943, the Führer's fascist ally in Italy, Mussolini, fell ignominiously from power. In the midst of growing unrest over economic hardship and the Anglo-American landings on Sicily, the Duce was summoned to the king's presence, summarily dismissed, and packed off to jail in an ambulance. Within a matter of weeks the new Italian Government, under Marshal Pietro Badoglio, had signed an armistice with the Allied Powers. The Germans were still in control of some two-thirds of the Italian peninsula but on 3 September, Allied troops landed on the coast of southern Italy proper. In a daring but futile attempt to reverse the course of events, on 13 September the Germans pulled off a stunning rescue of Mussolini by glider-borne SS troops. The miniature state Mussolini attempted to create in the north, the so-called 'Republic of Saló', was little more than salve for the bombastic dictator's wounded dignity. As an ideological and military ally to Germany, Italy was finished. US and British troops were now on the European continent.

Above: 'Operation Bagration', the Soviet offensive which drove the Germans out of Belorussia, saw some of the bitterest and most destructive fighting of the war. Here a 7.5cm (2.95in) Pak 40 sits abandoned.

Below: As the Eastern Front began to crumble, the Germans remained confident that their Western flank was protected by the 'Atlantic Wall'. Here a MG-34 machine gun team scans the Atlantic horizon.

Worse was to come during the following year. By the summer of 1943, the Germans had already lost their supremacy over the Atlantic to the combined British and American navies. This little-heralded Allied victory not only cost the Germans dearly in destroyed vessels, it also ensured that the United States' massive industrial capabilities could now supply the war effort, something that Germany simply had no hope of countering. During this period, the bombing raids on German cities were stepped up. The meaning of 'Total War' was brought home to the German people as never before, as the British and American bombers unloaded hundreds of thousands of tons of explosives not only on military and industrial targets, but also on civilian populations. The aim was to destroy both the German state's ability to conduct the war, and the German people's willingness to support it. It was working. Propaganda Minister Josef Goebbels noted in his diary on 25 May 1943, after a series of devastating bombing raids in the Ruhr industrial region: 'The people in the West are gradually beginning to lose courage. Hell like that is hard to bear ... In the evening I received a report on Dortmund. Destruction is virtually total. Hardly a house is habitable.' The bombing campaign reached a sort of ghastly crescendo in mid-February 1945, when the intensity of the bombing of Dresden

ignited the first urban fire-storm in recorded history, killing roughly 135,000 civilians, 57,000 more than were killed at Hiroshima six months later. It was during that spring and summer of 1943 that the bombing of Berlin also began in earnest. By the end of 1943, some 200,000 tons (or over 400 million pounds) of bombs had been dropped on Germany.

On 6 June 1944, British and American forces, supported by troops from Canada, France, Poland, Czechoslovakia, the Netherlands, and virtually every other member of the United Nations alliance, launched an amphibious assault on the Normandy coast and, after a day of furious and exceptionally bloody fighting, succeeded in securing several beachheads in Nazi-held France.

The magnitude of their problem was apparently not immediately realised by the Germans. That evening the desperately embattled Seventh Army received an order from the Führer's HQ:

'16:55 hours. June 6, 1944

Chief of Staff Western Command emphasises the desire of the Supreme Command to have the enemy in the bridgehead annihilated by the evening of June 6 since there exists the danger of additional sea- and airborne landings for support ... The beachhead must be cleaned up by not later than tonight.'

Above: Two Red Air Force officers pause in front of the remains of a German JU-52 transport plane. By 1943 the German Luftwaffe no longer controlled the skies over the Soviet Union.

The beaches of Normandy were not going to be 'cleaned up' by the Germans, on the evening of 6 June, or any other day.

Things were beginning to go equally badly for the Germans in the East. Since 1938 Hitler and the German diplomats had been telling the world that they were fighting a purely defensive war; in 1944 that actually became true. By this time, the Red Army was a very different military organisation from that of 1941. Three years and many tough battles later, the Soviet Army possessed a sizeable officer corps of experience and genuine operational talent, a vast mechanised force, and a new, much more flexible and inventive tactical doctrine. The US Lend-Lease programme was crucial to Soviet survival during the war; nevertheless Soviet industry had recovered to the extent that in 1944 it produced 29,000 tanks and assault guns, 122,500 guns and mortars, 40,300 aircraft, and some 184 million shells, mines, and bombs. While it would be too simplistic to suggest that in 1944, Germany suffered from the same weaknesses vis-à-vis her enemies as

Above: Some of the estimated 86,000 German soldiers who ended up as Soviet prisoners of war. These men were captured by Marshal Konev's First Ukrainian Front in April 1944.

they had suffered *vis-à-vis* Germany between 1939 and 1943, it is nonetheless true that the German Army at this point was no match, on any level, for the Allies, including the Red Army. Since the end of the Cold War, it has been generally recognised that the Soviet victory over Germany was the result of much more than Soviet numerical superiority and that the German Army did not match the exemplary professional fighting force of many peoples' fantasies. The inter-departmental jealousies and rivalries which criss-crossed the Nazi state; an often conservative and unimaginative general staff which, despite some genuine brilliance, was for the most part hampered by an 'inability to understand war' (in the judgement of the Royal Military Academy's H.P. Willmot); a surprising patchiness in the army's modernisation (85 per cent of German units still depended on horse-drawn transport); and above all the dilettantism and outright irrationality of the Third Reich's leadership, which viewed the military establishment with suspicion and even hostility: all rendered the advantages that Germany had enjoyed from 1939 to 1943 moot in the new conditions of 1944 and 1945. Indeed, Willmot suggests that without a change in military doctrine, without increased mobility, and without a shortening of their lines and the concentration of a reserve, 'the Wehrmacht on the Eastern Front entered 1944 as little more than a disaster waiting to happen'.

Left: A propaganda shot of a girl offering refreshment to a Hitler Youth member. By 1945, Hitler Youth were conscripted to help clean up after air raids, do guard duty, man antiaircraft guns, and run supplies.

In the Soviet Union, 1944 is known as 'the Year of the 10 Victories'. For the fate of Berlin, however (and indeed for the war itself), the most crucial Soviet move in 1944 was the summer offensive directed against Belorussia: 'Operation Bagration'. This largest of all Soviet operations up to that time – what Soviet histories call 'the first modern offensive of the third phase of the war' – succeeded in virtually destroying the Wehrmacht's Army Group Centre and brought the Red Army deep into Poland, to the banks of the Vistula outside Warsaw, less than 300km (186 miles) from Germany's 1939 border. The offensive, which again caught German intelligence by surprise, was launched on 22 June (the anniversary of the German 'Operation Barbarossa') and involved four entire Soviet Fronts, commanding at least 1.2 million troops, 4000 tanks, 24,400 guns, and 5300 aircraft. The disadvantage in numbers faced by the Germans overall was on the order of 1:1.7; in certain key sectors it was closer to 1:10.

Within the first three weeks of the offensive the Germans had already lost 350,000 men killed, wounded, or captured. The breach in their lines was approximately 300km (186 miles). By early August, Zhukov's First Belorussian Front had established two bridgeheads on the river Vistula, not far from Warsaw. Army Group Centre, the largest German command in the East, suffered the encirclement and destruction of at least five corps-sized, or larger, units, and a loss of 840,000 men dead or missing. In terms of manpower, this represented double the loss being experienced at that time on the western front. Altogether, in 1944 Germany lost 106 divisions. The official US Army history of the operation comments that, 'in executing the breakthroughs Soviet forces showed elegance in their tactical conceptions, and control that did not fall short of the Germans' own performance in the early war years'.

Germany's rapidly disintegrating military situation was, without question, a contributing factor in the eleventh-hour conspiracy to assassinate Hitler at Rastenburg in East Prussia on 20 July 1944. The plot, which misfired when the Führer was saved from the full force of the bomb planted in his bunker by a fortuitous coincidence, involved a circle of German officers at the highest levels, including Field Marshal Rommel. Although the conspirators were hardly the sort of principled anti-Nazi lovers of democracy that they are sometimes made out to be, like many of their class they had been suspicious and contemptuous of Hitler and Nazism from the beginning. Now they believed that his refusal to consider a negotiated end to the war would be the ruin of Germany. When their assassination plan failed, over 7000 individuals were arrested by the Gestapo for real or imagined implication. Nearly 5000 were executed. Many chose suicide rather than allow themselves to be hauled before the farcical *Volksgericht* (People's Court). Rommel, because of his tremendous popularity and prior service to the war effort, was given the luxury of taking his own life without any public acknowledgment of his role in the plot, and his death was attributed to wounds from a strafing attack on his car three days before the assassination attempt.

The loss of so many well-placed military men, particularly 'old-school' military men with experience and talent, naturally did nothing to slow Germany's collapse. Most of those who had escaped implication

Below: Katyusha rocket launchers were among the most fearsome weapons in the Soviet arsenal. Each truck could fire sixteen rockets simultaneously, and were used extensively in the final phase of the war.

and punishment found themselves with no real influence. The 'Generals Plot' of 20 July was the final proof Hitler needed that his army officer corps was untrustworthy and incompetent at best, traitorous at worst. All eyewitness accounts agree that from 20 July until the final act of the tragedy in April of the following year, Hitler became a different person; or rather, certain personality traits which had always been there became magnified to an extreme. Increasingly paranoid, insisting on food tasters and rarely venturing into public, the Führer became more and more withdrawn, unconfident, irritable, and sickly. The blast at Rastenburg had bruised and cut him, punctured his eardrums, and temporarily paralysed one arm.

Even without the increasing military dilettantism and mismanagement on the German side, however, the advantage had shifted decisively in the Allies' favour. The successful Normandy landings were followed in quick order by the liberations of France, Belgium, Luxembourg, and the Netherlands. By early September, the Germans had lost most of the western European capitals they had occupied four years earlier, as well as over half a million men (most as prisoners) and nearly all their tanks, trucks, and artillery in the western theatre. By the second week in September, the Americans were at the borders of the Fatherland itself: Patton's US Third Army had reached the banks of the Moselle River, and General Courtney Hodges' First Army held the field just short of Aachen, near the German–Dutch–Belgian border. On 24 October, this ancient city, Charlemagne's imperial seat, became the first German city to surrender to an enemy force in over 130 years.

The Allied offensive began to slow at this point, unable to slug its way across the border to the Rhine. Hitler seized on the lull to go over on to the offensive. His plan was to punch a hole in the Allied line in the Ardennes in Belgium, drive through to the coast, and retake Antwerp. If successful, the plan would have split Patton's and Hodges' armies, isolated the British and Canadian units along the Dutch-Belgian border and, probably most importantly, would have denied the Allies their primary re-supply port. The 'Battle of the Bulge', from 16 December 1944 to 16 January 1945, could perhaps have changed the course of the war, had the German Army not been so weakened by the three and a half years of a double-front war. The battle was costly to both sides: the Germans lost 120,000 men killed, wounded and missing, 1600 aircraft, 600 tanks and assault guns, and 6000 vehicles; the four American divisions which met the brunt of the offensive lost 8000 men killed, 69,000 wounded, captured or missing, and 733 tanks and tank destroyers. But these numbers represent a much greater loss to the already severely stretched Germans than to the Americans. Ultimately, the Wehrmacht could not sustain the

Below: German troops captured by the British in the 'Falaise Pocket' in August 1944. Within a matter of weeks of the invasion on 6 June, almost the whole of northwestern France was in Allied hands.

Left: Adolf Hitler at the Wolfsschanze *(Wolf's Lair), his bunker near Rastenburg in East Prussia, on 15 July 1944. Five days later, a bomb planted by Klaus von Stauffenberg (far left) failed to kill the Führer.*

attack and had to withdraw to their original positions, now even weaker than before.

A few days before the collapse of the Germans' offensive, in an effort to take some of the pressure off the western Allies there, the Soviets launched their biggest offensive yet. On 12 January the First Belorussian and First Ukrainian Fronts burst out of their bridgeheads on the Vistula and Narew rivers, north and south of Warsaw. Each front commanded two tank and eight infantry armies, two cavalry corps, and at least two tank corps (the First Ukrainian had three). Over 2.2 million men, 6400 tanks, and 46,000 guns, heavy mortars and rocket launchers were thrown at Army Group A, which numbered 400,000 men, 1236 tanks, and 4100 guns. To the north, the Second and Third Belorussian Fronts, reinforced by a corps from the First Baltic Front, chewed into East Prussia and Army Group Centre, which it outnumbered by roughly 7:1. The advance was spectacular. The Red Army fought its way across the 450km (280 miles) from the Vistula, just opposite Warsaw, to the banks of the Oder, a mere 70km (44 miles) from Berlin, in just three weeks, advancing at an average rate of 19-22 km (12-14 miles) per day. Some units, like the Second Guards Tank Army, were able to drive ahead at rates approaching 88km (55 miles) a day. Marshal Zhukov, the new commander of the First Belorussian Front and hero of Moscow and Kursk, reported in his memoirs that, in an effort to check the Red Army's advance, the German High Command had transferred six armoured divisions from the west and from East Prussia, but that these 'were destroyed even before they could properly deploy for combat.' He went on: 'Our thrust was so swift and so stunning that the Germans gave up all hope of stopping the Soviet troops anywhere on Poland's territory.'

After the second day of the offensive, the Soviets could report the capture of 350 localities. By 19 January Marshal Ivan Konev's First Ukrainian Front had taken Kraków and Zhukov's First Belorussian Lódz; the following day General Cherniakhovsky's Third Belorussian Front captured Tilsit in East Prussia; on 23 January Konev struck into industry-rich Silesia and reached the Oder River along a 65km (40 mile) front; and on 29 January (less than three weeks after the drive began) Zhukov's forces crossed the pre-war borders into Germany southwest of Posen (Poznan), two days later driving into the province of Brandenburg not far from Frankfurt an der Oder. The first units to reach the river Oder were the Second and Third Battalions from the 1006th Rifle Regiment of General Nikolai Berzarin's Fifth Shock Army. Aided by the frozen ground and

Right: Urban combat became increasingly common as the Allies advanced. Here a German soldier, carrying a Panzerfaust antitank weapon darts in front of a Jagdpanzer IV tank killer.

Above: A Red Army infantryman covers his comrades as they advance. During the first two days of the Vistula-Oder Operation, in January 1945, the Soviets reported the capture of 350 towns in western Poland.

thick ice on the river, the Soviet troops were able to cross to the western bank and seize the village of Kienitz. The surprise at the speed of the Soviet advance was so complete that, as Zhukov wrote, 'When the detachment burst into the town of Kienitz, German soldiers walked around unperturbed, and officers were sitting at a restaurant. Trains on the Kienitz-Berlin line ran on schedule, and the communications were operating normally.' Within about an hour, the Soviets had succeeded in establishing a western bridgehead 4km (2.4 miles) wide and 2km (1.2 miles) deep. In the course of the day the Soviet position was strengthened and expanded, and by the next day two more substantial bridgeheads on the western side had been established at Göritz and Zellin.

Left: Soviet infantry on the attack. The Vistula-Oder offensive saw gains of 19–22km (12–14 miles) per day. Within three weeks the Soviets had established beachheads on the Oder River, inside Germany.

Zhukov's original intention had been to continue the drive beyond the Oder, reaching the heart of Berlin by mid-February. But a fierce blizzard at the end of January was followed by an early thaw which reduced the roads to mud and made negotiating the frozen river extremely treacherous. Then a German counter-offensive in the area of Stargard (Szczecinski) – 'Operation Sonnenwende' (Solstice) – though a limited success, convinced Stavka (Soviet High Command) to hold along the 150km (93 mile) stretch of the Oder, to allow their supply and communication lines to catch up with them. Thus did Hitler celebrate the twelfth anniversary of his coming to power: with Soviet troops on historically German soil.

With six Allied armies poised on their western border, more driving up the Italian peninsula, and four Soviet Fronts (some 200 divisions with 2.5 million men) already making gains into their homeland, those Germans not wholly blinded by ideology recognised that the war was almost over. Except amongst the true fanatics, there was now little talk of a German victory, only the terms of defeat. But while a great many Germans – military and civilian alike – were willing to contemplate some measure of submission to the West's demands, most were full of fear and hatred of the Russians. They desperately hoped to put all their efforts into holding out against the Soviets in the East until a settlement on the western front could bring some relief. Indeed, Hitler continued to nurse the expectation that the alliance of the Soviet Union and the West was on the verge of collapse, and that the latter could yet be recruited for a crusade against the Communists. It was not an entirely irrational hope, but it severely underestimated the Western Allies' commitment to the complete destruction of Nazi Germany. Underneath the German prayers for the dissolution of their enemies' unity was a grim understanding that those enemies were still calling in unison for the unconditional surrender of Germany.

The worst, most Germans understood, was still to come. A Lieutenant in the 21st Panzer Division fighting on the Eastern front described the view of the average German soldier of the way the war was going for Germany:

'Even the last soldier was aware that the war was lost. He was aiming to survive, and the only sense he could see was to protect the front in the East to save as many refugees as possible. He felt bitter to have to fight on German soil for the first time in this century, and he could not foresee any alternative but to stay put with his unit and to stick to his oath of allegiance. He realised that the attempt of 20 July against Hitler had failed and, despite the obvious facts, he was hoping for a political solution for ending the war, not knowing however what kind of solution. Last but not least, the demand for unconditional surrender left, in the light of self-respect, no alternative but to continue the hopeless fighting.'

He might as well have been describing Germany as a whole.

Below: A Hitler Youth unit detailed to prepare fortifications in East Prussia in September 1944. Most of these young men would in a few months time be drafted into the Volkssturm *(People's Storm) militia.*

626

CHAPTER TWO

The Race for the 'Main Prize'

Allied Plans for Berlin

The early months of 1945 saw the forces of the Western Allies and the Soviet Union preparing for the last push on Berlin itself. It seemed that the race was on between them for the Reich's capital, but Eisenhower had other ideas.

It has perhaps always been true that war is 'politics by other means', as the Prussian military theorist Carl von Clausewitz quipped; it certainly was for much of World War II. But never were the distinctions between political and military objectives and methods as blurred as during spring 1945, in the lead-up to the final phase of the war and the rush for the German capital city, Berlin. As the Allied armies surged into the heart of Germany in the first months of 1945, their commanders found themselves in a situation at once welcome and uncomfortable. There were three Anglo-American army groups under the command of the recently appointed Supreme Commander of the Allied Forces (SCAF), General of the Army Dwight D. Eisenhower, and three Soviet fronts under the commands of Marshals Konstantin Rokossovsky, Ivan Konev, and Georgi Zhukov. Both groups were making breathtaking progress in their two-pronged advance into Germany after the Western Allies had finally pushed back the Germans' Ardennes offensive in January. After reaching and bursting across the Rhine on 22 March, for example,

Left: Soviet IS-2 tanks make an assault crossing of the Dnieper River, 28 September 1943. The Red Army's combat engineers became highly skilled at erecting pontoon bridges under fire from the enemy.

Left: The face of a German soldier reflects the weariness and anxiety which most in the German military must have started to feel as they were pushed inexorably out of Russia, and back towards Germany.

Lieutenant General George Patton's US Third Army, part of the 12th Army Group under the command of General Omar N. Bradley, galloped eastward across central Germany at a rate of nearly 50km (31 miles) a day. So great was the speed of the advance, and so disorganised the German resistance, that when the Ninth Army's 82nd Reconnaissance Battalion paused to report its new position on 28 March, its tanks spread out on either side of a main railway line, a German train suddenly appeared, filled with troops, armoured vehicles and guns. Quoting the 82nd's commander Lieutenant Colonel Wheeler Merriam, Cornelius Ryan describes how the German and American soldiers stared at each other silently, dumbfounded and without firing a shot, as the German train chugged right through the ranks of the American tanks; the Germans were not even aware that the Allies had crossed the Rhine.

On the Eastern Front, where the Germans resisted much more fiercely, the advance had also been spectacular. By early February the Red Army's 'Vistula-Oder Operation' had succeeded in effectively destroying Army Group A and had driven through Poland and East Prussia to the Oder river, establishing substantial bridgeheads at three points, within 70km (43 miles) of Berlin. By late March, units of Zhukov's First Belorussian Front and Rokossovsky's Second Belorussian Front had cleared Pomerania of German forces to the north of their positions, Konev's front had secured Silesia and advanced to the Neisse river on the south, and Zhukov had managed to enlarge his bridgehead on the west bank of the Oder to a depth of nearly 10km (6 miles) and a breadth of almost 50km (31 miles).

These stunning military successes were creating problems of an entirely new nature. The gains on the ground were outpacing the ability of the planners to keep up. Disgruntled airborne units, whose planned missions were frequently scrubbed as the ground armies advanced past the proposed drop-zones, wondered if they'd ever get a chance to participate in this final push of the war. 'The way the ground forces are moving,' complained the US 101st Airborne Division's assistant commander, Brigadier General J. Higgins, 'they're going to put us out of business.' But even more problematic for the generals on the ground was the effect of these gains on the political calculations at the top levels of the increasingly delicate alliance. Before the Germans' disastrous Ardennes offensive in December 1944, which opened the way for the Allies' advances in spring 1945, there had been little need for anything more than a vague agreement on post-war objectives. But with the war's end now in sight, and with Allied troops occupying large tracts of German territory, it became necessary to make concrete plans for the disposition of the occupation forces and the government of a defeated Germany. The general agreement on unconditional surrender and the physical occupation of German territory now required plans for zonal boundaries. The issue was given added urgency by the military leaderships' fears of what could result from an unexpected meeting of the Anglo-American and Soviet armies as they rushed headlong in each other's directions. A similar clash in 1939 in Poland between the Germans and the Soviets, despite their pact over the division of the

Above: Churchill, Roosevelt, and Stalin at Yalta in February 1945. The Allies affirmed their insistence on German unconditional surrender and made plans for the division of Germany into occupation zones.

Below: US Secretary of the Treasury, Henry Morgenthau, author of the 'Morgenthau Plan' which called for the division of post-war Germany into several smaller states, and the stripping of their industrial capacity.

country, had resulted in brief combat with fairly heavy casualties on both sides.

The greatest tension, however, existed between the British and the Americans. It was clear to everyone that the Soviets should be responsible for eastern Germany, but as early as October 1943, British and American politicians were at loggerheads over control of the population- and industry-rich north-western sector of Germany, which also contained the most important ports at Hamburg, Bremen, and Bremerhaven. President Roosevelt was adamant that the US zone should stretch from Germany's north-western borders, down the Rhine as far as Mainz, then east to the Czechoslovak border, from there up to Leipzig, and north-east to Stettin and the Baltic. Berlin, which all agreed should be jointly occupied by all three allies, was strategically placed exactly on the line between the Soviet and American zones. Prime Minister Churchill just as adamantly insisted that by rights of geography and military action (Field Marshal Sir Bernard L. Montgomery's 21st Army Group held the northernmost flank of the three army groups under Eisenhower's command), responsibility for Germany's north-western zone should fall to Britain. The British proposal also gave to the Soviet Union a much bigger piece of the German pie than did Roosevelt's: nearly 40 per cent of Germany's total area (pre-1939). It also placed Berlin, while still

Above: General of the Army Dwight Eisenhower, the non-political Supreme Commander of Allied Forces in Europe, with Field Marshal Bernard Montgomery (left) and Air Chief Marshal Arthur Tedder.

jointly occupied, securely within the boundaries of the Soviet zone. Of course, Stalin quickly agreed to this at the European Advisory Commission's meeting on 18 February 1944, while the Americans continued to oppose it.

Roosevelt and the US State Department's position was made significantly more difficult by the fact that their own military authorities disagreed. It has often been suggested that, unlike British (and for that matter Soviet) military leaders, American generals tended to be trained to discount political goals and motivations in their strategies. Eisenhower, in particular, saw his role even as Allied Supreme Commander as purely military: his mandate from the Combined Chiefs of Staff, to 'enter the continent of Europe and, in conjunction with the other United Nations, undertake operations aimed at the heart of Germany and the destruction of her armed forces', he interpreted as requiring those actions which would ensure the speediest defeat of Germany with the smallest Allied losses. The political disposition of Germany after the war and the relations among the victors, he believed, were not his responsibility. Thus it seemed to Eisenhower, and to most of the American military brass, that since the US Army groups had been quartered in Northern Ireland and the south of England, and had made their landings on the western flank of the D-Day operation, they should hold their southern position relative to the British. In August 1944, he had cabled the Combined Chiefs of Staff on the prospect of an early occupation of Germany: 'All we can do is approach the problem on a purely military basis.' This would mean, he urged, maintaining 'the present deployment of our armies ... Unless we receive instructions to the contrary, we must assume this solution is acceptable ... considering the situation which may confront us and the absence of basic decisions as to the zones of occupation.' And so the military authorities proceeded. The political tug of war at the higher levels continued until September 1944, when a visibly declining Roosevelt, meeting with Churchill at Québec, agreed to the British-Soviet plan, including the assignment of the southern zone to the United States.

At the same time, the Supreme Commander's attitude towards Berlin had been undergoing a vital change. Ever since the Allies' agreement on the goal of the complete destruction of Nazi Germany, and in accordance with traditional political, as well as military, thinking, it was assumed that Berlin was, as Eisenhower said, 'the main prize'. As the Anglo-American and Soviet armies squeezed the German forces from both sides, commanders and foot soldiers alike felt they were engaged in a great race for Berlin. Perhaps more than anyone else, the politically savvy – and popular – Montgomery wanted those laurels, a desire further fuelled by the growing Allied, and particularly British, concern over Soviet intentions. On 27 March 1945, Montgomery sent a cable to the Supreme Headquarters of the Allied Expeditionary Force (SHAEF), pleading with Eisenhower for permission to lead a single, 'powerful and full-blooded thrust toward Berlin'. But the SCAF continued to stand by his strategy of a broad front, proceeding more deliberately, a preference which had been powerfully reinforced by the failure of a single, narrow thrust at Arnhem in September 1944 during Operation 'Market Garden'. Moreover, while he felt that Berlin would eventually be taken, Eisenhower had come to the conclusion that the speed of the Allied gains and the prospect of Germany's imminent collapse or surrender had lessened Berlin's strategic importance.

Right: Under constant enemy fire, US infantrymen cross the Rhine River. Although inside Germany territory, the Rhine formed a kind of symbolic and psychological last bastion on the Western front.

Below: M4 Sherman tanks from the US First Army roll across the Remagen bridge over the Rhine, 11 March 1945. The bridge was captured intact, giving the Allies their first bridgehead across the Rhine.

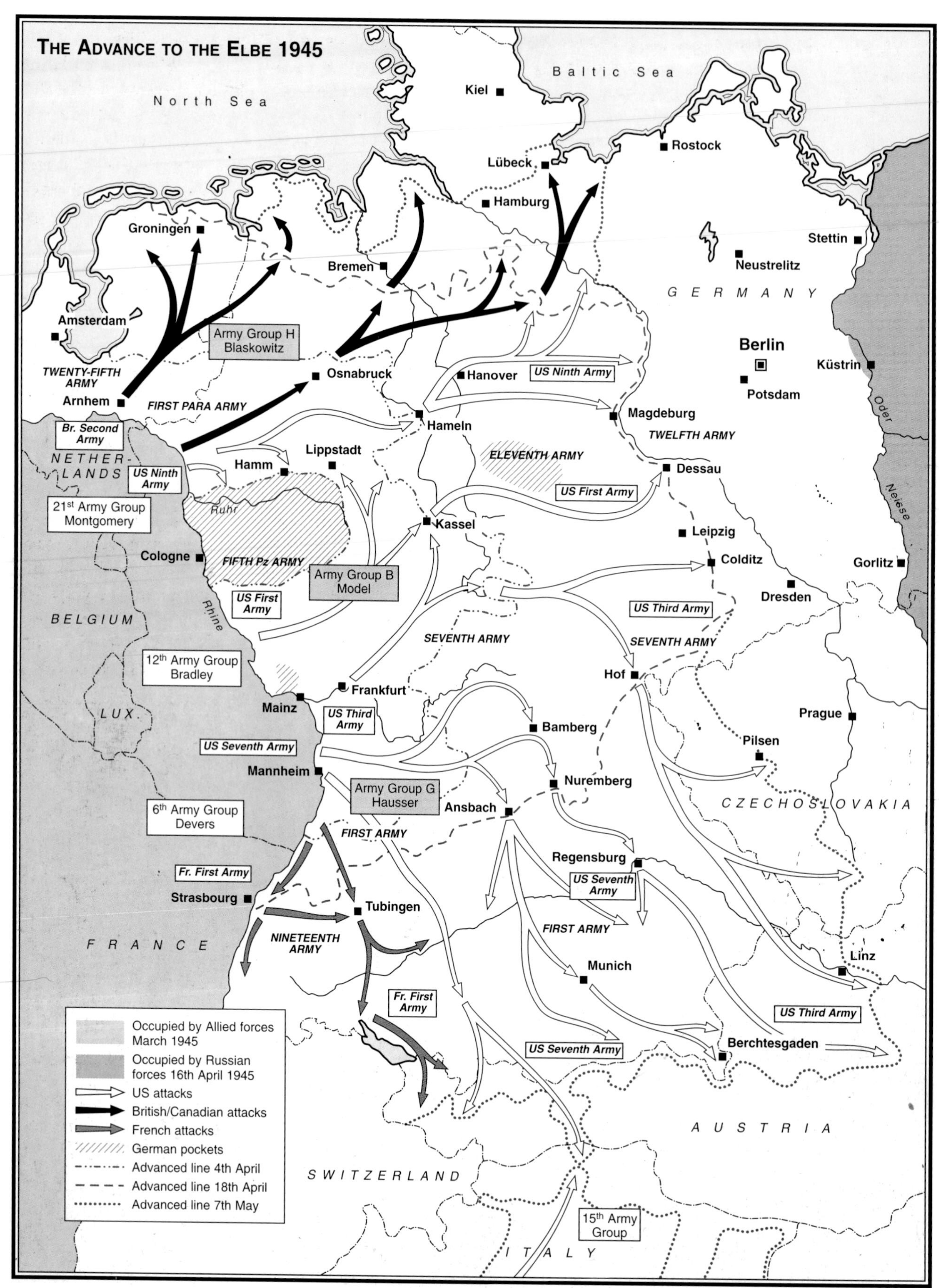
THE ADVANCE TO THE ELBE 1945
North Sea
Baltic Sea
Kiel
Rostock
Lübeck
Hamburg
Groningen
Bremen
Stettin
Neustrelitz
GERMANY
Amsterdam
Army Group H
Blaskowitz
Berlin
Küstrin
TWENTY-FIFTH ARMY
Osnabruck
Hanover
US Ninth Army
Potsdam
Arnhem
FIRST PARA ARMY
Oder
Br. Second Army
Magdeburg
Hameln
TWELFTH ARMY
NETHERLANDS
Lippstadt
Hamm
US Ninth Army
ELEVENTH ARMY
Dessau
21st Army Group
Montgomery
Ruhr
US First Army
Neisse
Kassel
Leipzig
Cologne
FIFTH Pz ARMY
Colditz
Gorlitz
Army Group B
Model
Dresden
US First Army
BELGIUM
Rhine
US Third Army
SEVENTH ARMY
SEVENTH ARMY
12th Army Group
Bradley
Hof
Frankfurt
LUX.
Mainz
US Third Army
Prague
Bamberg
Pilsen
US Seventh Army
Mannheim
Nuremberg
Army Group G
Hausser
Ansbach
CZECHOSLOVAKIA
6th Army Group
Devers
FIRST ARMY
Regensburg
Fr. First Army
US Seventh Army
Strasbourg
Tubingen
FIRST ARMY
FRANCE
NINETEENTH ARMY
Linz
Munich
Fr. First Army
US Third Army
Occupied by Allied forces March 1945
Occupied by Russian forces 16th April 1945
US attacks
British/Canadian attacks
French attacks
German pockets
Advanced line 4th April
Advanced line 18th April
Advanced line 7th May
US Seventh Army
Berchtesgaden
AUSTRIA
SWITZERLAND
15th Army Group
ITALY

Left: The Western Allies' advance from the Rhine to the Elbe was achieved at a rapid pace, aided by the propensity of most German units to surrender as soon as the Allies arrived at their position.

Two main considerations influenced Eisenhower's decision. The first was the Soviets' unexpectedly rapid advance across Poland and Prussia. Because of the Germans' surprise offensive in the Ardennes during the previous winter. the Soviets had agreed to launch their offensive earlier than planned. Despite the severe strain this put on their supply and communication lines, the Soviets surged through western Poland and into the heart of Germany's Mark Brandenburg in less than three weeks, successfully establishing bridgeheads along the Oder River by early February. The three Red Army Fronts had been holding there for nearly two months by the time of Montgomery's cable; indeed, on 11 March Eisenhower's headquarters in Rheims had received intelligence (faulty, as it turned out) that Zhukov's First Belorussian Front had advanced as far as Seelow, on the western side of the Oder, a mere 45km (28 miles) from Berlin. But while this was a welcome contribution to the Allied war effort, SHAEF had astonishingly little knowledge of the Red Army's planning and objectives. Indeed, there was no formal protocol for contact and co-ordination between the Anglo-American and Soviet forces below the highest political levels. Even Eisenhower, as Supreme Commander, was expected to go through regular diplomatic channels in order to communicate with his Soviet counterparts.

Below: Wehrmacht soldiers surrendering to an American GI. The faces on these young conscripts show their relief at having managed to surrender to the Americans or British, rather than to the Soviets.

Under such circumstances it would have been difficult to co-ordinate a joint advance on Berlin among the best of allies; but between the Soviets and the Western Allies there was already a good deal of suspicion and mistrust. Although it is anachronistic to interpret the East–West relationship at this point through a Cold War lens, it is nonetheless true that the alliance between the Soviets and the Anglo-American West had always been more a marriage of convenience than one of true affection. Tensions were apparent at the Yalta summit, which took place between 4 and 11 February. With victory in sight, the Allies' political leaders had to begin making plans for post-war Europe. The 'Big Three' – Josef Stalin, Winston Churchill, and Franklin Roosevelt – discussed the final provisions for zonal occupation of

Above: Civilian casualties were appallingly high on both sides during the Soviets' long drive from Stalingrad and Moscow to Berlin. The line between civilians and military combatants became somewhat blurred.

Germany, the inclusion of France in the occupation, the principle of reparations, and the question of Poland's new government. But with combat still being waged against a stubbornly resisting enemy in Germany, and the United States and Great Britain hoping to persuade the Soviet Union to enter the war against Japan, agreements were limited to general principles on the most contentious issues, like the disposition of Poland.

As Alexander Werth has shown in his masterful history, *Russia at War*, the Yalta agreements were seen at the time almost universally as a great triumph for 'Big Three Unity' and particularly for the Western allies, who had managed to secure far more concessions from Stalin than he had from them. Between Stalin and the Western allies, particularly Churchill, there remained a good deal of suspicion of each other's motives and post-war intentions. The Soviets were well aware that the British and Americans differed over strategy towards Berlin, and they knew, too, that most German troops were hoping mainly to surrender to the Anglo-American forces rather than to the Red Army. There was a deeply rooted suspicion prevalent at many levels of Soviet society that the Western, capitalist allies were secretly counting on the Soviets' to bear the brunt of the German resistance, and that the Soviet Union would be bled to a position of weakness vis-à-vis the West. Stalin had (true) reports that the Germans were floating proposals for a separate peace with the West, and that some allied commanders urged driving on to Berlin to limit Soviet gains and occupation zones. In his memoirs, Zhukov voiced this suspicion, particularly about Churchill. 'In his letters one could sense a lack of sincerity, secret intentions, and a persistent desire to seize Germany's central parts. This, naturally, compelled certain caution on the part of the Soviet government.' In these circumstances an unplanned meeting of Anglo-American and Red Army forces in the heat of battle for the 'main prize' could prove to be disastrous.

At the beginning of 1945 the Soviets were much closer to Berlin than any British or American troops – a mere 70km (43.5 miles) compared to roughly 500km (310.7 miles) – and had far more men ready to be thrown into battle than the Western Allies. Eisenhower considered Montgomery's bold call for a single powerful thrust into Berlin far too risky. It was estimated that an assault on Berlin would cost some 100,000 Allied casualties. The SCAF was also concerned that a single thrust would require the commitment of so many forces that the other axes of advance into northern and southern Germany would be left undermanned and would be stymied; this would prolong Germany's ability to continue fighting, even if Berlin were successfully taken. From a strictly military perspective it seemed better to allow Zhukov to take Berlin, and to direct Montgomery's 21st Army Group to secure Hamburg and Hannover. Bradley's 12th and Lieutenant General Jacob Devers' 6th Army Group on the southernmost flank would seal off the Ruhr, the industrial heart of Germany, which Eisenhower considered more important to the Germans' continued war effort than Berlin.

Right: Red Army soldiers erect a new border post on the re-established frontier between the Soviet Union and Romania, March 1944. Under the fascist dictator Antonescu, Romania had supported Germany.

Below: A Soviet 45mm anti-tank team take up a position in front of a Gasthaus somewhere in East Prussia. The Red Army crossed the pre-war border into German East Prussia in January 1945.

Reinforcing this sense of Berlin's lessening importance were disquieting intelligence reports on a reputed Nazi 'National Redoubt', a plan to move the top echelons of the Nazi leadership to a series of mountain fortresses in the rugged Alpine region between Munich and northern Italy. Centred on Hitler's mountain retreat near Berchtesgaden, this *Alpenfestung* (alpine fortress) was believed to cover roughly 32,000 km^2 (12,355 square miles). It was further believed to contain huge stocks of supplies, weapons, ammunition, and sophisticated communications; enough to hold out for two years. Most disturbing of all were the reports of large numbers of elite troops streaming south, and the rumours of Himmler's *Werwölfe* (Werewolves), specially trained guerilla units which were expected to harass and sabotage the occupation. The information on the purported redoubt was sketchy at best, and there were those who were sceptical. Nevertheless, it was plausible. Intelligence units in Lieutenant General Alexander Patch's US 7th Army on the Allied southern flank, for example, furnished SHAEF with reports of a large force, 'predominantly SS and mountain troops, of between 200,000 and 300,000 men' arriving in the redoubt area, along with as many as 'three to five very long trains each week' including supplies and 'a new type of gun'. SHAEF intelligence described the frightening scenario in the 'practically impenetrable' Alpine mountains in a report on 11 March:

'Here, defended by nature and by the most efficient secret weapons yet invented, the powers that have hitherto guided Germany will survive to reorganise her resurrection; here armaments will be manufactured in bombproof factories, food and equipment will be stored in vast underground caverns and a specially selected corps of young men

Below: Weary but alert Wehrmacht soldiers ride through a German town. Despite Hitler's designation of certain key cities as 'Fortress-Cities' which were never to surrender, the Germans continued to retreat.

Right: Having borne some of the most ferocious and brutal assaults that Germany had inflicted in any theatre of the war, Soviet soldiers were determined to push their retaliatory drive all the way into Berlin.

will be trained in guerilla warfare, so that a whole underground army can be fitted and directed to liberate Germany from the occupying forces.'

The US Office of Strategic Services (OSS, precursor of the CIA), while cautioning against excessive alarmism, took the threat seriously enough to urge a revision of operational planning. British Major General Kenneth W.D. Strong, Eisenhower's chief of intelligence, summarised in a report: 'The redoubt may not be there, but we have to take steps to prevent it being there.'

Thus, on 28 March, with these concerns and pressures mounting, Eisenhower made a command decision which was to become one of the most closely examined and controversial military decisions of the war. After first sending an unprecedented 'Personal Message to Marshal Stalin' in which he outlined his operational plans and requested information on the Soviet forces' plans, the Supreme Commander drafted a cable to his immediate superior, US Chief of Staff General of the Army George C. Marshall, and immediately after that, one in response to Field Marshal Montgomery. In them, Eisenhower made his new orders clear. Montgomery's 21st Army Group was to link up with Bradley's 12th east of the Ruhr, at which point the major role would become Bradley's. Operational control of the US 9th Army under Lieutenant General William H. Simpson would be taken over from Montgomery by Bradley, and the expanded 12th Army Group would be expected to mop up the Ruhr, 'and with the minimum delay will deliver his main thrust on the axis Erfurt–Leipzig–Dresden to join hands with the Russians' near Dresden, roughly 160km (100 miles) south of Berlin, thus effectively dividing Germany in half, and preventing any further German military or political withdrawal to the south. Montgomery, in the meantime, was ordered to advance to the Elbe, at which point command of the 9th might revert back to him, and hold there. In a defence of his plan several days later, Eisenhower explained:

'Berlin itself is no longer a particularly important objective. Its usefulness to the German has been largely destroyed and even his government is preparing to move to another area. What is now important is to gather up our forces for a single drive, and this will more quickly bring about the fall of Berlin, the relief of Norway and the acquisition of the shipping and the Swedish ports than will the scattering around of our effort.'

Left: Waffen-SS officers of the Sixth SS Panzer Army during planning for the 'Spring Awakening' offensive in Hungary in March 1945, aimed at relieving Budapest. It was to be the last German offensive.

Above: The 76mm (3in) gun was the backbone of Soviet field artillery. Small enough to allow relatively easy mobility and use in a variety of types of terrain, the 76mm still had a range of roughly 12km (7.5 miles).

The decision set off a furious debate between Washington, London, and the modest former technical college in Rheims that was serving as the SCAF's headquarters. Churchill, in particular, was incensed that Eisenhower had violated protocol and the chain of command by approaching Stalin directly, that his plan would relegate the British 'to an almost static role in the North', leaving the Americans to garner all the glory, and above all that he was underestimating the continued importance of Berlin which, in Churchill's view, could both prolong the war and seriously complicate an Allied post-war settlement if the Soviets were allowed to take the city unassisted. In a personal cable to Eisenhower, the vexed Prime Minister put his point as strongly as he could:

'If the enemy's position should weaken, as you evidently expect ... why should we not cross the Elbe and advance as far eastward as possible? This has an important political bearing, as the Russian army ... seems certain to enter Vienna and overrun Austria. If we deliberately leave Berlin to them, even if it should be in our grasp, the double event may strengthen their conviction, already apparent, that they have done everything. Further, I do not consider that Berlin has lost its military and certainly not its political significance. The fall of Berlin would have a profound psychological effect on German resistance in every part of the Reich. While Berlin holds out, great masses of Germans will feel it their duty to go down fighting. The idea that the capture of Dresden and the juncture with the Russians there would be a superior gain does not commend itself to me ... Whilst Berlin remains under the German flag, it cannot in my opinion fail to be the most decisive point in Germany.'

Churchill was not alone; much of the British Chiefs of Staff agreed, and so did Field Marshal Montgomery, who sent a cable of protest. Eisenhower's relationship with Montgomery had always been rather strained, but now the normally diplomatic Supreme Commander was rapidly becoming exasperated by the reaction to his decision. In an interview years later, Eisenhower described his irritation: 'Montgomery was becoming so personal in his efforts to make sure that the Americans – and me, in particular – got no credit, that, in fact, we hardly had anything to do with the war, that I finally stopped talking to him.' There was a general sense at SHAEF that 'Monty' was too concerned with personal glory. The British Deputy Chief of Staff at SHAEF, Lieutenant General Sir Frederick Morgan, wrote: 'At that moment, Monty was the last person Ike would have chosen for a drive on Berlin – Monty would have needed at least six months to prepare.' His anger rising, Eisenhower responded to Montgomery's protest with firmness:

'I must adhere to my decision about Ninth Army passing to Bradley's command ... As I have already told you, it appears from this distance that an American formation will again pass to you at a later stage for operations beyond the Elbe. You will note that in none of this do I mention Berlin. That place has become, as far as I am concerned, nothing but a geographical location, and I have never been interested in these. My purpose is to destroy the enemy's forces.'

To Churchill, he had already bluntly stated, 'Berlin is no longer a major military objective.' Although the dispute continued for some days, the US Combined Chiefs of Staff gave Eisenhower their unqualified support on 31 March, discounting the British leadership's second-guessing of Eisenhower's judgement:

'The battle of Germany is now at the point where the Commander in the Field is the best judge of the measures which offer the earliest prospect of destroying the German armies or their power to resist ... General Eisenhower should continue to be free to communicate with the Commander-in-Chief of the Soviet Army ... The single objective should be quick and complete victory.'

The decision had been made, but the British remained unhappy. Churchill's concerns increased when he saw Stalin's reply to Eisenhower's cable. On 1 April, the Soviet leader had conferred with his two top field commanders, Marshals Zhukov and Konev, and the seven-member State Defence Committee. Before discussing the concrete plans for the capture of Berlin, Stalin wanted to air his concern that the *soyuznichki* (little allies), despite their Yalta promises, intended to seize Berlin ahead of the Red Army. He showed them reports from unnamed sources which cited the divisions over the issue in the Anglo-American camp. They claimed further that two Allied airborne divisions were being prepared for an assault on Berlin, and that Montgomery was developing plans to enable his 21st Army Group to race across northern Germany to take Berlin. These reports were, of course, strictly speaking, true, and the Soviet leaders were justifiably wary of Allied, and particularly British, intentions. But the Soviets also had other reasons for wanting to get to Berlin. The Russians and other peoples of the Soviet Union had suffered grievously at the hands of the Germans, and the lust for revenge was understandably strong. The Soviet PoWs liberated by the Red Army frequently told horror stories about the way they had been treated. Units of the Fourth Guards Rifle Corps from Colonel General Vassily Chuikov's Eighth Guards Army, among the first to reach the Oder south of Küstrin on 1 February, stumbled upon a Gestapo prison at Sonnenburg whose 700 inmates had been executed by the fleeing Germans.

Stalin gave Zhukov and Konev 48 hours to develop plans for the conquest of Berlin, which he indicated he wanted to commence in mid-April, and then crafted his response to Eisenhower. He expressed his agreement with the SCAF's proposal for cutting the German forces in two through a meeting of the eastern and western Allies around Dresden-Leipzig. Churchill's suspicions were raised particularly by the portion of the cable which indicated that 'the main blow of the Soviet Forces' would be directed to the Dresden-Leipzig area, rather than towards Berlin. 'Berlin has lost its former strategic importance,' Stalin explained. 'The Soviet High Command therefore plans to allot [only] secondary

Left: Soviet artillerymen ready their self-propelled gun (SPG) for another pounding of German positions. SPGs were used by all sides, but were an important factor in the speed of the Soviet advances.

Left: Dead German children in uniform, photographed by an American war correspondent in the Hürtgenwald forest. Allied soldiers were horrified at having to fight and kill children as young as ten.

forces in the direction of Berlin.' The timing for the Soviet offensive, he informed Eisenhower, would be 'approximately the second half of May'. Churchill was given to doubt the intentions of the Soviets, but even if what Stalin had written were true, he explained in another telegram to Eisenhower, 'I am all the more impressed with the importance of entering Berlin which may well be open to us by the reply from Moscow to you ... [it is] highly important that we should shake hands with the Russians as far to the east as possible.' A few days later Eisenhower sent a small sop to the British, conceding that if Germany were to suddenly collapse, then the western Allies would rush forward to Berlin. 'Naturally if I can get a chance to take Berlin cheaply, I shall do so,' he added.

So began an undeclared race to the German capital. As Marshals Konev and Zhukov were developing their plans for Berlin's conquest, the Allied troops in the West, unaware of the decision at the top levels which reduced Berlin's strategic importance, continued to battle their way forward. General Bradley's 12th Army Group, now with the US Ninth Army numbering nearly one million men, completed the encirclement of the Ruhr on 2 April, trapping Field Marshal Walter Model's Army Group B, with 325,000 men. Leaving a part of the Ninth and the First to clean up the Ruhr pocket, the rest of Bradley's Group drove through central Germany, heading toward the Elbe and Leipzig-Dresden. Eisenhower's instructions to Bradley ordered him to exploit any opportunity to seize a bridgehead on the Elbe, 'and be prepared to conduct operations beyond the Elbe'. Bradley's orders to the Ninth Army's Lieutenant General William Simpson went a step further: 'and be prepared to continue the advance on BERLIN'. General Simpson, 'Big Simp', was elated. 'My people were keyed up. We'd been the first to the Rhine and now we were going to be the first to Berlin. All along we thought of just one thing – capturing Berlin, going through and meeting the Russians on the other side.' His plan was to reach Hildesheim, southeast of Hannover, within a few days, and then 'get an armored and an infantry division set up on the autobahn running just above Magdeburg on the Elbe to Potsdam, where we'll be ready to close in on Berlin.'

Below: Gauleiter Hofer (right) oversees planning for the Alpenfestung, *or 'Alpine Fortress' – intended to be the site of the Nazis' last stand deep in the German and Austrian Alps – at the end of January 1945.*

Above: A wrecked 8.8cm (3.45in) Flak 18 anti-aircraft gun sits abandoned. Its wheels have been removed, as rubber was in critically short supply, and the tyres have probably been scavenged.

The commander of just about every other unit in the Group had his own ideas. The Second Armored 'Hell on Wheels' Divison, the 'Rag-Tag Circus' of the 83rd Infantry Division, the Fifth Armored 'Victory' Division, the British Seventh Armoured 'Desert Rats' Division: all wanted the kill for themselves. The competition was so fierce that it sometimes resulted in furious arguments between the various commanders and their subordinates. When units of the 83rd Infantry and the Second Armored Divisions reached the Weser river at the same time on 5 April, a bitter row erupted over which one would cross it first. The two commanders finally reached a compromise: they would cross simultaneously, their units sandwiched together. But the commander of the 'Hell on Wheels' division, Major General Isaac White, was still incensed. 'No damned infantry division is going to beat my outfit to the Elbe!'

Their anticipation was heightened by the speed of the Allied troops' advance, and by the relatively light resistance. Not that the advance was without risk; some of the engagements were as ferocious as anything these soldiers had encountered since Normandy. But the resistance was very uneven. Some areas surrendered with hardly a fight. Civilian authorities in particular hoped to avoid the destruction of attempts to resist the inevitable capitulation. Other units, especially the SS, put up a tenacious struggle, exacting stiff Allied casualties. The city of Detmold in the Teutoburger Woods, for example, was the scene of some prolonged and very bloody combat before the American infantry units succeeded in pacifying it; to their chagrin they had discovered that Detmold was the home of a large SS training centre. But for much of the campaign, the Allied advance met only very sporadic, unorganised, and dispirited resistance. For most troops of the German 12th Army, which bore the brunt of this central Allied thrust, the war was next to over, and they were only too happy to have the opportunity to surrender to the British and Americans rather than to the Soviets. Captain Ben Rose of the US 113th Mechanized Cavalry Group recalled how during their drive to the east, he witnessed some German officers, in full dress uniform, jogging alongside the column, 'trying to get someone to notice them long enough to surrender their side arms'. The GIs, however, anxious to keep their momentum, simply waved the Germans to the rear.

The airborne units, too, though increasingly fearful that they would miss the action and be relegated to police duty – or worse, 'saved' for a drop on Tokyo – had their own plans for Berlin. On 25 March, the commanders of the US 82nd and 101st Airborne divisions and the British First Airborne Corps were briefed on a secret contingency operation for a drop on Berlin. The timing was uncertain, dependent on the speed of the ground forces' advance, but the 101st's Operations Chief, Colonel Harry Kinnard, thought that they could be in Berlin within five hours of receiving the green light. No one expected it to be easy; initial plans called for 1500 transport planes, 20,000 paratroopers, 3000 support fighters, and more than 1000 gliders.

The plans for a hostile drop were never put into operation. But the air forces were not left without any role to play in the defeat of Berlin. For over a year and a half, the city had been subjected to probably the most punishing continuous bombing campaign of the war. For the Royal Air Force, the 'Battle for Berlin' began on 23 August 1943, when 719 Lancaster bombers took off from airfields all over central England, flew to Berlin and dumped 1800 tons of bombs on the city. By the spring of 1944, the RAF alone had flown over 10,000 sorties over Berlin, dropping more than 30,000 tons of bombs on or near it. By that time, the US Army Air Force had joined in the attacks with daytime raids, while the British continued to bomb the city at night. Air Chief Marshal Sir Arthur Harris, head of the RAF's Bomber Command, firmly believed that an intensive bombing of the Reich's nerve centre and largest city could by itself bring about Germany's surrender, precluding the need for a prolonged land campaign. 'We can wreck Berlin from end to end if the USAAF will come in on it. It will cost between us 400 and 500 aircraft. It will cost Germany the war,' he had written to Churchill in November 1943. To his superior, Air Chief Marshal Sir Charles Portal, he wrote: 'It appears that the Lancaster force alone should be sufficient, but

Below: Powerful searchlights were utilized by all armies, primarily to highlight airborne targets for anti-aircraft fire. The Allied bombing raids had for years been taking a heavy toll on German cities.

Below: The 3.7cm (1.4in) Flak 18 anti-aircraft gun was withdrawn in 1936, having proved itself to be too cumbersome. In 1945, however, the Germans were forced to use whatever weapons they could find.

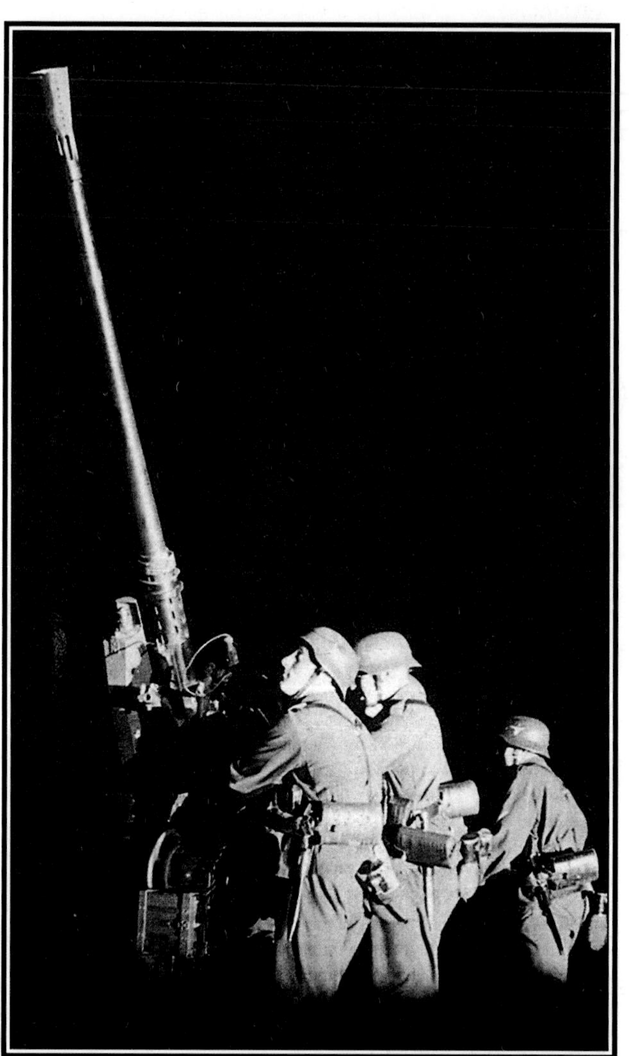

only just sufficient, to produce in Germany, by 1 April 1944, a state of devastation in which surrender is inevitable.' Harris was somewhat overly optimistic, and found virtually no agreement. In line with the Casablanca Directive of January 1943, the real goal in the bombing campaign was to destroy as much of Germany's military forces as possible and to demoralise the civilian population.

Even from the air, in any event, it was not an easy campaign. The sheer size of the city struck fear into every bomber crew that flew over her. Nicknamed simply 'the Big City' by flight crews, this was the third largest city in the world at the time, covering over 1400 km^2 (540 square miles). As Germany's capital and largest city, Berlin was naturally heavily defended; as the showcase for Hitler's grandiose 'Thousand-Year Reich', those defences were built on an equally grandiose, monumental scale. In 1940, Albert Speer, the state's chief architect and one of Hitler's closest personal advisors, had designed three massive, fortress-like buildings which became the centrepiece of the city's air defences. Each building covered an area of roughly a city block and was approximately 13 stories high, topped with gun platforms containing four pairs of 128mm (5in) guns capable of firing a salvo every 90 seconds to a ceiling of 14,800m (48,556ft), with a kill zone of 240m (260yds) across. The three *Flaktürme* (Flak Towers), located in the Tiergarten, Friedrichshain and Humboldthain districts, all had separate floors for ammunition stores, a hospital, and an air-raid shelter; the Tiergarten tower also had a floor for Berlin's most valuable art treasures. The Humboldthain tower was connected to the U-Bahn (subway) system; together, the tower and the subway station could hold up to 21,000 people during air-raids. So well-stocked were the towers, and so impregnable the 2.6m (8ft) thick, reinforced concrete walls with their steel-shuttered windows, that the 100-man Wehrmacht garrisons stationed in each one thought they could hold out for a year, whatever happened to the rest of Berlin. Indeed, after the war the Allies found the towers very difficult to destroy; the French tried, and failed, three times to blow up the tower in their sector. These towers and the other anti-aircraft systems organised in two rings around the city produced a flak area over the city measuring nearly 65km (40 miles) across, and the searchlight ring around it was over 95km (60 miles) wide. Martin Middlebrook quotes Flight Lieutenant R.B. Leigh from the 156th Squadron in his authoritative history of the British Bomber Command's Berlin campaign:

Above: A German 'Hausfrau' receives instruction in the use of a Panzerfaust. The Nazi leadership was loathe to mobilise the female population, as they believed a woman's place was in the home.

'Lying in the nose of a Lancaster on a visual bomb run over Berlin was probably the most frightening experience of my lifetime. Approaching the target, the city appeared to be surrounded by rings of searchlights, and the Flak was always intense. The run-up seemed endless, the minutes of flying 'straight and level' seemed like hours and every second I expected to be blown to pieces. I sweated with fear, and the perspiration seemed to freeze on my body.'

By the eve of the land battle, tens of thousands of bombing sorties, and the loss of hundreds of bombers and their crews later, Berlin was a badly pummelled city. Over 15km^2 (6 square miles) of the city lay in rubble; at least 52,000 Berliners had been killed. But the city's many factories continued to operate at 65 per cent capacity and, in the words of Cornelius Ryan, life in the city went on with 'a kind of lunatic normalcy'. However, with their government displaying an increasing level of lunacy, and with millions of enemy troops surging towards their city, for the Berliners, no amount of 'normal' daily routine could obscure that the end of the world as they knew it was at hand.

CHAPTER THREE

Gotterdämmerung in Berlin

As the Allies advanced, most Germans faced reality and hoped for a swift end to the fighting and conquest by the Western Allies rather than the Red Army. Only in Berlin was the talk of no surrender, or, at best, a deal with the Western Allies for joint strikes against 'their mutual Soviet enemy'.

For some 10 years, until the reverses of 1943 and 1944, the Nazis' dreams for Germany had been rather intoxicating to many Germans. The degree of active popular support for the Nazi regime has often been exaggerated; in reality, it was a dictatorship which oppressed ordinary Germans in many aspects of their daily lives even if they were not part of that group of German citizens (Jews, Romanys, Socialists, homosexuals, pacifists, the handicapped) who were targeted for special treatment. Still, whatever their distaste for and reservations about National Socialism, in a very short time the Nazis had succeeded in giving many Germans reason for celebration; jobs, consumer goods and, since Germany was again a powerful and globally important player, restored honour. As long as that could be maintained, many (though by no means all) Germans were prepared to tolerate the Nazis.

By the end of 1944, the Nazis' dream was backfiring in a horrific way. The war which they had started in order to achieve these things was rapidly coming home to roost. Germany was now threatened with levels of devastation and humiliation higher than anything it had experienced

Left: Hitler's Thousand-Year Reich falls apart. A government building in Berlin, showing the Nazi insignia – a fierce eagle, clutching a swastika emblazoned wreath, on top of the globe – lies in rubble.

Left: By 1945, Berlin was a city of women and children. Roughly two million of the city's nearly 3 million official inhabitants were female. There were only about 100,000 civilian men aged between 18 and 30.

in the years before the Nazis. The nearly simultaneous Allied offensives from the east and west during early 1945 were wreaking catastrophic destruction on the German armed forces, and the capture of territory was severely interrupting the German economy, as well as the ability of the remaining forces to maintain a sound defence. In February 1945, the Wehrmacht forces on the western front had been whittled down to an estimated 65 infantry and 12 Panzer divisions; in the east, 103 infantry and 32 Panzer and Panzer Grenadier divisions faced the massive Red Army fronts, whose reserves alone outnumbered them several times. German losses in the east were estimated by the Soviets to be 295,000 dead, 86,000 prisoners, 15,000 guns and mortars, 2995 tanks, 26,000 machine guns, 34,000 motor vehicles and 552 aircraft. By the end of March, the only territory west of the Rhine still held by the Germans was the rapidly diminishing salient near Landau in the Palatinate, north-west of Karlsruhe. In the east, Kurland and East Prussia, with 51 divisions between them, had effectively been written off, cut off and surrounded by the Soviets.

Albert Speer, Hitler's chief architect and Minister for Armaments and War Production – one of the most intelligent and practically-minded of the Nazi inner circle – delivered a memorandum to Hitler on 30 January 1945, in which he stated quite bluntly: 'The war is lost.' With the Ruhr in ruins from the continual bombing and Silesia now under the Soviets, Speer reported, Germany had at best a two-week supply of coal for railways, factories, and powerplants; production capabilities for 1945 were one quarter what they had been in 1944 for coal, and one sixth for steel. Fuel was in such short supply that a fighter group with over 37 aircraft stationed at Krefeld could fly only sorties of 100km (60 miles) one out of three days, and then with only 20 of its planes. Speer told of seeing a column of 150 trucks from the 10th Army in northern Italy in October 1944 being pulled by oxen. In his memorandum, Speer concluded: 'After the loss of Upper Silesia, the German armaments industry will no longer be able even approximately to cover the requirements of the front for ammunition, ordinance, and tanks ... From now on, the material preponderance of the enemy can no longer be compensated for by the bravery of our soldiers.' Most of the major German cities were subjected to terrifying air attacks and Berlin was almost constantly bombed, from the Americans during the day and the British at night.

Clear-headed military authorities and Berliners believed that enemy troops could be in the city within weeks. In fact, by this time, most of them were beginning to hope, not that the Wehrmacht could yet achieve some sort of victory, but that the Americans and British, rather than the Soviets, would conquer them. Berliners thus followed the news of the Anglo-American advances across Germany with a mixture of despair and anticipation. Maria Kückler, a 45-year-old housewife in 1945, told the writer Cornelius Ryan that she had been 'ready to go out and fight to hold back the Reds until the Amis [Americans] get here'. This was even what most of the OKH General Staff was hoping for. It was widely believed within the Nazi leadership that the Western Allies' alliance with the Soviet Union was bound to disintegrate.

H.R. Trevor-Roper, the first Allied historian to chronicle the collapse of the Third Reich, has emphasised the importance in National Socialist ideology of hostility to both Communism and the Russians. Although it would be wrong to minimise the German animosity to the West and the nations which stood in Hitler's way – particularly the French

– it is nevertheless true that in both racial ideology and geopolitics, the Nazis nurtured a special animus towards the Russians. While they considered Britain, France, and the United States to be hopelessly bourgeois and Judaised states, they found it inconceivable that their leaders and people would not eventually wake up to realise that the Communist Russians were more alien to them, and a much greater threat, than were the Nazi Germans. While the German leadership was quite accurate in their perception of geopolitical tensions between the Soviet Union and the Western Allies, the degree of wilful blindness on Hitler's part about the anti-German alliance is revealed in Führer conference notes from 27 January, the day Zhukov's Belorussian Front reached and crossed the Oder:

Hitler: 'Do you think the English are enthusiastic about all the Russian developments?'

Göring: 'They certainly didn't plan that we hold them off while the Russians conquer all of Germany ... They had not counted on our ... holding them off like madmen while the Russians drive deeper and deeper into Germany, and practically have all of Germany now.'

Jodl: 'They have always regarded the Russians with suspicion.'

Göring: 'If this goes on we will get a telegram [from the British] in a few days.'

The telegram never came. Instead, a number of elements within the German armed forces and some in the Nazi party hierarchy began efforts of their own to contact the British and Americans with peace proposals. The most notorious was Rudolf Hess' rather bizarre, and still partly inexplicable, solo flight in a Messerschmitt 110 fighter to Scotland in May 1941. Since the turning of the military tide between 1942 and 1943, and now in the spring of 1945, with the Red Army almost literally at the gates of Berlin, the number of such plots increased. Two days before the Führer conference, OKH Chief of Staff General Guderian had contacted Foreign Minister Joachim

Below: The Red Army were greeted with relief in eastern Europe. Here a delirious crowd in Sofia, Bulgaria, cheers the entrance of Soviet troops. The sign reads: 'Welcome our Liberators'.

von Ribbentrop and pleaded with him to attempt to secure an immediate armistice with the West, so that Germany's remaining resources could be diverted to the east, and Berlin spared. However, Ribbentrop quickly tattled on the general, which led to another of Hitler's frequent eruptions of vitriol against his treasonous general staff. Albert Speer, too, was by this time searching for a way to end the war before Germany was utterly destroyed and occupied by the Russians. So desperate was he that he actually initiated a scheme in mid-February – eventually abandoned – to assassinate Hitler, Göring, Hitler's personal secretary Martin Bormann, and Robert Ley, the head of the Party Political Organisation.

Such eleventh-hour efforts to end the war, of course, came to naught. The Allies insisted unanimously on Germany's unconditional surrender. There is perhaps some truth in the argument that by insisting so stubbornly on this principle, the West prolonged the war. But it is doubtful that, even in these dire straits, Hitler would have considered any of the necessary means to end the war and remove Germany as a military threat to the West. Never was the dilettantism and military incompetence of the Third Reich's highest leadership as apparent and disastrous as in this last phase of the war. Hitler, who had assumed overall command of the army in November 1941, liked to think of himself as a genius of the bold tactical thrust. In military studies, he spurned the professionals' and experts' advice to exercise caution or consider practical realities. His failed gambit in the Ardennes forests in Belgium and northern Luxembourg in December 1944 – ordered despite the warnings of his generals – had left most of western Germany highly vulnerable, with its remaining forces stretched dangerously thin. Even more worrying, however, was the effect of the offensive's failure on the Eastern Front. Hitler's general staff had warned that an offensive of the size he demanded would mean committing huge numbers of reserve troops and tanks which, as well as risking them in a venture which could fail, would deprive the hard-pressed army groups trying to hold on to the Vistula and Narew in Poland and East Prussia of their much-needed reinforcements. A massive Russian offensive was expected at any time: 225 divisions and 22 armoured corps, estimated Guderian's chief of intelligence, Reinhard Gehlen. 'Who prepared this rubbish?' shrieked Hitler, according to Guderian. 'Whoever he is he should be shut up in a lunatic asylum!' At this point, Guderian lost his temper (a frequent event in those last months) and screamed back: 'If you want General Gehlen sent to a lunatic asylum then you had better have me certified as well!'

Above: A little bit of home in the middle of a war-torn country. Soviet soldiers relax around a piano in the half-destroyed piano room of an East Prussian house in February 1945.

Below: Marshal Ivan Konev, seated, had been one of the heroes in the routing of the German Sixth Army at Stalingrad in 1943. His First Ukrainian Front was one of the two key army groups closing in on Berlin.

In fact it was neither Gehlen nor Guderian who required psychiatric help. Across the length of the front, the Soviet Union had six million men facing just over two million Germans and their allies. On 12 January, as Guderian had feared, Konev's Ukrainian and Zhukov's First Belorussian Fronts – 163 divisions in Poland and East Prussia alone – had broken out of their bridgeheads and surged across the Vistula, taking Warsaw by 17 January and over-running the Silesian coalfields (by then producing 60 per cent of Germany's coal). By 27 January, the Red Army had reached the Oder, Zhukov's forces making the first bridgehead on the western bank at Lüben; by the end of the following month they had occupied a 150km (93 mile) line along the river.

This disaster was followed by the Anglo-American counter-offensive in the west and the inevitable collapse of the Western border. For the first time since Napoleon had careered across Europe in the early-nineteenth century, German soldiers were faced with fighting the enemy on their own soil. Despite the pretensions of Nazi ideology, this was not something that the Germans were prepared for. For all his imitation of Mussolini's totalitarian state, Hitler had always been reluctant to order a total mobilisation of all Germany's economic and social resources for the war effort. He had insisted on the maintenance of a fairly high output of consumer goods, in a wise effort to keep civilian morale up during the war. In the last years of the war, the domestic servants in Germany numbered the same as they had before the war. Hitler had also rejected plans to mobilise women into the economy. Women belonged in the home, Nazi ideology taught, producing Aryan babies. 'The sacrifice of our most cherished ideals is too great a price,' Hitler explained to Speer, when the latter had proposed enlisting women for the industrial sector. While Great Britain had managed to call two-and-a-quarter million women into economic service, only just over 180,000 were similarly employed in Germany.

However, sending old men and young boys to their deaths was apparently no sacrifice of a cherished ideal to the Nazis. During autumn 1944, the conscription age was amended to include boys between 15 and 18, and men between 50 and 60. This produced half a million more men for the Wehrmacht, most of whom were placed in the 25 new *Volksgrenadier* and *Volkspanzer* divisions to supplement the regular army units in the West. The hopeless inexperience of these civil reserve units thrown into the bitter combat is illustrated by Speer's account of his visit to a Panzer unit stationed near Bitburg in September 1944. The newly formed *Volkspanzer* brigade had just withdrawn from a disastrous engagement with the Americans. Its division commander, an experienced tank officer, told Speer that the unit had destroyed 10 of its own 32 brand-new tanks by poor driving. The remaining 22 tanks deployed themselves so ineptly on an open battlefield that the American anti-tank unit effortlessly picked off 15, leaving only seven of the original 32 tanks after a relatively minor engagement. In addition, in a real sign of the Germans' desperation, *Reichsführer* SS Himmler was given the task of creating a civilian militia, the *Volkssturm* (People's Storm), made up in many cases of old men and adolescent *Hitlerjugend* (Hitler Youth) members, to help with the battle on the home front. The size of the *Volkssturm* eventually reached one-and-a-half million.

Some of the first serious action the *Volksstürmer* saw was in the desperate German attempts to throw back the Soviet bridgeheads on the Oder in February 1945. One such unit, the 7/108th Franconian Volkssturm Battalion, had been hastily put together and issued with desert boots and brown uniforms which stood out magnificently against the snow and

Right: A Red Army soldier charges through a forest, carrying the standard issue PPSh submachine gun. These lightweight, easy to manufacture weapons were commonly used by Soviet infantry in place of rifles.

Above: A propaganda photograph showing Robert Ley, Reich Organization Leader, and head of the German Labour Front (the Nazi 'union') helping collect for the German Winter Aid in Berlin.

made them liable to be mistaken for Soviet soldiers by the regular Wehrmacht units. They were given only old Italian rifles and a few grenades, with no fuses. Although many of the men were World War I veterans, they had received no training for the battle. When another such *Volkssturm* battalion lost its positions to the Soviets, the commander of the Ninth Army, Busse, ordered its 60-year-old commander to be court-martialled and executed (although in the chaos of those last months, the order was never carried out). Even on the western front, Allied troops were often horrified to discover that they were fighting, and killing, women and children. Lieutenant Colonel Roland Kolb of the US 84th Division battling toward the Elbe reported coming across boys aged 12 and even younger, manning artillery pieces. 'Rather than surrender, the boys fought until killed,' he remembered. Major James Hollingsworth of the US Second Armored Division recalled with horror another incident near Bielefeld in which, during a tank battle with a Panzer training unit, his .50 calibre machine-gun shot up a truck loaded with soldiers all of which, when they looked at the ripped-up bodies, were found to be women.

The final battle was coming; the only question for the political and military leaderships of the crumbling Thousand Year Reich was their response to the onslaught. Hitler and his closest cronies, in the past always fantastical, now became delusional. The historical research of the past few decades shows conclusively that many of the most powerful Nazi leaders were opportunists who used the Nazi ideology as a vehicle for national and personal advancement. Nevertheless, there were those at the top with Hitler – namely the propaganda minister, Goebbels, and head of the SS, Himmler – for whom the prospect of defeat and capitulation were inconceivable.

Ever since the so-called 'Generals' Plot' of 20 July 1944, Hitler had been a near-recluse, scurrying from one of his six Headquarter Bunkers to the next. After 16 January 1945, he had been holed up in the Reichschancellery in Berlin. A great deal has been written about those last months in the Berlin Führerbunker. It was, by all accounts, a surreal place. In this cramped, foul-smelling and gloomy concrete vault, Hitler's manic-depressive tendencies were magnified to psychotic dimensions. The Führer had never been accustomed to countenance any discussion of defeat or even retreat. At the bloody battle for Stalingrad during the winter of 1942–43, he had infamously ordered General Paulus's Sixth Army to 'hold their positions to the last man and the last round and by their heroic endurance ... make an unforgettable contribution toward the ... salvation of the Western world', thereby consciously condemning over 285,000 men to death or the prison camp. By the spring of 1945, facing almost daily briefings of cities and men lost, Hitler found himself constantly remonstrating with his generals, throwing around accusations of treason as frequently and passionately as a preacher denouncing wickedness in a brothel. Those who survived the last days in the bunker described him later as having been physically and mentally wrecked, his almost-permanent daze broken only by

Below: In the expanded conscription of the autumn of 1944, 500,000 men between the ages of 15 and 18, and 50 and 60, were added to the ranks of the Wehrmacht – most in the Volksgrenadier *units.*

Above: A field soup-kitchen erected to feed the civilians evacuated from an area near the front. German policy forbade citizens from attempting to leave their official town of residence until evacuated to the rear.

his screaming fits, directed usually at Guderian, the OKH Chief of Staff. Guderian described one of these fits, after some bad news on 13 February:

'His fists raised, his cheeks flushed with rage, his whole body trembling, the man stood there in front of me, beside himself with fury and having lost all self-control. After each outburst Hitler would stride up and down the carpet edge, then suddenly stop immediately before me and hurl his next accusation in my face. He was almost screaming, his eyes seemed to pop out of his head and the veins stood out in his temples.'

The outburst went on for two hours, while his embarrassed generals fidgeted nearby, unwilling or unable to interrupt. Even Hitler's favourite, Albert Speer, a fellow artist – a higher order of person in Hitler's view – had taken to bringing him bad news. After the 30 January memorandum, Hitler refused to see Speer alone anymore, telling his generals, 'He always has something unpleasant to say to me. I can't bear that.' The conduct of military operations was even more seriously hampered, at a time of extreme crisis, by Hitler's *Führerbefehl* (Führer-Order) of 19 January 1945. With the stroke of a pen, it tied the hands of every German commander, from the divisional level up. They were required by the order to clear every plan and movement, whether offensive or defensive, with Hitler personally. 'They must ensure that I have time to intervene in this decision if I think fit, and that my counter-orders can reach the frontline in time.' By the middle of March, however, as the Americans prepared for a break-through across the Rhine, and with the massive Soviet build-up along the Oder, even Hitler and Goebbels were beginning to see what was happening. In keeping with the social-darwinian, teutonic fantasy at the heart of their Nazi ideology, however, the warlords determined that, just as Wagner's operatic gods 'cleansed' the world through their self-immolation, Germany's eventual defeat should loose a final, apocalyptic conflagration; a *Gotterdämmerung* (Twilight of the Gods) which would destroy Germany along with much of the rest of the world. In response to another of Speer's reports from 15 March that the war was lost, Hitler replied that 'If the war is lost, then the nation will also perish.' It was not really a change in his thinking.

Although his colossal self-possession had, until now, called for supreme confidence, he had from the beginning given hints of his view of the war's nature. Meeting with his *Gauleiter* (district party bosses) in August 1944, he stated: 'If the German people was to be conquered in the struggle, then it would be too weak to face the test of history, and

Above: Wehrmacht pioneers prepare a house in the southern part of Breslau for defence against the Soviet advance by creating loopholes and machine gun positions.

was fit only for destruction.' In 1934, Hitler had described the purposes of such a war: 'Even if we could not conquer, we should drag half the world into destruction with us, and leave no one to triumph over Germany ... We shall not capitulate! No, never! We may be destroyed, but if we are, we shall drag a world with us! A world in flames.' In September 1944, with German territory seriously threatened, Hitler issued a brutal scorched-earth directive. 'The amenities of civilisation', in the words of Speer, 'were to be destroyed in those areas about to be over-run by the enemy. The industrial plants, the gas, water, electrical works and the telephone exchanges would be completely smashed. Everything essential to the maintenance of life would be destroyed: ration-card records, files of marriage and resident registries, records of bank accounts. In addition, food supplies were to be destroyed, farms burned down and cattle killed. Not even those works of art spared by the bombs were to be preserved. Monuments, palaces, castles and churches, theatres and opera houses were also to be levelled.' The German inhabitants in those areas were instructed to leave; no German was to live in territory occupied by the enemy. An editorial in the *Völkischer Beobachter*, the Nazi newspaper, had appeared on 7 September 1944: 'Not a German stalk of wheat is to feed the enemy, not a German mouth to give him information, not a German hand to give him help. He is to find every footbridge destroyed, every road blocked! Nothing but death, annihilation, and hatred will meet.' The policy was to be carried out by the Nazi party *Gauleiters* and Commissars for Defence in conjunction with the Wehrmacht. 'All directives opposing this,' Hitler added, 'are invalid.' This last line was clearly in direct response to Speer's recent and open efforts to ensure that the basics of German life survived after the war. 'There is no necessity to take into consideration the basis which the people will need to continue [even] a most primitive existence', Hitler had insisted to Speer the evening before, after receiving the latter's 15 March memorandum. 'On the contrary, it will be better to destroy these things ourselves because this nation will have proved to be the weaker one and the future will belong solely to the stronger eastern nation. Besides, those who will remain after the battle are only the inferior ones, for the good ones have been killed.' As if to guarantee an even more theatrical closing act in this grim, apocalyptic opera, on 23 March, Bormann issued a directive that, if obeyed, would have seen the majority of the rapidly diminishing Reich's population, as well as foreign workers and prisoners of war, converging in the centre of Germany for the last stand.

The German people were spared Hitler's nightmare scenario by the determined efforts of a handful of military commanders, especially Speer. Now convinced that Hitler was mad, Speer went immediately into action. For several days, he flew, drove and telephoned all over the country to persuade, wheedle, cajole, and bribe Gauleiters and provincial officials to disregard Hitler's and Bormann's orders, or at least to await implementation orders. In most cases, Speer prevailed, either because of fear, conviction that the war was lost and that Hitler had lost his mind, or simple organisational confusion. In Düsseldorf, the unusually fanatical and dutiful Gauleiters were dissuaded from setting the city on fire only by the very real prospect that they would be lynched by the populace if they carried out the orders. Indeed, the American soldier and later historian James P. O'Donnell reports that many towns near the western front sent out citizens' committees to the Wehrmacht units to ask if they would be so kind as to move on and let the town fall peacefully to the advancing Allied troops.

The mood in Berlin, however, was quite different. If there was no widespread panic in the city, it was not because there was no fear, nor because the population wished the war to be over as quickly as possible, if that meant, as it did, the entry of Soviet troops into their city. Terrorised by daily quantities of Nazi propaganda, as well as by eye-witness accounts from the thousands of refugees pouring through the city from the east, Berliners had a desperate fear of the Russians. They saw them as blood-thirsty Mongols who would torture civilians for sadistic pleasure. Some rumours told of clergymen incinerated alive with flame-throwers, nuns gang-raped then marched through the streets naked, and people whose tongues were nailed to tables. The rumours were given ample fuel by the Soviets' own propaganda, meant both to bolster the fighting spirit of the Red Army and to terrify the German population. Most dreadful of all were the howling, anti-German manifestoes written by Ilya Ehrenburg. 'Germany is a witch,' he ranted in one article. 'We are in Germany. German towns are burning; I am happy ... Germany, you can now whirl round in circles, and burn, and howl in your deathly agony; the hour of revenge has struck!' In another leaflet distributed to Red Army soldiers which achieved infamy among the Germans in their path, Ehrenburg exhorted these soldiers to 'Kill! Kill! In the German race there is nothing but evil! ... Follow the precepts of Comrade Stalin. Stamp out the fascist beast once and for all in its lair! Use force and break the racial pride of these Germanic women. Take them as your lawful booty. Kill! As you storm onward, kill! You gallant soldiers of the Red Army.' Those who had personally witnessed Red Army brutality in the conquered territory, or who had personal knowledge of the atrocities committed by the German troops during their advance in Russia, expected the worst.

Below: Königsberg, the East Prussian capital, was one of those cities designated by Hitler as a 'Fortress-City', never to capitulate. The sign reads: 'We shall hold Königsberg.' In April 1945, the city surrendered.

However, a significant portion of the stories were the results of Goebbels' Ministry for Public Enlightenment and Propaganda, which aimed to frighten the population into supporting the costly war effort. 'Our propaganda as to what the Russians are like, as to what the population can expect from them in Berlin, has been so successful that we have reduced the Berliners to a state of sheer terror,' admitted Goebbels' assistant, Dr Werner Naumann, at the end of 1944. Referring to the large numbers of citizens attempting to flee the city, as well to the greatly increased number of military desertions, he added glumly: 'We have overdone it; our propaganda has ricocheted against us.' Even as Hitler and his cronies continued to cling to their teutonic illusions deep in the Führerbunker, and his top military staff groped for a way out of the 'fantastic mess' (as Guderian put it), Berlin's civilian population went grimly about their business, waiting for the dreadful end to the drama which, for the most part, they had welcomed. Berliners have always had a reputation for a sarcastic, stubborn toughness. Now, in the midst of a disaster far worse than those of the 1930s, they responded in character. A variety of derisive and macabre jokes and other forms of black humour were as active as the black market. 'Enjoy the war:' went one example, 'the peace will be terrible.'

Before the war, Berlin was one of Europe' s great capital cities. The third largest in the world, with a population of some 4.3 million, it was thoroughly modern. With its broad avenues, imposing neo-classical architecture, and bawdy nightlife, it was the showcase for the eager, bustling modernism of the young German Reich. But now, after 314 air raids on the city by 21 March 1945 – 85 in the previous 11 weeks alone – much of the city was in rubble. Almost one half of all the housing in the city was in some way damaged, a third of it uninhabitable. The mutilated shell of the Kaiser Wilhelm Memorial

Church now loomed grotesquely over the Kürfstendamm; the beautiful, world-famous *Tiergarten* (zoological gardens) was now an ugly eye-sore of burned trees, craters and demolished animal houses; the famous Brandenburg Gate, charred and pockmarked, straddled the Unter den Linden Straße which was lined with half-destroyed government buildings. The city of glorious monuments had become a city of *Trümmerhaufen* (rubble piles). Roughly 16sq/km (6 square miles) of the city had been destroyed, ten times the area of London destroyed in the Blitz in 1940, filling the city with nearly one billion cubic metres (three billion cubic feet) of debris. And yet, as if fate had a twisted sense of humour, the graceful winged figure on the top of the *Siegesäule*, Germany's 'Victory Column', still stood watch, entirely unharmed, over the devastated city. This city was boastfully called *Festung Berlin* (Fortress Berlin) by the Nazi authorities; the city for which Hitler and Speer had such grandiose plans after the war. Berlin was to be almost completely rebuilt by Speer, the centerpiece a huge copper dome with standing room for 160,000 spectators, so vast that it would produce its own interior meteorological system, including clouds. The new city was to be called 'Germania', the symbol of Germany triumphant. Now, in March 1945, it was daily being pounded into rubble.

As the end of the war approached, Berlin's population was shrinking drastically. The city's defenders estimated in January 1945 that the pre-war high of 4.3 million had sunk to about 2.9 million. At least 52,000 had been killed in the air raids, and twice that number injured. But most of the missing 1.4 million Berliners had either fled the destruction or were in the military. Under Goebbel's direction – besides being the Third Reich's propaganda chief, he was also Gauleiter of Berlin and a Reich Defence Commissioner – the government had made it a crime for certain categories of person to leave the beleaguered city without permission. Thousands still fled, their numbers swollen by the huge numbers of ministerial employees mainly moving south, either as part of an official relocation, to the National Redoubt, or as a private effort to save their skins. However, in the summer of 1943, shortly after the bombing raids on Hamburg and their massive civilian casualties, Goebbels had ordered that children and young mothers leave the capital city; some 790,000 did so. And yet most Berliners remained, grimly determined to see their city through to the end, and whatever came after. Erna Sänger, a Berlin housewife and mother of six, wrote in her diary in early spring 1945: 'Oh Germany, Germany, my Fatherland. Trust brings disappointment. To believe faithfully means to be stupid and blind ... but I'll stay

Below: As the war dragged on, much of Germany's civilian population was reduced to the kind of primitive existence which had not been experienced since the end of World War I.

Above: General Dwight Eisenhower (left), the Allied commander, jokes with General George Patton (second from left), commander of the US Third Army. Generals Bradley and Hodges stand behind him.

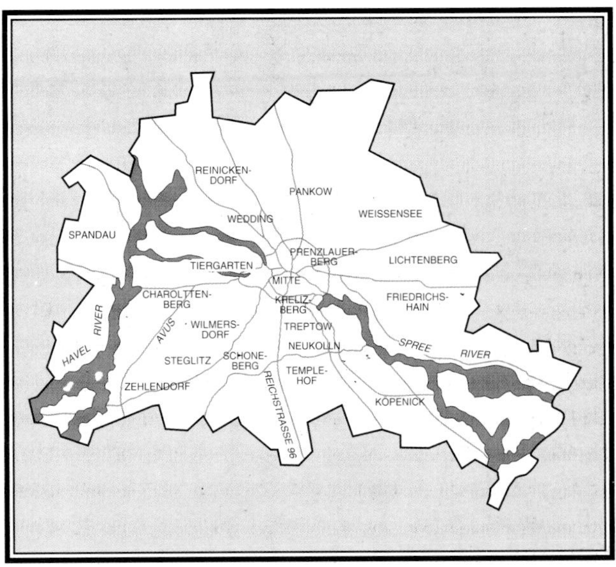

Above: A map showing the main districts of Berlin and significant roads in and out of the capital. 'Mitte' is the central district where the key Nazi buildings were located.

in Berlin. If everyone left like the neighbours the enemy would have what he wants. No – we don't want that kind of defeat!' In fact, despite the official effort to evacuate them, Berlin had become a city of women and children. More than two million of the remaining population was female; and apart from the Wehrmacht units stationed in the capital, the number of males aged between 18 and 30 was only about 100,000; most of those were wounded or otherwise unfit for battle.

Somewhat ironically, even as some people were desperately trying to get out of the city, other thousands were trying to get in. They too had to fight the Nazi state's prohibitions to do so. Since the beginning of the Soviet drive westwards in January, the roads into Berlin had been clogged with refugees. In vehicles, on foot, carrying their belongings on their backs or in pushcarts, driving cows, horses, and chickens before them, they streamed west. The bombed-out city could not possibly provide for the refugees; they were allowed to remain in the city a maximum of 48 hours, mostly in camps on the outskirts of town, before they were forced to resume their trek west. During the three-and-a-half months that Hitler spent holed up in his bunker, from mid-January to the end of April 1945, an estimated one million *Ostvertriebene* (eastern refugees) passed through Berlin. Many did manage, through the myriad of extra-legal tricks which seem to thrive under authoritarian regimes, to stay in the city, perhaps as many as tens of thousands.

Another category of refugee of sorts – persons who would much rather not be in Berlin, but were forced to – was the *Fremdarbeiter* (foreign workers). In order to meet the enormous labour needs required by the Third Reich's war effort, the Germans had adopted a policy of conscripting labour in the countries they had over-run. Nearly seven million of these – Poles, Czechs, Danes, Norwegians, Dutch, Belgians, French, Yugoslavs, Italians, Greeks, Russians – were sent to Germany to work as secretaries, maids (Russian girls were especially in demand by the Nazi elite), mechanics, clerks, drivers and menial labourers. Many of them, it is true, were voluntary foreign workers, those who truly believed that National Socialism was the wave of the future, or who sought to make a profit in the one place in Europe where that seemed most likely. But the majority were little better than slave labourers. Berlin had been allotted over 100,000 of these *Fremdarbeiter*, mostly French and Russians. They were even being used in ministerial offices, so critical was Germany's manpower shortage becoming.

By this last spring of the war, even prisoners-of-war were being pressed into labour service. Since the Soviet Union was not a signatory to the Geneva Convention, the Germans did not hesitate to treat Red Army prisoners-of-war the same as slave

Above: German infantry carrying automatic rifles and machine guns and wearing winter snow camouflage suits walk alongside a fearsome Tiger II tank through a quiet village in eastern Germany.

labourers, though they placed even more restrictions on them. In many cases, they were forced to work on the anti-aircraft batteries. Despite the danger they were in, however, by the spring of 1945 prisoners-of-war were beginning to feel more optimistic than most Germans. At the Alkett factory in the Ruhleben district, the 2500 largely French *Fremdarbeiter* producing German tanks spent their free time talking excitedly about French food and singing Maurice Chevalier tunes. Even their work gave them cause for cheer: they had been sabotaging the ball-bearing parts they made for years.

Between the beleaguered city and the three Red Army Fronts on the River Oder stood Army Group Vistula. All through the autumn of 1944, General Guderian had been trying to convince Hitler and his sycophants that the greatest danger lay on the Eastern front, and that drastic measures were necessary. Guderian, who had been one of the architects of the *Blitzkrieg* and a leader in the assault on Moscow, had intelligence that the Red Army had twice as many divisions facing the Germans as the Western Allies; the Wehrmacht had fewer divisions fighting the Russians than they did in the West. The reports showed the Germans could be outnumbered by 11 to 1 in infantry, 7 to 1 in armour, and at least 20 to 1 in artillery and aircraft. Guderian called for a transfer of resources east, and a shortening of lines, including a strategic withdrawal from the Balkans, Italy, Norway, and especially from the Baltic states. In Kurland (today's Latvia), 30 divisions were in danger of being completely cut off. But Hitler would not hear of it, angrily dismissing the intelligence as rubbish. Despite all the talk around him of a separate peace and alliance with the West against the Soviet Union, there is a good deal of evidence that Hitler would have settled for nothing less than total victory over Germany's traditional western rivals and the chief authors of her humiliation in 1918.

When the Soviets launched their Vistula-Oder offensive on 12 January, they struck at the weakest part of the German line. The *Oberkommando der Wehrmacht* (OKW: High Command of the Armed Forces) had expected the main thrust to be directed south to the Hungarian oilfields, or north to the Panzer units in Kurland. On the north, the remnants of Army Group Centre – under the command of Colonel General Reinhardt and reinforced to a relatively healthy strength of 580,000 troops, with seven Panzer divisions – clung to the Baltic coast, including Kurland and the strategically and symbolically important city of Danzig (Gdansk). Holding on to Hungary and the Balkans was the desperately-embattled Army Group South. Determined to keep Budapest at all costs, Hitler had ordered the transfer of some of the Wehrmacht's best resources south. For example, Herbert Gille's IV SS Panzer Corps was ordered from its position north of Warsaw to Budapest, leaving the German position in Poland even more vulnerable.

This middle sector, stretching from northern Poland to the Carpathian mountains, was held by Colonel General Harpe's Army Group A. At the beginning of 1945, Harpe commanded five armies, with a total of 400,000 troops, 4100 artillery pieces, 1236 tanks and assault guns, and 515 aircraft. The weakest section was Harpe's northernmost sector along the Vistula river, where the Fourth Panzer Army and the Ninth Army had between them only four Panzer divisions and two Panzer Grenadier divisions. The official Soviet military history of the Great Patriotic War reports that 'the First Belorussian and First Ukrainian Fronts had 163 divisions, 32,143 guns and mortars, 6460 tanks and mobile guns and 4772 aircraft; in total, 2.2 million men. Thus the Allies had in the Warsaw-Berlin direction 5.5 times more men than Germany, 7.8 times more guns, 5.7 times more tanks, and 17.6 times more planes.' Under this onslaught the Germans' Polish front crumbled within days.

At this point, Guderian urged the reorganisation of the remaining resources to create Army Group Vistula as a last bastion between the Soviets and the German heartland. Guderian had suggested the able Field Marshal von Weichs to command this vitally important unit, but Hitler considered him too old and appointed Himmler, despite the fact that Guderian, 'argued and pleaded against the appalling and preposterous appointment'. Himmler, already Minister of the Interior and Chief of the Gestapo as well as the police and the security services, head of the SS, and Commander of the Training Army, had neither the experience of commanding troops in battle, nor any real inclination for battlefield conditions. Under Himmler's command and due partly to the High Command's miscalculations of Soviet plans, Army Group Vistula's defensive line all but completely collapsed.

Once the Soviets broke across the Vistula, part of their forces swung north and captured Danzig, cutting off scores of German divisions in East Prussia and the Baltics, while the main body of Zhukov's and Konev's forces ground their way into Pomerania and Upper Silesia, reaching the Oder and Neisse rivers by late January. German losses in that single drive amounted to 2995 tanks, 15,000 guns and mortars,

Below: A Soviet 45mm (1.77in) gun crew in Budapest, in front of the famous bridge across the Danube. The Hungarian capital was captured by the Red Army in February 1945.

Above: Soviet infantry, covered by a Lend-Lease armoured car, race across a street in Vienna in April 1945. Annexed by Hitler's expansionist Third Reich in 1938, Austria became part of Nazi Germany.

26,000 machine guns, 552 aircraft, 34,000 motorised vehicles, 147,000 prisoners, and 295,000 dead.

On 20 March a desperate Guderian convinced Himmler to give up command of the army group, arguing that his multiple responsibilities left him overtaxed. Hitler reluctantly agreed and, at Guderian's suggestion, appointed Colonel General Gotthard Heinrici as the new commander. The 58-year-old Heinrici was a German officer of the old school. The son of a Protestant minister, he read his Bible daily and insisted on Sunday church parades for his troops, none of which sat very well with the Nazi authorities. But Heinrici was one of Germany's most brilliant defensive tacticians. His unglamourous job was to take over when things were going wrong, to hold the line for as long as possible, and then to manage the retreat. In January 1942, he had been given command of the remnants of the Fourth Army after the assault on Moscow had faltered. The Fourth held the key position, directly facing Moscow. Ordered to hold the line at all costs in anticipation of the next assault which 'would surely take the city', they lasted for nearly 10 weeks in the brutal Russian winter, which claimed nearly as many of Heinrici's soldiers as the Red Army did, before beginning the long, staggered retreat back to Poland. The slight Heinrici, nicknamed '*unser Giftzwerg*' (literally, 'our poisonous dwarf') by enemies and admirers alike, was a tough, stubborn commander, but he had the respect of his troops. He was known to be a crafty and creative defender and to stand for no nonsense from either his troops or 'the Nazi court jesters'.

On 22 March 1945, Heinrici arrived from his most recent post in northern Hungary at Maybach I, the OKH Headquarters near Zossen, 38km (23 miles) south of Berlin. There he was briefed by Guderian. 'The mess we're in is fantastic. The way the war is being run is unbelievable. Unbelievable!' Using maps, Guderian traced for the new commander of Army Group Vistula the line he was to defend. It stretched roughly 280km (175 miles) from the Baltic

Left: Guderian awards decorations on 27 March 1945, shortly before the Soviet offensive against Küstrin. The Edelweiss badge on the side of the cap identifies these men as members of an elite mountain unit.

south along the Oder to its confluence with the Neisse River in Silesia. Most of the front actually already lay on the western side of the Oder, but there were still three important bridgeheads on the eastern bank: in the north at the Pomeranian capital Stettin, and in the south at Frankfurt an der Oder and Küstrin. To repel the coming Soviet assault, Army Group Vistula had two armies: the Third Panzer Army commanded by General Hasso von Manteuffel, one of the greatest tank generals in Germany, holding the northern flank from Stettin to just north-east of Berlin, where the Hohenzollern canal flows into the Oder; and on the south, General Busse's Ninth Army. Both armies were supplemented by remnants of the decimated Fourth Panzer and Twelfth Armies.

The key to the success of the defence, Heinrici quickly realised, was at Küstrin, in Busse's sector. The Soviets were concentrating their forces on this portion of the line, and throughout March they had been sending out sorties to cross the Oder to try to seize footholds on the other bank, managing to hold on to two substantial bridgeheads on either side of Küstrin. Only a single, narrow corridor linked the units in the town to the rest of the Ninth Army, and kept the Soviets from the ideal launching point for a drive on Berlin, just over 60km (38 miles) down Reichsstraße 1. Since early February the Soviets had been trying to link the two bridgeheads and cut Küstrin off. It was a dangerous situation. But Guderian and Heinrici both considered Hitler's plan to wipe out the Soviet bridgeheads even more dangerous. According to their later recollections, the Führer was insisting on sending five Panzer Grenadier divisions out to cross over the river in Frankfurt, 21km (13 miles) below Küstrin, then drive up the eastern bank of the Oder to Küstrin and knock out the Soviet bridgehead from the rear. It would have been, in keeping with Hitler's opinion of himself, a bold and quite unorthodox move. The problem, as Guderian and Heinrici could clearly see on the map, was that it had no chance of success. 'Quite impossible,' Heinrici told Guderian. There is only one bridge connecting the two sectors of Frankfurt across the Oder, and it was much too small to accommodate five Panzer divisions with any kind of security. Guderian calculated that the tanks would have to roll across the bridge one by one. The resulting 24km (15 mile) long column of men and tanks would be easy pickings for the Soviet artillery massed in the hills which loomed up on the eastern bank of the river, the direction in which the Germans would have to move.

As it happened, Hitler's plan was never executed. No sooner had Heinrici arrived on 22 March at his

Below: Volkssturm *(home guard) training with dummy Panzerfaust anti-tank rockets. Allied troops were often horrified during the final stage of the war to find themselves fighting boys and elderly men.*

new HQ at Birkenhain, 80km (50 miles) north of Berlin, and taken over command from the clearly bored Himmler, than he received the news that Küstrin had been lost. The Soviets had detected General Busse's preparations for the attack and had struck hard, closing the pincers around Küstrin and cutting off 20th Panzer Division inside. The Germans were now entirely on the defensive. On the very same evening that Heinrici received the news of Küstrin's loss, General George S. Patton's US Third Army had burst across the Rhine, followed the next day by Field Marshal Montgomery and, within days, by the rest of the three Anglo-American Army Groups driving at Germany's western flank. On 23 March, Heinrici sent Busse's Ninth Army twice on the attack to attempt to break through to the isolated unit inside Küstrin, hoping to dislodge the Soviets before they had a chance to consolidate their gain; both attacks ended in failure. Five days later, although feeling that the only hope was for the Küstrin defenders to break out, he acceded to Hitler's and Guderian's orders, and sent Busse again. Despite a fierce effort by the Germans and the successful breakthrough of some Panzer units, the attempt ended again in a rout. 'The attack is a massacre,' fumed Heinrici. 'The Ninth Army has suffered incredible losses for absolutely nothing.' Nearly an entire division, 8000 men, had been lost.

The failure of the Küstrin offensive had far-reaching consequences for the defence of Berlin. The next day, 28 March, at the Führer's normal mid-day conference in the bunker, General Busse was ordered to appear and report on the failure. What followed has been described by most of those in attendance who survived the war; it was by all accounts one of the most bizarre scenes ever to take place in that surreal and strange place. Midway through Busse's report, Hitler suddenly yelled at him, 'Why did the attack fail? Because of incompetence! Because of negligence!' He began to heap abuse on the army general staff, especially Busse and Guderian. When Guderian attempted to explain what had prevented the attack's success, Hitler cut him off. 'Explanations! Excuses! That's all you give me!' The rant was a fairly common occurrence that spring in the Führerbunker; what was not so common was Guderian's reaction. In the middle of Hitler's raving, he suddenly lost all restraint, bellowing, 'Nonsense! This is nonsense!' His face red, spitting out the words, the Chief of the General Staff jumped to defend his subordinates. 'Busse is not to blame! I've told you that! He followed orders! Busse used all the ammunition that was available to him! All that he had! To say that the troops are to blame! Look at the casualties! Look at the losses! The troops did their duty! Their self-sacrifice proves it!' When Hitler shrieked 'They failed! They failed!' Guderian roared, 'I must ask you ... I must ask you not to level any further accusations at Busse or his troops!'

The other officers present, including OKW Chief of Staff Field Marshal Wilhelm Keitel, Chief of Operations Colonel General Alfred Jodl, Hitler's adjutant General Wilhelm Burgdorf, and several others, were stunned, and unable to react. The shouting between the two men continued for several minutes. Hitler flung invective in all directions, calling his commanders 'fools, fatheads, spineless, incompetent, traitorous'. Guderian challenged every accusation, suggesting not so subtly that Hitler was the incompetent one. Reminding him of Gehlen's intelligence reports about Soviet strength that Hitler had dismissed as rubbish, Guderian demanded, 'Who has misled you?' Finally, the other officers intervened. Jodl grabbed Guderian by the arm and pulled him to one side, while Burgdorf and Keitel attempted to calm Hitler. Guderian's terrified aide, Major Freytag von Loringhoven, telephoned Guderian's Chief of Staff, Lieutenant General Hans Krebs at Zossen, to tell him what was happening. They managed to get a still-furious Guderian to the phone to talk to Krebs on the pretence of some urgent developments at the front, just long enough for him to regain control of his emotions.

When Guderian returned some 15 minutes later, Hitler, too, had calmed down. He continued with the briefing. However, after everyone but Guderian and Keitel had left, Hitler stated flatly, 'Generaloberst Guderian, your physical health requires that you immediately take six weeks convalescent leave.' Guderian agreed to go. His sacking left the High Command now without any of Germany's best military minds, precisely at the moment of the country's greatest danger.

On that very day, 28 March, just before 1100 hours, as the leaders of the Third Reich were hurling abuse at each other deep below the city, the people of Berlin were startled by the wailing of air-raid sirens. Air raids were not in themselves a startling occurrence; they had been taking place with oppressive regularity for months. But the timing of this one was odd. The Berliners generally knew when to expect

Above: The fate of Germany now rested in the hands of young Hitlerjugend *like the one seen here meeting Himmler. Himmler's own attempt at reversing the Soviet tide had met with ignominious failure.*

the raids: the Americans around 0900 hours, and again toward 1200 hours, and the British after nightfall. But this time the planes were coming from the east, with red stars on their wingtips.

The Soviets' tactics were terrifying. Instead of heavy bombers like the Lancasters, or B-17 Flying Fortresses, these were Shturmovik fighter-bombers, streaking in at just above rooftop level, and raking the Berlin streets with machine-gun fire. As wave after wave of the low-flying fighters hit the city, the anti-aircraft gunners were forced to aim just above rooftop level. Many of the Berliners killed that morning were hit by German anti-aircraft shrapnel. It was the beginning of the final act in the Third Reich *Gotterdämmerung* tragedy: the Battle for Berlin.

By the second week of April, the situation looked exceedingly bleak. On 11 April the US Second Armored Division successfully took Magdeburg, on the Elbe river, 140km (87 miles) south-west of Berlin. On 13 April Vienna fell to the Soviets, leaving of the Reich cities only Prague, Munich, and Berlin still in German hands. And the Red Army continued to build up on the Oder. After the disastrous attempts to break through the Küstrin pocket, Army Group Vistula was left with fewer than 480,000 troops, facing a Soviet army which intelligence estimated could be as many as three million men (though, in fact, Zhukov and Konev had just over one-and-a-half million). Heinrici had almost no reserves, and was desperately short of tanks, artillery, gasoline, ammunition, and even rifles. Some replacement units had been sent to him with hand-held anti-tank weapons, rather like small bazookas, instead of rifles, and with only one rocket per weapon. To make matters worse, Hitler had become convinced that the massive Soviet build-up at Küstrin was nothing but a ruse, and that the main assault would be directed at Prague, roughly 200 km (120 miles) to the south. Perhaps out of a desire to have his forces increased, Colonel General Ferdinand Schörner, the commander of the army group on the southern flank of Army Group Vistula, had warned Hitler: 'It is written in history. Remember Bismarck's words, Whoever holds Prague, holds Europe.' Ever the afficionado of a bold, imaginative plan, Hitler was convinced and, after quickly promoting Schörner to Field Marshal, on 5 April transferred four of Heinrici's panzer units to defend Prague. The *Giftzwerg* could do nothing but make the best of the few resources he had and wait for the assault.

CHAPTER FOUR

Preparing for the Battle

The preparations for the final Soviet offensive on Berlin were carried out in the by-now customary professional manner by Zhukov, Konev and their subordinates. However all realised that the Germans would not give up their territory easily, and would, in many cases, fight to the death.

To the Red Army soldiers massing along the Oder and Neisse rivers, as much as to the Soviet leadership, the desire to conquer Berlin and bring the Nazi state to its knees was a force so compelling as almost to override every other consideration. Although weary of the war, one thing impelled them all: the desire to reach Berlin, to plant their flag atop the Reichstag, and to forever humble the Germanic *Herrenvolk*. Marshal Konev described their motivation: 'Berlin was for us the object of such ardent desire that everyone, from soldier to general, wanted to see Berlin with their own eyes, to capture it by force of arms. This too was my ardent desire ... I was overflowing with it.'

It was principally to Marshal Georgi Konstantinovich Zhukov that the task of crafting this final attack fell. Born at the tail-end of the previous century into a poor rural family, Zhukov had begun his military career as a regular cavalryman in the Tsar's army during World War I. In February 1917, as the first phase of the revolution was breaking out, Zhukov's unit in the 10th Dragoon

Left: A Soviet infantrymen peers intently through the sights of his machine gun. The Battle for Berlin was one of the most intensively prepared for of the war. Both sides understood that it would be a desperate struggle.

Novgorod Regiment quickly sided with the more radical Bolsheviks; Zhukov was unanimously elected chairman of his squadron's Soviet. His scrupulous attention to detail and hands-on approach; his stubborn refusal to accept anything short of their best effort from his subordinates; and his ability to inspire equal amounts of fear and loyalty bordering on love in his troops: all fueled Zhukov's rapid rise through the ranks of the Red Army. His successes, including during the Soviet participation in the Spanish Civil War, were such that in 1936 he was distinguished with the Order of Lenin, one of the highest decorations given by the Soviet Government. Having survived the brutal purges of the officer corps which emasculated the Red Army during 1937 and 1938, Zhukov again distinguished himself during the brief war with Japan along the Manchurian and Mongolian borders. By the time the Germans launched 'Operation Barbarossa' on 22 June 1941, Zhukov had been promoted to chief of the Soviet General Staff. He was responsible for the successful defence of Moscow in 1941, and also for the defeat of the Germans in the largest tank battle in history at Kursk in July 1943. As the Stavka representative in the field, Zhukov also had the primary responsibility for 'Operation Bagration', the Belorussian offensive which cleared the Germans from Soviet territory and began the long chase to Berlin. It was thus more as a reward than a demotion that, in November 1944, he was given field command of the First Belorussian Front, one of the two army groups which had been designated the spearheads of the final assault on Berlin.

The other spearhead unit, the First Ukrainian Front, was commanded by Marshal Ivan Stepanovich Konev. Konev and Zhukov were in at least one basic respect different types of men: while the latter had risen to his position from humble beginnings through the military ranks, Konev had begun his career as a political officer, responsible solely for the political education and reliability of the troops. It was only relatively late in his career, in the mid-1920s, that he switched over to the military officer corps. Konev always retained a certain ease with the political world and, unlike Zhukov, he had a gift for glib expression and political-diplomatic niceties. He was also probably more a master of large-picture strategic analysis than was Zhukov, while Zhukov was arguably the better field tactician. But in other ways they were remarkably similar. Intensely ambitious and jealous of each other, both had been awarded their country's highest honour, Hero of the Soviet Union, three times already. And they were both exceptionally good commanders, with the same attention to detail and respect from their soldiers.

Below: Red Army troops wearing standard-issue greatcoats and fur-lined caps set up a 45mm (1.77in) gun in a Danzig street in March 1945. In 1939 Danzig had been reincorporated into the Third Reich.

Above: Soviet troops advance after clearing a bunker near the German frontier in East Prussia. Cut off from the rest of Germany, after the war East Prussia was divided between Poland and the Soviet Union.

Even before the plans for the Berlin operation were finalised at the Moscow conference at the beginning of April, Zhukov was convinced that the town of Küstrin, 60km (38 miles) straight down Reichsstraße 1 from Berlin, would be absolutely crucial to any assault. A medium-sized industrial town, dominated by the medieval castle rising from the Altstadt (Old Town), Küstrin had been designated a *Festung-Stadt* (Fortress City) by Hitler: a defensive bastion to which would be committed all necessary resources, and which was to be defended to the last man. The fortress numbered some 16,800 people, of which 10,000 were part of the military garrison; of these, 900 were members of the local *Volkssturm* unit. Virtually all branches of the German Wehrmacht, as well as the Waffen-SS and anti-aircraft and police units were represented. Heavy armaments included an estimated 102 artillery pieces, 30 anti-aircraft guns, 25 self-propelled guns, 50 mortars, and 10 Katyusha rocket launchers ('Stalin Organs' to the Germans). Colonel General Vassily Chuikov, the commander of the Eighth Guards Army, described the difficulties faced by the attackers:

'The citadel itself was set on an island formed by the Oder and Warthe rivers. The spring flood had submerged all the approaches to the island. The only links between the citadel and the surrounding land were dykes and roads fanning out towards Berlin, Frankfurt, Posen and Stettin. Needless to say, the enemy had taken care to block these roads securely,

Right: The conqueror of Berlin: Marshal Georgi Zhukov (left) with Marshal Rokossovsky. Zhukov had risen through the ranks of the regular army. Both feared and loved by his men, he was a soldier's soldier.

Above: Urban combat was a relatively new phenomenon in this war. Every soldier feared it, and every commander hoped to avoid it by engaging and vanquishing the enemy at the approaches to the city.

Below: Many of the Soviet troops had already had extensive experience in urban combat at Stalingrad. Eighth Guards Tank Army, for example, had produced a booklet on urban warfare for the Berlin assault.

covering the dykes and embankments with dugouts, pillboxes, trenches, caponiers, barbed wire, minefields and other defences. Our small subunits managed to come so close to the enemy fortifications that hand grenade and Panzerfaust exchanges went on almost round the clock. But we were unable to deploy large forces here since a single tank took up the whole width of a dyke.'

The town was by any measure a difficult military objective. At the same time, however, it was the ideal location for the launching of the Soviets' attack on Berlin.

By the beginning of February, the Soviets had succeeded in establishing two bridgeheads on either side of Küstrin: at Kienitz and Göritz. Zhukov's Fifth Shock, Eighth Guards, and 69th Armies had tried all through February and the first half of March to close the pincers and cut off Küstrin, but without success. The 21st Panzer Division and (after 9 February) the 25th Panzergrenadier Division managed to maintain a 3-5km (1.8-3 mile) wide corridor into the town. Though traversable only at night by tracked vehicles, 'the pipeline' was indispensable to Küstrin's long-term survival. On 22 March, the day Generaloberst Gotthard Heinrici took command of Army Group

Vistula, it was finally lost and the pincers closed, though not without considerable cost to the Soviets; the defending Ninth Army claimed 116 Soviet tanks that day.

It took still another week before the town itself was finally conquered. It had been subjected to devastating artillery, mortar, and Katyusha rocket attacks since February, and the Soviets had attempted a number of assaults on it, including at least two attempts in inflatable boats. On 8 March they had finally succeeded in capturing the industrial Neustadt (New Town) along with a sizeable number of the defending troops, at which point the Germans blew up the remaining bridges across the Warthe to the heavily fortified Altstadt. The German counter-attack of 27 March had failed to relieve the besieged town, and on that same day the Soviets succeeded in using rafts and barges to cross the flooded old Warthe and establish themselves on the railroad tracks leading into the town from the south-east. Reinefarth's radioed request to General Busse, commander of the Ninth Army, for permission to break out of their position – effectively abandoning the *Festung-Stadt* – was the catalyst to Guderian's dismissal in the Führerbunker as OKH Chief of Staff, and orders from Hitler that Reinefarth be arrested and court-martialed. After a day of fierce hand-to-hand fighting near the Oder 'Cow Bridge', the garrison's officers agreed among themselves to attempt a break-out, although in view of Hitler's orders it was to be entirely voluntary for the soldiers. The attempt was launched at around 2300 hours on 29 March, and after fighting through six lines of Soviet trenches, 1318 men, including Reinefarth and 118 *Volkssturm* members, succeeded in getting through to their own lines. Another 135 *Volkssturmer* remained behind to negotiate a surrender to the Soviets. Altogether, the defence and attempted relief of Küstrin cost the Germans an estimated 5000 killed, 9000 wounded, and 6000 taken prisoner; the Soviets also lost 5000 killed and 15,000 wounded. Ultimately, however, Zhukov gained an ideal platform for an assault on Berlin.

On the same day that Küstrin fell, Zhukov arrived in Moscow to go over the plans for the operation with Stalin. On 1 April, Zhukov and Konev met with Stalin and the members of the State Defence Committee.

'So, who is going to take Berlin,' demanded Stalin. 'Us or the *soyuznichki* [little allies]?' The

Above: Some of the several thousand tanks shipped to the Oder for the attack on Berlin. Dozens of trainloads of tanks and other supplies arrived at the Küstrin bridgehead every day until 16 April.

question was meant more than a little rhetorically, for he quickly made it clear that he wanted the Red Army to be in Berlin no later than 1 May, 'May Day', International Workers' Day and the biggest holiday in the socialist world. The operation was to commence no later than 16 April and be completed within 12 to 15 days. Major General A.I. Antonov, from the Stavka's General Staff, presented the basic operational plan. It called for a colossal assault carried out on a very broad front, along several axes of attack. The idea was for the German capital to be encircled from the north and south by three Red Army Fronts, cutting off any attempt to escape to the southern Alpine redoubt, while fixing actions in Czechoslovakia and Hungary would prevent the diversion of German forces from those regions to Berlin. The Soviet forces designated for the attack were to penetrate the outer German defences and cut them up into isolated sections, wiping them out piecemeal. The Ninth Army was to be destroyed outside the city; serious urban combat inside the city, it was hoped, could thus be avoided as the experience of Stalingrad was not something anyone wished to repeat. Once the perimeter defences had been breached, the city was expected to fall quickly.

This plan was very similar to that which Zhukov had already discussed with Stalin. In November 1944, Stalin had singled out the First Belorussian Front, with Zhukov in command, for the honour of taking Berlin, and the current plan showed lines of demarcation between the participating Fronts' operational zones which would give the First Belorussian the only direct access to the city. But Antonov and the other members of the Defence Committee worried that an objective of the size and symbolic importance of Berlin, extremely well fortified, which may yet have to be taken street by street, would be beyond the capabilities of one Front. Konev was eager to agree. His First Ukrainian Front had been given the task of clearing the area south of Berlin, destroying the Fourth Panzer Army around Cottbus and then proceeding in a west-northwesterly direction to the Elbe and Dresden. Konev argued vehemently against any *a priori* exclusion of his troops from Berlin, urging that at least one or two of his tank armies should drive directly for Berlin's south-western suburbs. According to several reports from that meeting, Stalin looked at the map, then quietly erased the part of the demarcation between the First Ukrainian and First Belorussian which ran from Lübben to Potsdam, leaving Konev a 65km (40 mile) opening towards Berlin. He then looked at his field commanders and said, 'Whoever breaks in first, let him take Berlin.' Konev was then asked to develop an 'operational variant' which would require the Third and Fourth Guards Tank Armies to strike at the heart of Berlin from the southern suburbs. It was a typically Stalinesque resolution – setting his commanders in competition with each other – but it was also probably the only militarily sound solution.

Below: In the Germans' retreat, damaged equipment or vehicles for which there was no fuel were simply abandoned. Some of it was able to be put to good use by the Soviets, but most of it was simply ignored.

Zhukov's orders called for three separate attack axes in an 88km (55 mile) sector between the Oder-Spree rivers and the Hohenzollern Canal at the approach to Berlin. Here, it was expected, the main body of the Ninth Army would be destroyed. The First Belorussian consisted of one Polish and seven Soviet combined-arms armies, two tank armies, and four separate mobile corps. Its main assault would be launched by four rifle armies and two tank armies from the freshly secured Küstrin bridgehead. Two supporting attacks, each employing two armies, would be launched simultaneously heading north-west, to Eberswalde-Fehrbellin, and south-west towards Fürstenwalde, Potsdam, and Brandenburg. Konev's First Ukrainian Front was only slightly weaker, with five Soviet and one Polish combined-arms armies, two tank armies, and four mobile corps. The third Front slated for the Berlin operation was Marshal Konstantin Rokossovsky's Second Belorussian Front, with five combined-arms armies and five mobile corps located on Zhukov's right flank up to the Baltic coast. The Second Belorussian's primary responsibility during the Berlin operation would be to clear Pomerania and northern Brandenburg of the enemy and prevent the Third Panzer Army from reaching Berlin. In an

Above: A Russian scout proudly poses with his PPSh-41 submachine gun. Like many of his comrades, he had seen action all the way from Stalingrad to Berlin, a factor responsible for their high motivation and morale.

Below: Red Army tank corps men inspect their spoils after capturing a town in western Hungary, spring 1945. The neat parking of these German tanks suggest they were abandoned due to a lack of fuel.

Above: A German half-track observes the Soviet build-up across the Oder in the early spring of 1945. The danger from Soviet aircraft has forced the half-track to seek what shelter it can from the barren trees.

Below: It was widely assumed in the West that the Soviet success was due to their superior numbers and sheer, brute attrition. In fact, it was a well-led, modern professional army which conquered the Germans.

effort to allow the First Belorussian to concentrate on the main prize, Rokossovsky's armies were also to take over a chunk of the former's sector, from Kolberg to Schwedt, thereby reducing Zhukov's frontline by some 160km (100 miles). In addition, two of Rokossovky's armies were to be transferred to Konev.

Rather than the typical frontal penetration assault which had characterised the Soviet offensives since 'Operation Bagration' in the summer of 1944, Berlin was to be taken with a series of flanking attacks. First Belorussian's right flank would sweep around north and north-west, while First Ukrainian's right flank would swing around and up from the south. At the same time, the left flank of First Belorussian would strike at the bulk of the defending army in the southern suburbs. If successful, the plan would not only split the German defence up into manageable pieces, but would also cut off the bulk of the regular Wehrmacht units – the Ninth Army and Fourth and Third Panzer Armies – from the fighting in the city proper. The total number of resources committed to the planned offensive were 2.06 million Soviet combat troops, 155,900 Polish troops, 6250 tanks and self-propelled guns, 41,600 field artillery pieces and mortars, and 7500 combat aircraft. They would be opposed by an estimated 766,750 regular German front-line troops, 1159 tanks and assault guns, 9303 guns and mortars, and at least two million civilians, many of whom would fight alongside the army.

The plan was agreeable to the two main field commanders, but it presented them with a logistical

Above: The burned out hulk of a streetcar sits on a rubble strewn street in a German city. The constant pounding of Germany's cities by the Allied air forces seriously hampered the Wehrmacht's war effort.

nightmare. In only 14 days, they would have to develop detailed unit plans and brief their officers; they would also have to undertake gargantuan resupply, reinforcement, and redeployment operations. None of the three fronts involved were at their full operational strength. Reinforcements were forthcoming, but they would have to be properly deployed and integrated into the command and supply structure, and many of them were still quite distant. Two of the armies which Konev was counting on to deliver his promised strike at Berlin – the 28th and 31st from the Third Belorussian Front – couldn't possibly reach the staging area by the beginning of the offensive, and would have to be thrown cold into the progressing battle as soon as they arrived. The existing units also had to be brought back up to strength after the long winter of fighting. Although in better shape than Germany, after over three and a half years of war, the Soviet Union was close to reaching its limits in manpower. For the first time, repatriated prisoners of war were being rearmed and distributed back into the front lines. Huge amounts of equipment, ammunition, food, and medical supplies also had to be repaired, overhauled, and stockpiled. The fuel requirements were enormous: in addition to the tanks and aircraft, 'Operation Berlin' was to involve 85,000 trucks and 10,000 towing vehicles, also requiring fuel. As for artillery ammunition, the planners expected to use over one million shells out of a stockpile of just over seven million on the first day alone. In the event, 1.23 million shells (98,000 tons, delivered in 2450 railway wagon loads) were hurled at the Germans as the offensive opened. Zhukov commented about the logistical operation:

'The nature of the operation required a steady stream of ammunition from front depots to the troops, bypassing the intermediate links such as army and divisional depots. The railway line was converted to the Russian gauge and ammunition was brought up almost to the very bank of the Oder. To picture the scale of these transport operations it suffices to say that if the trains used to carry these supplies were stretched out buffer to buffer they would have extended over a distance exceeding 1200 km [746 miles].'

In the midst of this deployment and stockpiling, the bridgehead from which the attack was to be launched had to be readied. Most of the bridges into and out of Küstrin had been destroyed by the Germans; in any event, they would hardly have been large or numerous enough to carry the traffic the Soviets had planned. A total of 27 engineering and 13 pontoon battalions went immediately to work and, under nearly constant enemy fire, constructed 21 bridges at Küstrin – 19 of them from scratch – and five more at other points across the Warthe and Oder. The bridge at Göritz was reportedly demolished by the Germans 20 times during its construction, and the one at Zellin cost 387 casualties (201 deaths) during the seven days of construction. It was a prodigious feat, involving bravery and resourcefulness. The construction teams earned a reputation for being masters of underwater bridge-building when rising floods submerged some of their bridges, which they proceeded to mark out with poles so that they could still be used. The bridges and around 40 ferries which supplemented them began immediately to carry a constant stream of traffic. The five bridges and three ferries into the Fifth Shock Army's sector of the bridgehead, for example, were put to use on the night of 8 April. The traffic of artillery was so high – roughly the equivalent of a brigade a night – that a traffic control system had to be improvised. Starting on 11 April, the tanks started crossing into the sector at a rate of 75-90 per night, crossing at 300m (328yds) intervals. By 7 April, the protection of the bridges was significantly eased by the arrival of the Dnieper Flotilla. Two entire brigades, each consisting of 18 armoured boats, 20 minesweepers, six floating barriers, two gun-boats, and 20 semi-hydrofoils, provided security for the bridges and offered additional anti-aircraft power as well.

Konev's First Ukrainian Front didn't receive nearly as much in the way of materiel and support troops as did Zhukov's First Belorussian. But he had no

Below: Berliners line up to collect drinking water, as the sewerage system had been destroyed by the bombing. The Nazi leadership had made virtually no plans for the care or evacuation of the people of Berlin.

cause for complaint. At least 125 combat engineer battalions were deployed to his positions, where they constructed 136 bridges, 14,700 bunkers and command posts, and 11,780 machine-gun nests. Ultimately, his position was to receive 7733 field guns. For the First Ukrainian, lacking First Belorussian's foothold on the western bank of the river, the bridges were even more crucial; all of their troops and weapons would have to be brought across the river during the initial assault. In addition to the fixed bridges, each rifle regiment was issued with two light assault bridges, each division with two three-tonne pontoon bridges, and each corps with one 16-tonne pontoon bridge, which were intended for use on the Spree once Berlin had been penetrated. In total, the three Fronts massed along the 376km (235 mile) Oder–Neisse line counted over 190 heavily armed divisions, and 16,716 assault guns, with an ammunition stockpile of over seven million shells.

This tremendous build-up and frenetic activity along the central Oder front had, of course, to be accomplished with the greatest possible secrecy. It would be too much for the Soviets to suppose that the enemy had no inkling of their intentions. That Berlin was the ultimate target few in Germany could doubt, and the hard-won Küstrin bridgehead was too ideally suited for such an attack to be left unused. But the Soviets could try to keep secret the precise timing of the assault, and its main axis of advance. Zhukov accordingly placed a premium on elaborate mechanisms of deception. Troop and supply transports were permitted only during the night, without lights or radios. The same was true for the digging and road-construction operations. All traces of the work had to be removed, or camouflaged, by the break of daylight. Zhukov wrote:

'The bridgehead would usually be deserted in the day-time, coming alive only by night. Thousands of men armed with spades and pickaxes would start noiselessly digging the ground. The work was rendered more difficult by underground spring waters close to the surface, and by the spring thaw. During these night sessions over 1,800,000 cubic metres [2,354,400 cubic yards] of earth were dug out. By morning no traces of this colossal work were to be seen. Everything was camouflaged as carefully as possible.'

The dozens of trainloads of combat equipment and troops arriving every day were disguised as loads of wood and hay, and in an effort to convince the Germans that no imminent major action could be expected, four open trainloads of tanks and artillery were sent daily to the rear, only to return the next night disguised as a load of hay. Zhukov even concocted an elaborate phony attack plan, complete with dummy staging areas, river-crossing preparations, radio traffic, and reconnaissance raids, to make the Germans believe that the attack would take the form of a classic pincer movement launched from positions near Stettin and south of Frankfurt, more than 50km (30 miles) to either side of Küstrin. Clearly relishing the vast masquerade, Zhukov went to the extent of distributing dummy newspapers and fake documents announcing that he had been replaced by General Vasily Sokolovsky, which would again suggest that nothing major was being planned in that sector.

Above: Civilians collecting firewood pass the air-raid damaged Reich Air Ministry building in Berlin in the late spring of 1945. The building (minus its Nazi eagles) survived the war and still exists today.

The Germans, meanwhile, were well aware that something could be expected in the not-too-distant future. Common sense dictated that the Soviets would want to follow up the Vistula–Oder operation with an assault on Berlin as soon as practicable. And as ingenious and well executed as the Soviet *maskirovka* efforts may have been, they could not entirely obscure that there was a great deal of large-scale preparation taking place all along the Oder front, including in Küstrin. General Heinrici, the consummate defender, had an uncanny ability to sense the timing and direction of an imminent attack. Since the beginning of April he had been making daily flights over the Soviet positions in a small reconnaissance plane and studying the intelligence reports and prisoner interrogations. He was convinced that the main force of the attack would be launched directly at Berlin from Küstrin, with a secondary assault directed towards Schwedt, roughly 100km (60 miles) northeast of Berlin. But he did not yet know exactly when the attack would be launched, or how well his troops would be able to resist.

At a Führer-conference in the Reichschancellery bunker on 4 April, Heinrici painstakingly detailed the alarming situation along his 160km (100 mile) front. 'My Führer, I must tell you that the enemy is preparing an attack of unusual strength and unusual force.' It was clear to him, he went on, that 'the main attack will hit Busse's Ninth Army' in the central sector around Küstrin, and 'the southern flank of von Manteuffel's Third Panzer Army around Schwedt'. He said:

'While the Ninth Army is now in better shape than it was, the Third Panzer Army is in no state to fight

Above: Two elderly men sit in front of bombed buildings in the Französische Street in Berlin, April 1945. Berliners have an acerbic sense of humour: 'Enjoy the war,' went one joke: 'the peace will be terrible.'

Below: The once elegant streets of Berlin had been reduced by the spring of 1945 to a city of 'Trümmerhaufen' (rubble piles). Some 16 sq. km (6 sq. miles) of the city lay completely destroyed.

at all. The potential of von Manteuffel's troops, at least in the middle and northern sectors of his front, is low. They have no artillery whatsoever. Anti-aircraft guns cannot replace artillery and, in any case, there is insufficient ammunition even for these.'

He explained that even the relatively healthy looking numbers for the Ninth were misleading since the newly created Army Group Vistula was a patchwork of various units – some of them already badly battered – which had never fought together before. In fact many of the troops – the *Volkssturm* and *Volkswehr* – had never fought at all. It also contained a number of allied armies, including for a time General Vlasov's 'Russian Liberation Army', whose reliability in defending the German capital was dubious. Heinrici concluded, with characteristic bluntness:

'My Führer, I do not believe that the forces on the Oder front will be able to resist the extremely heavy Russian attacks which will be made upon them… I must tell you that since the transfer of the armoured units to Schörner [in Prague], all my troops – good and bad – must be used as front-line troops. There are no reserves. None. Will they resist the heavy shelling preceding the attack? Will they withstand the initial impact? For a time, perhaps, yes. But, against the kind of attack we expect, every one of our divisions will lose a battalion a day. This means that all along the battle front we will lose divisions themselves at the rate of one per week. We cannot sustain such losses. We have nothing to replace them with. My Führer, the fact is that, at best, we can hold out for just a few days. Then, it must come all to an end.'

In an effort to shore up his badly stretched lines, he urged the Führer to allow the abandonment of Frankfurt an der Oder, one of those cities designated a *Festung-Stadt.* Hitler, with equally characteristic obstinacy, refused. Instead, to Heinrici's disgust, the leaders of the various branches of the armed forces began trying to outbid each other in offering

Below: Under a large Nazi party flag, city and party authorities collect clothing and other supplies for refugees. The word 'Volksopfer', on the signs on the wall, translates roughly as 'the people's sacrifice'.

reinforcements to the defence of the Oder–Berlin sector: Göring 100,000 from the Luftwaffe, Himmler 25,000 from the Waffen SS, and Grand Admiral Dönitz 12,000 from the Kriegsmarine (navy). Heinrici knew that in their efforts to ingratiate themselves with Hitler, these commanders probably had no idea if they had these numbers of men at their disposal or not. In any event, he was hardly impressed by the idea of sailors attempting to fight against Soviet tanks. But Hitler was satisfied. 'All right,' he said. 'We will place these reserve troops in the second line about eight kilometres behind the first. The front line will absorb the shock of the Russian preparatory artillery fire. Meanwhile, the reserves will grow accustomed to battle and if the Russians break through, they will then fight.' Finally, Hitler explained to Heinrici that the Soviet preparations on the Oder were a colossal ruse, and that the main attack would be directed instead against Prague, and that he would not receive the armoured units he had requested back from that sector. Exhorting the Giftzwerg to trust in the power of faith, Hitler rhapsodised about the glories awaiting them: 'I tell you, Generaloberst, if you are conscious of the fact that this battle should be won, it will be won! If your troops are given the same belief – then you will achieve victory, and the greatest success of the war!'

Such faith, while perhaps the prerogative of messianic leaders, scarcely recommends itself to experienced military men, and the General Staff of Army Group Vistula were not inclined to leave the defence of the approaches to Berlin to such abstractions. Before the Vistula-Oder operation, strong forward defence had generally been the Germans' preferred philosophy, but during the Vistula-Oder offensive, which saw the Germans lose some 450km (280 miles) of ground in three weeks, the Soviets had consistently managed to shatter both the Germans' front lines and their mobile reserves with fierce opening artillery and air bombardments, before punching through with armoured units and overrunning the rear defences. In response, the OKH now adopted the defence-in-depth philosophy for which Heinrici was already known. The main idea was to construct multiple consecutive defensive 'strips' and to pull back the troops from the forward-most line just before the enemy's initial barrage. Heinrici, who had used the technique to great effect in the retreat from Moscow, described the effect as causing the enemy to waste their artillery barrage on empty

Below: The bazooka-like Panzerschreck *('tank's terror') anti-tank weapon, wielded by a soldier in the Kurland region of East Prussia – now Latvia – where thirty divisions had been trapped in a pocket.*

Above: This photograph of a cinema illustrates both the huge predominance of women and children in the city's population by 1945, and the Berliners' penchant for continuing 'normality' as long as possible.

positions, 'like hitting an empty bag', after which the unharmed troops could reoccupy their front-line positions and offer fresh resistance to the attempted advance. On 30 March, Hitler approved the new tactic with a detailed order. Additional orders from Heinrici placed special attention on the preparation of alternate and dummy artillery positions, in addition to the primary positions.

Under these guidelines, Army Group Vistula's defensive preparations came to comprise three separate 'defensive strips', each consisting of a number of 'defensive lines' of fortified locations and barrier zones, extending to a depth of 40km (24 miles). The first one, the 'Forward Combat Zone' was, despite the intention to abandon part of it during the opening bombardment, a formidable defensive complex. It was located on the western bank of the Oder, just below the Seelow Heights, a chain of steep bluffs rising 40-50m (130-165ft) up from the floor of the Oder valley, approximately 12-15km (7-9 miles) from the river and stretching roughly 20km (12 miles) in front of the attackers. In the boggy zone between the heights and the river, Heinrici directed the construction of three defensive lines, each 1-3km (0.6-1.8 miles) deep for a total depth of 8-10km (4.8-6 miles). Twelve divisions of troops manned the extensive networks of concealed trenches and machine-gun nests in the Forward Combat Zone, and they were supported by a number of fortified points, including the Frankfurt 'Fortress-City', which sported a number of tank turrets in its fortifications.

The Second Defensive Strip, in keeping with the new defence philosophy, was accorded the same importance and resources as the first position; indeed, as the 'Main Combat Zone', it was possibly considered even more important. This zone took maximum advantage of the natural benefit provided by the terrain to the defenders. Much of the Seelow escarpment was too steep for the tanks, and the numerous draws and ravines were ideal for concealed gun positions with a commanding view over the river and valley floor.

Above: A 15cm (5.87in) heavy artillery piece in action in East Prussia. The sIG 33 was one of the Germans' most powerful and reliable infantry field howitzers, but was difficult to manoeuvre due to its heavy weight.

The forward line of this Second Position, called the 'Hardenberg-Stellung' (Hardenberg Position), ran along the lip of the bluffs and the Alte Oder and again consisted of between two and three lines of concealed trenches reinforced by machine-gun nests. The town of Seelow became another fortified city, with a battalion-sized garrison blocking the highway to Berlin. Artillery positions were dug in on the reverse slopes, providing effective cover even as they provided excellent field of fire and observation.

While the first two 'strips' were intended to be the main theatre of the battle, a Third Defensive Strip was constructed along a line from the western edge of Scharmützel Lake, near Buckow, to the eastern edge of Fürstenwalde, generally no more than 30km (18 miles) east of Berlin. This was the 'Wotan-Stellung' and consisted of a string of heavily fortified towns (most importantly Fürstenwalde, Müncheberg, Sternebeck, and Eberswalde) linked by anti-tank barricades and fields of fire. From this position, if necessary, artillery, tanks, SPGs, and tank-hunters would be able to coordinate their fire and so prevent a breakout by Soviet armour. In between the last two strips, blocking positions were constructed to cover both the Küstrin-Berlin and Frankfurt-Berlin *Autobahnen* (motorways).

Though this was an enviably strong position, aided by the natural obstacles presented by the flooding Oder and Seelow escarpment, General Busse was concerned by his shortfall in heavy weaponry, particularly artillery, and the woeful shortage of military manpower. Of the 137,000 reserve troops so eagerly promised by Göring, Himmler, and Dönitz, only 30,000 completely unequipped and inexperienced men ever materialised, for whom, as it turned out, only 1000 rifles could be found by Army Group Vistula. The Ninth Army was partially filled out with replacements and reinforcements from sundry depot, guard, and training units and by a number of Volkssturm battalions raised in Berlin, Potsdam, Stettin, and elsewhere. The civilian population also lent a hand. Civilians had been evacuated from the most forward area back in February, although all healthy adult males were expected to remain to participate in the defence preparations. The villages and towns in the Second and Third Defensive Strips, however, seem to have remained fully inhabited right up until the attack.

Right: By the spring of 1945, Hitler was almost never seen in public. In his 'Führerbunker', Hitler was described as being increasingly delusional, alternating between manic confidence and suicidal depression.

By the eve of the battle, Ninth Army consisted of four corps and an army reserve division, totalling about 200,000 men, as well as 512 operational tanks, SPGs, and tank-hunters, and 658 artillery and flak batteries with 2625 guns with scant ammunition. There was also a sort of bizarre, jury-rigged armoured train – the 'Berlin' – which consisted of five flatcars carrying tanks for which there was no fuel. This 'Zug-Panzer' ran back and forth out of the Seelow station. The Army could also count on some air support from the Fourth Air Division of the Sixth Air Fleet. The division's 300 aircraft (of a total of some 3000 left to the Germans over the whole of the eastern front) were allocated exclusively to Army Group Vistula. But the critical shortage of fuel and the dwindling number of serviceable airfields seriously reduced the number of sorties which could be mounted at any one time. Not all the planes, however, needed much fuel: fantastically, the Luftwaffe had by this time even created its own kamikaze unit – the 'Special Operations Unit' – which was manned by 39 volunteer pilots and operated from Jüterbog.

In addition to these units of Army Group Vistula, the Fourth Panzer Army of Schörner's Army Group Centre, with two corps, defended the southern approach to Berlin along the Dresden–Neisse River axis. And finally, the confines of the city itself were defended by the so-called 'Berlin Garrison', a collection of forces under the immediate control not of the Wehrmacht hierarchy, but of Berlin's *Gauleiter*, Josef Goebbels. This garrison included the 56th Panzer

Below: The terrain approaching Berlin favoured the defenders. The marshy field of the Oderbruch was an obstacle for Soviet armour, while the Seelow Heights allowed the Germans to observe the Soviet advance.

Above: The last public appearance of Heinrich Himmler before the war's end, inspecting troops of Army Group Vistula. Guderian finally convinced Hitler to replace Himmler with General Gotthardt Heinrici.

Below: Army Group Vistula suffered from serious manpower shortages. Impressive on paper, in reality many units were severely understrength or manned by young, untested troops, like this teenage soldier.

corps with five or six divisions, more than 50 *Volkssturm* battalions, and a few units of 'Alarm Troops', which were made up primarily of clerks, cooks, and other non-combat personnel. The garrison's commander was Major General Helmuth Reymann. Only appointed a few weeks previously on 6 March, Reymann was not enthusiastic about his position. He had been trying for over a month to convince Goebbels to authorise comprehensive measures for the care and protection of the city's civilian population. In the face of Goebbels' stubborn refusal to order more than the most cursory paper plans, Reymann decided that their only hope would be for the Berlin Defence Region to come under the command of Heinrici's Army Group Vistula, and so benefit from the general's greater resources and defensive talents. He had learned that the OKH had tentative plans to eventually do just that, although the Giftzwerg was less than enthusiastic about the proposal. 'It's absurd!' he had complained to his staff. On 15 April Reymann met with General Heinrici to try to convince him to take the city under his wing and bolster its defensive preparations. But Heinrici made clear that his hard-pressed units could offer very little to the city. He hoped to

Above: Few Germans in 1945 expected to win the war. Nevertheless, the Germans built extensive defensive fortifications, like these tank traps, meant to slow down the Soviet advance.

mount a successful enough defence so that there would be no need for any kind of serious fighting within the city, but if it came to that, he told Reymann 'not to depend on the Army Group Vistula for support. Of course, I may be ordered to send units into Berlin, but you should not depend on it.' Fortunately, if somewhat perversely, in one way Reymann actually benefitted from the Reich's overall weakness. In this last ditch battle, with the amount of territory to defend rapidly dwindling, he was able to muster thousands of now-redundant anti-aircraft batteries to use as ground artillery.

The 'Berlin Defensive Region', extending to the city's suburban outskirts, was, rather like the Ninth Army's position on the Oder across from Küstrin, divided into three concentric rings, which were further subdivided into a total of nine defensive sectors. An extensive communications system linked all sectors with each other and with the OKW's huge and sophisticated telecommunications switchboard (perhaps the largest in all of Europe) in Zossen. The city's U-Bahn subway system was used to move troops and materiel around undetected. The central sector, in the heart of the governmental quarter near the Tiergarten, was the most heavily fortified and contained the greatest concentration of troops. The centre of it all, the nerve centre of the entire crumbling Third Reich, was the *Führerhauptquartier* (Führer Headquarters: FHQ), located 16.7m (55ft) below the garden of the old Reichschancellery building, surrounded by concrete bulkheads 1.8m (6ft) thick and protected by a massive 4.8m (16ft) thick ceiling, with its own ventilation system. This was the last of Hitler's 13 Führerbunkers scattered around the country, into which he had descended on 16 January 1945. He would never see another full day above ground.

While the Germans fully expected the main threat to come from the Soviets in the east, they were aware as well of the Anglo-American troops driving towards them from the West. Although many of them nursed a clandestine hope that the Western Allies would beat the Soviets to Berlin, they weren't going to leave the capital's western approach undefended. In early April, General Walther Wenck, formerly Chief of Staff to General Guderian at the OKH and then briefly Himmler's Chief of Staff at Army Group Vistula, was called back from convalescent leave for wounds sustained in a February automobile accident to take command of the newly organised 12th Army. He was given a two-part mission. His primary task was to shore up the rapidly receding western front between the armies of Field Marshals Ernst Busch

Above: The Reich Minister for Propaganda and Enlightenment, as well as the party's Gauleiter *for Berlin and therefore responsible for the city's defence, Josef Goebbels played a key role in the preparation for the battle.*

and Albrecht Kesselring, Commanders in Chief North-west and West respectively, now taking a severe beating from the British and North American forces racing eastwards with barely a pause since the landings at Normandy in June 1944. But Hitler had also envisioned a plan whereby Wenck's 12th Army would launch a massive counter-attack against General Bradley's 12th Army Group, now making rapid progress toward the Elbe. The idea was to slice a 320km (200 mile) swath straight through General William Simpson's Ninth Army to the Ruhr pocket, thereby releasing the 300,000 men of Model's Army Group B and splitting the armies of Montgomery and Bradley. Hitler wanted to achieve this improbable feat by appropriating a Soviet trick. He instructed the officers of the new 12th Army to round up 200 nondescript Volkswagen automobiles and use them to infiltrate the enemy lines and disrupt the rear to effect the breakthrough.

Even if the plan had been realistic when formulated, it never got the chance to be tested: the front was moving too rapidly eastwards. Indeed, Wenck had some trouble catching up with his new headquarters as it continually retreated to the East. He received a rude shock, and a quick education in the reality of the military situation when, on his way to assuming his new command, he attempted to stop in his hometown of Weimar to withdraw his family's savings from the bank: American tanks from General George S. Patton's Third Army were already there. Within two days of Hitler's elaboration of his plan, on 13 April, the Allies succeeded in cutting Model's forces in the Ruhr pocket in two and capturing the eastern half. Model had already told his troops that he was dissolving Army Group B on his own authority to save them the humiliation of surrender; it was left to each man whether to surrender individually, continue fighting, or attempt to make his way home through the Allied lines.

Wenck finally caught up with his headquarters near Rosslau, some 75km (46 miles) south-west of Berlin. Positioned along a 200km (125 miles) front from Wittenberge down the River Elbe to Leipzig, the 12th Army was supposed to have been made up of 10 divisions, some 200,000 soldiers, composed of Panzer Training Corps officers, cadets, *Volksstürmer*, and the remains of 11th Army, which had been involved in some ferocious fighting in the Harz mountains. But much of Wenck's army, he quickly discovered, existed only on paper. Some of the units were still in the process of being organised but, at most, he had at his disposal roughly five and a half divisions, with 55,000 men. These were equipped with a few self-propelled guns, about 40 personnel carriers, and a number of fixed artillery positions at bridges and around cities like Magdeburg. The outlook was not encouraging. But the situation throughout what remained of the Reich was bleak, and Wenck, the Wehrmacht's youngest general, faced it with surprising vigour and imagination. Determined to hold the Western Allies at the Elbe for as long as possible, while at the same time freeing up as many men as possible to help shield Berlin from the Soviets, he intended to use the most experienced of the 12th's few and green forces as a sort of mobile shock troop, shuttling them from crisis to crisis. To this end he positioned his best forces in Magdeburg and other centrally located urban centres.

Wenck's instincts for focusing on the cities were sound, though it didn't require too much military genius to understand that this last stage of the war would be fought predominantly in large, urban areas. There had been some significant city battles fought already in this war, most notably in Stalingrad and Warsaw. But for the most part it had been a war of large-scale, mobile operations conducted in open terrain or before cites; the kind of warfare best suited to the era's fascination with tanks and other mobile armour. But in April 1945, on the eve of the war's final act, with Germany's room for manoeuvring and building reserves rapidly disappearing, that kind of operational depth was no longer available. Inevitably, particularly given the Allies' insistence on Germany's unconditional surrender and Hitler's inability to consider any kind of retreat or surrender, the final battle would almost certainly have to be fought inside the Third Reich's capital.

Though they were eager to enter Berlin as conquerors, an urban battle was not a prospect looked forward to by the Soviet soldiers. Urban warfare is both terrifying and unpredictable. And, as the Germans discovered at Stalingrad, the normal defenders' advantage is tremendously magnified in a battle for a large city. With a greatly shortened frontline to defend, and with a tremendous population of reservists, cadets, Volksstürmer, and paramilitary Hitler Youth to reinforce the hard core of experienced Wehrmacht soldiers – not to mention a vast civilian population which could be counted on to resist the enemy in innumerable small ways in defence of their homes and streets – the Germans could promise a difficult and costly fight. The Soviet plan called for the annihilation of the main body of Busse's Ninth Army outside the city, but even if that

Right: Members of the Volkssturm *move to set up a machine-gun position. The* Volkssturm *had no standard uniform, beyond the armband seen here on these men.*

was accomplished, there was a very good chance that resistance, however diminished, would move into the city. Even with luck, it was sure to be a desperate fight.

The massive assembling of men, weapons, and supplies which the Soviets had been undertaking along the Oder since the beginning of April would, it was hoped, even the odds somewhat and enable the Red Army to overcome the German resistance before the May Day holiday. In addition, to help prepare the troops for the peculiar rigours and tactics of city fighting, Colonel General V.I. Chuikov of the Eighth Guards Army – the headquarters unit at the Battle of Stalingrad – had his staff prepare a pamphlet on the special problems of urban warfare for distribution throughout the First Belorussian Front. Zhukov also required every rifle division in the Front to form a special unit to train specifically for street warfare while the rest of the Front rehearsed river crossings.

Below: An aerial view of Pariser Platz and the Brandenburg Gate, with the Tiergarten behind it, in April 1945. The extent of the damage inflicted on the city by Allied bombing raids is clearly visible.

As the second week of April drew to a close, the Red Army troops all along the Oder front made last-minute preparations for battle. Several thousand aerial reconnaissance missions were flown over the city and photographic maps of the city and its defences assembled. Utilising those maps, as well as captured documents and prisoner interrogations, a team of Red Army engineers produced an exact-scale model of the city to use in planning the assault. Each unit was given specific and detailed orders. The Third and Fifth Shock Armies with the Eighth Guards, the core of the Küstrin formation, were assigned the spearhead role of smashing Heinrici's defensive positions and opening up a corridor for the armour; by day six they were to be at the eastern shore of Lake Havel in the Hennigsdorf-Gatow sector, on the far western side of the city. The 47th Army was ordered to sweep around on the city from the north-west, and attack at Nauen-Rathenow, reaching Schönhausen on the Elbe by day 11.

The chief tactical obstacle was the Seelow Heights. Steep, cut by numerous ravines, and heavily defended by artillery and machine-gun positions, the heights were no place for tank battles. It was

Above: Preparing for the Russians. Men and women dig anti-tank trenches on the outskirts of Berlin on 9 April 1945. The Soviet assault on the city began only a week later.

clear to Zhukov that his tank armies could be committed on this line only after the heights had been captured, but in the event of strong German resistance and a delay in the main strike force's momentum, he did not want his tanks idling in the rear. He therefore decided on a revision to the original plan developed with Stavka in Moscow. Instead of deploying the First and Second Guards Tank Armies with the main strike force, he now instructed them to perform flanking movements north and south of the city, squeezing the defending armies between their pincers, to 'rip the defences wide open', as the main force punched in from the east. Marshal M.E. Katukov's First Guards Tank Army, with Major-General Yushchuk's 11th Tank Corps, would move from their position on the southern flank into the breach opened up by Chuikov's Eighth Guards Army and seize the Köpenick-Friedrichshafen-Neuenhagen area by the second day. Meanwhile, Marshal S.I. Bogdanov's Second Guards Tank Army, coming in from the northern flank, would drive into the breach made by the Fifth Shock Army and continue on to the Havel River in the Oranienburg-Hennigsdorf sector. At that point the two tank armies were to meet up and together take the Zehlendorf and Charlottenburg districts in the western part of the city. To cover these primary assaults on Berlin, Zhukov ordered four of his armies to conduct two supporting attacks to the north and south. The 61st and First Polish were to attack north-west through Liebenwalde and from there reach the Elbe no later than 11 days after the start of the operation. At the same time, the 69th and 33rd Armies were supposed to launch a southern assault, breaking the German defences around Frankfurt, and head towards Fürstenwalde-Potsdam-Brandenburg on the southern and south-western outskirts of Berlin, thus effectively preventing the German Ninth Army from coming to Berlin's defence.

The objectives assigned to the First Ukrainian Front were not quite as straightforward as those assigned to Zhukov's First Belorussian. Its primary mission was to launch an assault on a southerly axis towards Cottbus, there engaging the Third Panzer Army to prevent it from moving to Busse's defence, and then moving towards Dresden and a rendezvous with the Western Allies. But, in an apparent effort to stimulate some 'socialist competition' between his two top commanders, Stalin had also instructed Konev to prepare an 'operational variant' which would throw some of his forces into the Berlin battle. As Zhukov's long-time rival, Konev very much hoped that his First Ukrainian would be able to join in that final, spotlight effort, but the task of being ready to go with two different plans, on top of his near-overwhelming logistical hurdles, seemed like an impossibility. He finally realised that it would greatly simplify his predicament and strengthen his chances of joining the conquest of Berlin – while remaining faithful to the spirit of Stalin's instructions – if he simply merged the two plans, integrating into the original mission a turn towards Berlin by some of his forces.

Accordingly, his final plan called for a strong main strike-force from Triebel to smash through all German front-line defences in the area of Forst-Muskau and drive on to the Spree River and Cottbus by the second day, which would enable a couple of units to wheel to the north and enter Berlin's southern suburbs in time for the main battle. The rest of the force would drive through to the Beelitz-Wittenberg line and from there on to the Elbe. Taking part in the main assault would be the Third, Fifth, and 13th Guards Rifle Armies, and the Third and Fourth Guards Tank Armies. Once the Spree was gained, the operation would unfold in a way similar to Zhukov's plan. The rifle armies were instructed to open up breaches in the defence for the tank armies, which were then to plunge through to their objectives. The Third Guards Tank Army, commanded by Marshal P.S. Rybalko, had orders to enter the breach opened by the Third Guards south of Cottbus, secure the Trebin-Treuenbritzen-Luckenwalde sector by the fifth day, and seize Brandenburg by the sixth. Rybalko was also instructed to 'bear in mind' the possibility of sending forces up to attack Berlin at that point: a reinforced tank corps, joined by one of the Third Guards' rifle corps had been pre-designated for this. General D.D. Lelyushenko's Fourth Guards Tank Army, meanwhile, following closely behind Zhadov's Fifth Guards, was also to swing north-west after jumping off from the Spree and secure the Finsterwalde area by day three, and the Niemegk-Wittenberg-Arnsdorf line by day five, finally seizing Rathenow and Dessau by the sixth day. As a cover for the main assault, Konev directed the Second Polish Army and right-flank divisions of the 52nd Army to launch an all-out drive in the direction of Dresden.

Below: Soviet armour rumbles towards the main final confrontation. In a departure from the standard Soviet tactic of frontal assault, the battle for Berlin was planned as a series of flanking penetrations.

Above: German preparations involved a series of defensive strips, each one in theory capable of providing stiff resistance to the enemy's advance. Volkssturm *conscripts were heavily relied on for the rearmost strips.*

Below: A Soviet gun crew survey the ground ahead. The two Fronts committed to the Berlin offensive were able to mobilise over 6200 tanks and guns, outnumbering the defenders by well over five to one.

The third Front commander involved in the Berlin operation, Marshal Rokossovsky of the Second Belorussian, was less engaged in this kind of precise pre-battle planning than his colleagues in the First Belorussian and First Ukrainian. His forces, badly depreciated by reassignments and nearly constant combat, had been engaged, with a couple reinforcement units from the First Belorussian Front, in a major offensive operation right up until early April to take Danzig and Gdynia, and to clear Pomerania of German forces. Positioned now on the northern flank of the Red Army's Oder-Neisse front, along more than 350km (218 mile) from Danzig to Stettin, the Second Belorussian Front urgently needed to regroup and resupply its forces which comprised four rifle armies, three tank and one mechanised corps, numbering approximately 314,000 men with some 597 tanks. At the same time, it would have to turn its units from the recently completed eastward-moving operations against Danzig and Gdynia to the west and south in order to take over the northern part of the First Belorussian's sector, thereby freeing Zhukov's troops for the concentrated assault on Berlin. Over 300km (200 miles) of completely devastated terrain had to be covered in a couple of weeks. Tanks were carried by train, which could proceed only very slowly due to the overwhelming

Above: The 76.2mm (3in) Model 1942 ZiZ-3 field gun was one of the best examples of its type ever built. It could knock out most tanks, and captured guns were used in large numbers by the Germans.

destruction in the region. Other units moved equally slowly by truck, or on foot, marching with full gear and weaponry at a pace of 30km (20 miles) a day. Once the redeployment was accomplished, the Front had orders to commence offensive operations, forcing a crossing of the Oder near Schwedt and preventing the German Third Panzer Army from coming to Berlin's aid. After a good deal of argument by Rokossovsky, the Second Belorussian was given until 20 April (four days after Zhukov's and Konev's main assaults were to have begun) to complete its redeployment and commence its attack.

On 13 April the first of Rokossovksy's armies, the 65th Army commanded by General P.I. Batov, arrived in its new positions along the Altdamm-Ferdinandstein line, and the preparations for the final assault entered their final phase. For weeks, Zhukov and Konev had been moving up supplies, briefing their officers, and staging exercises. The attack, Zhukov had decided, would commence in the middle of the night, two hours before dawn on 16 April. To ensure his troops could see what they were doing and, he hoped, to blind and confuse the enemy, he took the unorthodox measure of employing 143 huge searchlights which, on his orders, would all be snapped on at the exact moment the artillery began pounding the German positions. The plan was not without its detractors, including Konev, who felt that the lights would blind their own troops as well as the Germans. Nevertheless, after testing the idea in war games, Zhukov was confident that the blinding lights would work only to his advantage. The searchlights were accordingly brought in from the Front Searchlight Company and the Fifth Air Defence Corps, manned by all-female crews who arrived on 15 April. They were placed at 366-9144m (400-1000yds) from the front line, at 183m (200yd) intervals, and had a range of 4.8km (3 miles). Konev, on the other hand, who still had to gain a crossing of the Neisse at the beginning of the attack, decided that the darkness would work to his benefit, and planned to maximise it with a dense smokescreen and a massive, 145-minute artillery barrage.

While the Soviets prepared for their Berlin offensive, the Anglo-American forces continued to race eastwards across north-central Germany. By 11 April the US Second Armored Division had reached the River Elbe at Magdeburg. The advance had been so swift that the forward reconnaissance units, reaching the western suburbs, had careened right into crowds of terrified shoppers. To the north of Magdeburg, the US Fifth Armored Division was poised to seize Tangermünde, just over 60km (38 miles) from the western edge of Berlin. To the south, American forces had succeeded in crossing the Elbe at two points. The Second Armored Division had gained Schönebeck, although not before the Germans blew the bridge. Taking Combat Command D, Brigadier General Sidney Hinds managed to force a crossing at nearby Westerhüsen, putting three battalions across by the evening of the 12th and attempting to reinforce the bridgehead via an improvised cable ferry. On the morning of the 14th, however, armoured units of General Wenck's 12th Army suddenly attacked with ferocious intensity. Wenck's idea for mobile shock forces proved to be very effective, as his inexperienced but eager soldiers wreaked havoc on the Americans' newly won positions. With the cable ferry knocked out in one of the first salvoes, the desperate GIs radioed for air support. Few planes were forthcoming, however, as the advance had been so swift that the airstrips had been left too far behind for effective support. By midday, General Hinds ordered a full retreat from the Elbe's eastern bank, though it took days for all of the survivors to trickle back to the western bank. In the end, 304 men had been lost.

Below: Katyusha rockets are loaded onto their firing platforms. The solid-propellant-driven rockets' impact and penetration ability were relatively low, but they were much feared for their sheer volume of fire.

Slightly further south, at Barby, roughly 24km (15 miles) south-east of Magdeburg, another American unit had a good deal more success. On 13 April, soldiers of the 83rd Infantry Division threw a battalion across the river on pontoons and, virtually unopposed, hurriedly began construction of a treadway bridge. It was completed by the end of the day and a painted sign honouring the new American president, sworn in the night before, graced its western approach: 'Truman Bridge. Gateway to Berlin. Courtesy of the 83rd Infantry Division'. Word of Eisenhower's determination not to use AEF (Allied Expeditionary Force) troops in the capture of Berlin had not yet been given to the commanders on the ground, and the men of the 83rd, like all Allied units closing in on the Elbe, were pumped up for the drive to the 'Jerry' capital. Although Eisenhower believed that Berlin's value as a military objective had diminished significantly, he had told Montgomery and Churchill that if an opportunity presented itself to take the capital ahead of the Soviets without excessive costs, it would be taken. The 83rd's new bridgehead on the Elbe seemed to present just such a

possibility. General Simpson's Ninth Army was now barely 100km (60 miles) from Berlin; somewhat further than the Red Army, but facing unexpectedly light resistance. When he was apprised of the 83rd's success by General Bradley, commander of the 12th Army Group, Eisenhower asked, 'Brad, what do you think it might cost us to break through from the Elbe and take Berlin?' Bradley was sure that the drive from the bridgehead to the outskirts of Berlin would not be too costly, but he was convinced that the battle for the city itself would be brutal. And, like the SCAF, he was concerned about penetrating too deeply into the future Soviet zone of occupation and committing men to gain positions from which they would have to withdraw. 'I estimate that it might cost us 100,000 men,' he told Eisenhower, adding, 'It would be a pretty stiff price to pay for a prestige objective, especially when we know that we've got to pull back and let the other fellow take over.'

Eisenhower was also disinclined to order a drive on Berlin because of his forces' rapid advance. Their supply lines were stretched dangerously thin. Land transport was practically non-existent; all but one railroad line across the Rhine were destroyed. To supply the advancing armies by air, the Troop Carrier Command had to keep hundreds of C-47s flying round the clock. Furthermore, it wasn't only the Allied military forces that SHAEF now had to concern itself with. As they pushed deeper and deeper into German territory, the Allies found themselves faced with the new role of occupation government: hundreds of thousands of German PoWs and civilians had to be fed and cared for medically; policing duties had to be arranged for; the repair and maintenance of roads, housing, and water supply had to be organised; and, most unexpectedly, hundreds of thousands of newly liberated, emaciated concentration camp inmates had to be cared for. All of these considerations convinced Eisenhower that his initial decision to leave Berlin to the Red Army was correct. Convinced that the most likely

Below: Exhausted Red Army soldiers attempt to gain some much needed rest near the body of a German civilian killed in the fighting. The Soviets had been advancing almost without a break since August 1943.

Left: 'Stalin Organs' were typically loaded with rockets weighing 17.5lb (7.9kg), with a range of just under five km (three miles). A 30lb (13.6kg) version of the rocket had a range of nearly 10km (six miles).

spots for a German last stand were in the alpine 'National Redoubt' and Norway, and that the Soviets could best handle Berlin, the Supreme Commander issued a three-part order: to 'hold a firm front in the central area on the Elbe'; to dispatch Montgomery's forces north from Hamburg to Lübeck and Denmark; and to 'initiate a powerful thrust' by the Sixth Army Group south to meet Soviet forces in the Danube valley and destroy the Nazis' Bavarian redoubt. 'Since the thrust on Berlin must await the outcome of the first three above, I do not include it as a part of my plan.'

On 15 April Eisenhower's orders were transmitted by Bradley to the commander of the Ninth Army, Lieutenant General William Simpson. 'You must stop on the Elbe. You are not to advance any farther in the direction of Berlin. I'm sorry, Simp, but there it is.' Simpson was stunned, and, as he later recalled, 'heartbroken'. He passed the orders down to his Second Armored Division commander, General Hinds, who already had troops back on the eastern side of the Elbe, this time thanks to the 83rd's 'Truman Bridge'. Hinds was reportedly so flummoxed that he momentarily forgot his military discipline. 'No sir,' he exclaimed. 'That's not right. We're going to Berlin.' Simpson was deeply pained to have to throw water on his officer's enthusiasm. He told Hinds that he could keep some of his men in their eastern bank positions, but added that they were not to go any farther. 'This is the end of the war for us,' he said.

The death of US President Franklin D. Roosevelt just days before the Allies thought victory was in their hands had no effect on operational planning but deeply affected all involved in the conflict. The Americans were understandably grieved to learn of the death of their commander-in-chief and president for the last 16 years. He was the only president many of the GIs had ever really known and many wept openly. But the Soviets, leaders and soldiers alike, were also profoundly saddened by the news. Roosevelt had been considered by most, including Stalin, as a leader they could trust, with whom they could cooperate to both sides' mutual benefit. They distrusted Chruchill, and President Truman was unknown to them. However, Roosevelt was, as an emotional Foreign Minister Molotov told US Ambassador William Averell

Right: Hitler confers with General Theodor Busse (far right), commander of the Ninth Army. The Ninth held the key position in Army Group Vistula, directly facing Zhukov's massive build-up on the Oder.

Harriman, as cited by John Erickson, 'a true friend of Russia'. Even many ordinary Germans expressed a certain sadness at the news of the passing of a man they ultimately admired.

The German leadership, on the other hand, was positively giddy. 'My Führer, I congratulate you!' Goebbels crowed into the telephone to Hitler. 'Roosevelt is dead! It is written in the stars. The last half of April will be the turning point for us. This is Friday, April 13th. It is the turning point!' He then ordered champagne for the entire staff of the Propaganda Ministry. Earlier in the month Goebbels had two astrological horoscopes prepared for Hitler, both of which, he claimed in his diary, predicted a series of devastating reversals at the beginning of 1945, followed by a decisive turn in Germany's favour in the second half of April. His superstitious mind had been inflamed by reading Thomas Carlyle's *History of Friedrich II of Prussia*, which described how, during the Seven Years' War (1756-1763), having battled against a coalition of France, Austria and Russia, Prussia had been saved in the sixth year by the death of Czarina Elizabeth, and had emerged victorious. Now, in the sixth year of World War II, Roosevelt had died. For weeks Goebbels had been predicting to Hitler that something like the 'miracle of the House of Brandenburg' would intervene to save them. Now, eerily, Hitler's destiny seemed to be proved. 'This news will provoke a complete change in the entire German people's morale, for one can and must consider this event a manifestation of fate and justice!' Goebbels told the finance minister Count Schwerin von Krosigk. Krosigk agreed, writing in his diary that 'This was the Angel of History! We felt its wings flutter through the room. Was that not the turn of fortune we awaited so anxiously?' But at the same time he cautioned Goebbels to 'take the press into tow at once. New possibilities may now arise, and the press must not spoil them by clumsiness.' That very day Goebbels issued instructions to the press to avoid rejoicing over Roosevelt's death and to write entirely noncommittally about Truman, so as to preserve the possibility of a negotiated peace with the Americans.

Hitler was every bit as superstitious as Goebbels, and he seized on the news of Roosevelt's death as vindication of his refusal to surrender. Still, the elation was markedly tempered by the emotional depression and physical debility which had been increasingly affecting the Führer for the past months. Ever more suspicious, morose, and fatalistic, on 15

Below: Soviet artillery in action. As the preparations for the assault on Berlin were finalised, Red Army troops were rallied to the effort: 'The time has come to inflict the final defeat on the enemy.'

April Hitler allowed his long-time mistress, Eva Braun, to join him in the bunker; a sign that he considered the end near. Nevertheless, Goebbels' news buoyed him up at least long enough to compose a strident proclamation to his troops, the last he would ever write.

'SOLDIERS OF THE EASTERN FRONT!

Our mortal enemy – the Jewish Bolshevik – has begun his final massive attack. He hopes to smash Germany and wipe out our people ...

If in the coming days and weeks every soldier on the eastern front does his duty, Asia's last assault will fail ...

Berlin remains German, Vienna [which had fallen to the Soviets on 13 April] shall once more be German, and Europe shall never be Russian ... At this hour the entire German population looks to you, my fighters of the east, and hopes only that through your tenacity, your fanaticism, by your weapons and under your leadership the Bolshevik attack will drown in a bath of blood. At the very moment fate removed the greatest war criminal of all times [Roosevelt] from the world, the turning point of this war shall be determined.

Adolf Hitler'

Above: Germans wait for the onslaught which they know is coming. Zhukov's Front had succeeded in securing a bridgehead on the west bank, but the Germans still held long stretches of the Oder.

That same day, 15 April, back at the Oder front, Heinrici saw the signs of an impending assault. The Soviets had been making sporadic feints against his defences. He began to prepare orders for his men to fall-back to their secondary positions.

CHAPTER FIVE

Breakout from the Oder

When it finally came, in the early hours of 16 April, the Soviet assault was preceded by the largest artillery bombardment the war had yet seen. However, thanks to General Heinrici's cunning, most of the rounds fell harmlessly on German positions that had been emptied of their troops.

General Heinrici knew his enemy well. Despite the few innovations which Zhukov had incorporated into his plans for this, his greatest battle, he was basically following a well-tried Red Army attack plan. The *Voyenniie razvedky* (reconnaissances-in-force) tactic of probing the enemy's front lines for the emplacement and combat readiness of their defences was a Soviet favourite; it signalled to the savvy defender that a full-bore assault could be expected within the next 48 hours. All day on Saturday 14 April, reinforced rifle battalions of Zhukov's main forward-strike force – the 47th, Third Shock, Fifth Shock, and Eighth Guards Armies – had been making test feints into Ninth Army's positions. Supported by a few tanks, and covered by artillery fire, the units pushed towards Seelow, in places as far as 5km (3 miles). The reconnaissance forays succeeded in charting a number of minefields and creating some havoc with the German fire system. But they 'failed', in the judgement of historian John Erickson, inasmuch as neither Zhukov nor his subordinate commanders recognised that the second line of

Left: Shortly before dawn on 16 April, the First Ukrainian and First Belorussian Fronts opened offensives directed at Berlin from their positions on the Oder. Here Soviet soldiers wrestle a field gun across the river.

German defences was the crucial one. It was here at which the opening bombardment would have to be directed if the initial assault was not to be seriously stymied. In any event, the Germans were not misled by the Soviet feints; captured German soldiers confessed to their Soviet interrogators that their commanders had told them that the main assault would not come for another day or two.

Though the Battle of Berlin is usually portrayed as having begun in the early-morning hours of 16 April, it could be said to have actually begun the evening before. Early on the night of the 15th, aircraft of the Fourth and 16th Air Armies began to pound the Germans' first defensive strip. By then, however, Heinrici had already decided that the proper moment had arrived. Shortly after 2030 hours, the commander-in-chief of Army Group Vistula suddenly ceased his pacing at his field HQ. 'It was as though he had suddenly sniffed the very air,' said an aide. 'I believe the attack will take place in the early hours, tomorrow,' Heinrici told his staff, and issued a brief order to General Busse, commander of the Ninth Army: 'Move back and take up positions on the second line of defence.' Not all of his generals were pleased with the order to give up their front-line positions; to many it felt like they were retreating before the battle even began. To such complaints the *Giftzwerg* responded brusquely that in a steel mill one doesn't leave one's head under the trip hammer; one pulls it back in time. Under cover of darkness, the pull-back went off remarkably well. Only a handful of troops were left in well-fortified positions on the front line, many unaware that the bulk of their army was withdrawing to secondary positions.

Above: The lull before the storm. General Heinrici's intelligence, and his instincts, had been remarkably accurate regarding the timing of the Soviet attack, and he was not deceived by the Soviets' repeated feints.

Meanwhile, the Soviet troops were gathering for their customary last-minute pep-talks. In passionate speeches, genuinely emotional political officers mixed their traditional anti-fascist Party rhetoric with good old-fashioned patriotism and appeals to military camaraderie. At the end, the Red Army soldiers took turns swearing on oath on their red flags to fight with bravery and honour. In the words of Eighth Guards commander Colonel General Vassiliy

Chuikov, 'Lenin's face looked down as if alive from the scarlet banners on the soldier-liberators, as if summoning them to be resolute in the last fight with the hateful foe.'

In the pre-dawn darkness everyone waited tensely. At the stroke of 0400 hours, as Zhukov had ordered, over 40,000 field guns, mortars, and Katyusha rocket-launchers thundered into life. In a ferocious barrage unlike anything seen before in the war, over a million shells and rockets (over 100,000 tonnes) were spewed into the German positions. Eyewitnesses have described the deafening din and terrifying convulsions of the ground as forests and villages as far away as 8km (5 miles) burst into flame and disintegrated under the storm of steel and explosives. The bombardment, joined by hundreds of sorties by the Red Army's air forces, continued for half an hour. A few minutes before it ended, thousands of green and red flares illuminated the dark night sky. On that signal, the women soldiers operating the searchlights snapped on their huge instruments, instantly flooding the night with an artificial day of a hundred billion candlelight. The starkly lit up scene of the Seelow Heights being blown to bits in front of them was, Zhukov wrote later, 'an immensely fascinating and impressive sight, and never before in my life had I felt anything like what I felt then'. Captain Sergei Golbov, a front-line correspondent for the Red Army press, reported that the massive bombardment released a huge rush of pent-up energy and emotion in the Soviet troops. All around he saw 'troops cheering as though they were fighting the Germans hand-to-hand and everywhere men were firing whatever weapons they had even though they could see no target'.

As the aerial and artillery bombardment continued, shifting their range deeper into the German positions, the mechanised and infantry units were given the order to begin the assault. Cheering and yelling wildly, hundreds of thousands of men and machines charged across the Oder and towards the Seelow bluffs. The numbers still on the eastern bank of the river were so high, and the fighting spirit of the Soviet troops so great, that in many places, frustrated by the long waits to get across the clogged bridges and ferries, soldiers commandeered anything they could find – boats, barrels, pieces of wood, tree limbs – to paddle across the river, or simply threw themselves into the water, fully loaded down with weapons and gear, to swim across. Captain Golbov recalled seeing the regimental doctor, 'a huge man named Nicolaieff, running down the river bank dragging behind him a ridiculously small boat'. As a physician, Nicolaieff was 'supposed to stay behind the lines at the field hospital, but there he was in this tiny boat, rowing like hell'.

The Germans hardly fired back at all; only a few scattered machine-guns could be discerned from the other side. At first the assault made good progress. When the opening bombardment ended after 30 minutes and the first radio-phone reports began coming in, Chuikov could report that 'the first objectives have been taken' by his Eighth Guards Army. Zhukov, who had been observing the opening of the attack from Chuikov's command post with a perfect view of the Küstrin bridgehead, congratulated his subordinate warmly.

The Marshal's relief quickly gave way to frustration and anger, however, as the attack swiftly bogged down after just a couple kilometres on the approach to the Seelow Heights. Although in his memoirs Zhukov himself recounted no difficulties with them, part of the problem was the searchlights. Several of his sub-commanders reported that the lights hindered

Below: Flame trails from a load of Katyusha rockets light up the pre-dawn sky. The opening barrage of the Berlin offensive was unlike anything anybody in the war had ever seen before.

Above: Volkssturm *troops wait in their trenches for the first Soviet wave to cross the Oder. The Germans waited, hidden, until the tanks were very nearly on top of them, before firing from point-blank range.*

at least as much as they helped the advancing troops. Chuikov wrote in his own memoirs that, blinded and confused by the powerful beams, the troops in many sectors simply 'came to a halt in front of the streams and canals running across the Oder valley, waiting for the light of dawn to show them clearly the obstacles they had to overcome'. General Andreia Getman, corps commander in Katukov's First Guards Tank Army, had complained to Lieutenant General Nikolai Popiel, a member of Zhukov's general staff and a military historian, that, 'they didn't blind the main forces of the enemy. But I'll tell you what they did do – they absolutely spotlighted our tanks and infantry for the German gunners.' In other sectors, the searchlight operators were given orders to turn the lights off, only to have the orders almost immediately countermanded by higher-ups, resulting in a surreal strobe-light effect over the terrifying battlefield.

But other, more serious problems also slowed the attack. The marshy, boggy terrain, criss-crossed by flooded streams and irrigation canals, proved even more difficult than expected. Many of the SPGs and mechanised vehicles were mired down and started to lag behind, adding to the already chaotic traffic problem. Helplessly churning their wheels and tracks in the mud and water, the bogged-down vehicles were irresistible targets to the German artillery, which now began pounding the Soviets, completely destroying several tanks. The biggest obstacle was the *Hauptkanal* (Main Canal), located just before the Seelow Heights. The few bridges were under direct German artillery fire, and the banks were too steep for the vehicles to ford the canal which was too swollen by the spring thaw to be manoeuvrable. Here Chuikov's main axis of assault came to a dead stop, roughly 1.5km (1600yds) from its starting point.

Zhukov, not a commander known for gentleness or diplomacy, was furious. When informed by Chuikov that the advance had stalled, the commander of the First Belorussian Front exploded: 'What the hell do you mean – your troops are pinned down?' As the unflapped Chuikov explained what had happened, according to Popiel, Zhukov let loose with 'a stream of extremely forceful expressions' – no doubt a decided understatement of the earthy language of this peasant's son. Zhukov knew well that the attack would not be easy and that they were working under a preposterously short timetable for the conquest of a city the size of Berlin. He was under huge pressure from Stavka, and his leadership style had always been to keep the pressure on his subordinate commanders. But this outburst was clearly more than just a motivational tool: he hadn't anticipated such immediate difficulties. Zhukov and most of his general staff had fully expected the initial artillery and air bombardment to demolish the primary line of German defences, enabling them to gain the Heights and puncture the forward positions before the Germans had a chance to organise any kind of effective resistance. It was now becoming clear that the Germans had divined their intentions and pulled back most of their forces in time to escape the barrage; they were still almost entirely intact. 'Our artillery fire hit everything but the enemy,' was the bitter comment of the commander of the Third Shock Army, General Vasili Kuznetsov. 'As usual, we stuck to the book, and by now the Germans know our methods.'

At the same time, however, Heinrici knew he was in no position for self-congratulatory gloating. He went over the reports from the front with Busse, commander of the Ninth Army, in Army Group Vistula's command post in the Schönewalde forest north of Berlin. Though Busse had known what to expect, the opening bombardment had been truly terrifying; in his words, 'the worst ever'. After the first reports from the front, many in the command post assumed that their forward defences had been totally annihilated. But the *Giftzwerg*'s plan had worked well. At Frankfurt, defenders had even managed to repel the Soviets, throwing them back from their starting positions. But it had all cost the hard-strapped Germans significantly. Some of the Ninth's commanders reported that they were outnumbered ten to one. One of Busse's division commanders reported: 'They come at us in hordes, in wave after wave, without regard to loss of life. We fire our machine guns, often at point-blank range, until they turn red hot. My men are fighting until they run out of ammunition. Then they are simply wiped out or completely overrun. How long this can continue I don't know.' Heinrici knew that it was just a matter of time. He had neither the men nor the weapons to hold off the vast numbers of the enemy. And while Zhukov's assault was, for the moment, pinned down, he wondered what Konev to the south and

Above: Marshal Zhukov (right, foreground) observes the progress of the battle from a command post overlooking the Küstrin bridgehead. The Soviets quickly ran into difficulties, unable to adhere to Zhukov's plan.

Below: A Soviet assault gun division sweeping around Berlin's flank to encircle the city pauses to hear the order of the day from their commander before resuming their advance.

Rokossovsky in the north were up to. The answer was not long in coming.

At 0500 hours, exactly one hour after Zhukov's assault had begun, Konev gave the order to his First Ukrainian Front to start their assault crossing of the River Neisse. An artillery barrage opened the operation, but rather than the massive, carpet bombardment employed by his colleague, Konev's artillery batteries had painstakingly charted the exact position of the German defensive lines and strong-points and zeroed their guns in on those targets. Other batteries carefully blasted out corridors for the assault troops to take once they got across the river. In order to hide his troops' movements in the already breaking daylight, Konev chose, unlike Zhukov, to prolong the darkness as much as possible. To this end, a formation of specially equipped Shturmovik fighter planes flew in low over the river, laying a thick blanket of dense, white smoke. Braving the German anti-aircraft fire – although this was not very heavy – the planes roared up and down the river valley, 15.2m (50ft) above the surface, leaving a 400km (250 mile) section of the river with both its banks perfectly encased. Konev's plans called for an attack front of only 80km (50 miles), centred around Buchholz and

Above: Soviet troops with a Lend-Lease US M4 Sherman tank inside the suburbs of Berlin. Note the white flag, and the Soviet tanker speaking with the German civilian in the doorway.

Triebel, but if the smoke curtain held, it would prevent the Germans from knowing exactly where the attack came from. Fortunately the conditions were just right. Dry weather and a slight wind – a half a metre a second (just over a mile an hour), enough to help spread the smoke without dissipating it too quickly – combined with the black smoke from burning forests and villages to bring the smokescreen to a perfect consistency and altitude.

After 40 minutes of selective artillery and aerial bombardment, Konev gave the order for the troops to begin the crossing. At 150 different spots, hidden from German observation by smoke, assault boats carried the first soldiers across, towing small, portable bridges behind them. Combat engineers jumped into the neck-deep water to brace the bridge sections and bolt them together, and also raced to set up cable ferries in several locations. By shortly after 0600 hours, SPGs and 85mm anti-tank guns, followed by tanks and more infantry, were pouring across the bridges and ferries to strengthen the newly gained west-bank bridgeheads. By now the smoke-screen was beginning to scatter, but the Soviets had achieved what they needed to. By 0735 hours, with 133 of the 150 crossing points secured and operating, Konev received a report that advance units of Pukhov's 13th Army and Rybalko's Third Guards Tank Army were already engaging the enemy at Triebel, and had cracked through the centre of their defences. Meanwhile, supported by continued artillery fire from the eastern bank, the rest of the tanks and guns in the new bridgeheads went into action, providing the necessary cover for the engineers to erect the larger bridges for bringing across the heavy artillery. The first 30 tonne bridge was completed by 0800 hours, and at 1100 hours the first 60 tonne bridge was open for business.

That was the signal for the second echelon to go into action, to begin the drive into the German defences and, if Konev had his way, to Berlin. The 62nd Guards Tank Brigade, supported by armoured units from the 29th Guards Motor-Rifle Brigade, and the 16th Guards Mechanised Brigade – both from General D.D. Lelyushenko's Fourth Guards Tank Army – roared across the river at the stroke of noon, with orders to separate from the infantry as quickly as possible and barrel forward with all speed towards Berlin. Both Zhukov and the 'soyuznichki' had to be beaten to the 'main prize'.

At the moment, however, the First Belorussian was not in a position to offer much competition. Chuikov's Eighth Guards and the other units of the main strike force continued to fight stubbornly at the *Hauptkanal.* They had made some progress, clearing the first two lines in this Forward Defence Zone with the help of air strikes against the Germans' heavy artillery. But the third line, at the very base of the Seelow Heights and up onto its lower slopes, continued to hold out. The main brunt of the assault was being carried by the 47th Army, Fifth Shock, Third Shock, and Ninth Tank Corps. Forced to redeploy and fan out in an attempt to find an easier route up the rough incline, the Soviet tanks and soldiers time and again chewed their way forward a few thousand yards, only to run headlong into well-hidden and fortified German strong-points, or to be slammed back by fierce counter-attacks. Historian John Toland has reconstructed one part of the scene from the recollections of a young Luftwaffe soldier, Gerhard Cordes, who fought in that defensive line:

'The din of motors and clank of treads was tremendous. The earth trembled. He picked up a Panzerfaust. From behind came an abrupt, heavy-throated chorus; 88mm shells screeched overhead and smashed into the first tanks. Flames shot up,

Below: After capturing yet another German town on the approach to Berlin, Soviet infantrymen take the time to pose for a photo on their 'Stalin Organ', a truck mounting Katyusha rockets.

Above: Shturmovik bombers fly past the Ullstein-Haus in the Tempelhof district of Berlin. By the time of the battle for the city, the Red Army enjoyed almost completely unchallenged air superiority.

parts of metal and shell fragments rained over the foxholes. At least six tanks were on fire, but others kept coming on and on. In the reddish glare they stood out with clarity and were helpless before the withering fire of big guns. Red Army infantrymen began erupting from the middle of this massive conflagration. There must have been 800, and they scrambled up the hill shouting, Cordes thought, like madmen. The airmen fired rifles and burp guns, and hundreds of Russians toppled over. The rest came on, still yelling. More fell and at last, like a great wave that has shattered its strength against a jetty, the attackers fell back.'

As Cordes surveyed the scene around him, Toland continues, it seemed to him that at least 30 per cent of the Luftwaffe men left in the front lines to stall the enemy advance lay dead, and they only had two 88mm guns remaining. But, for the time being, they were holding the Soviets off.

By 1100 hours, seven hours after the attack began, with traffic jamming up behind the stalled forward-strike force, Zhukov could stand it no longer. Ignoring his own second thoughts, he now decided to throw his tank armies, which he had been saving until the treacherous Heights had been taken, immediately into the battle. There was no time to be lost in a lengthy siege of this forward defence position, so he intended to use brute force to bulldoze a path through to Berlin. His two top tank commanders, Colonel Generals Katukov and Bogdanov, were disturbed by the prospect of sending their tank units, the First and Second Guards Tank Armies respectively, onto the steep slopes; crisscrossed by ravines, minefields, and hidden German tank-busters, they left very little room for the kind of manoeuvring for which the tanks were made. Chuikov had in fact already ordered a renewed attack by his supporting infantry units to begin at 1300 hours. But Zhukov would not be dissuaded: the Heights must be taken by morning. By 1330 hours, the tank armies had been deployed into the Küstrin bridgehead and were advancing towards the final German defensive line before the Seelow Heights. Katukov's First Guards Tank Army was ordered to join Chuikov's Eighth Guards and blast open the heights, while Bogdanov and the Second Guards Tank Army were directed to co-operate with the Fifth Shock Army and attack in the direction of Neu Hardenberg-Bernau.

The tactic eventually succeeded, but only with great difficulty. The tank units added welcome muscle to Chuikov's main assault, but they made the jammed-up traffic even worse, leaving a large portion of the supporting infantry and artillery units – which would be needed for the consolidation of any gains by the armour – stranded on the boggy roadsides. Nevertheless, by 1800 hours, the Fourth Guards Corps, on the right flank of Chuikov's assault, had advanced against much resistance to the outskirts of Seelow itself. Zhukov insisted that the attack continue into the night, and by shortly before midnight on 16 April, Chuikov's infantry finally succeeded in capturing three houses on the northern

Below: Heinrici's fall-back strategy ran counter to the instincts of many of his soldiers, but it proved to be extremely effective in preserving the Germans' ability to resist the Soviet advance.

Above: Soviet armour advances through a forest near Berlin. It took Zhukov's forces nearly 24 hours to gain no more than 10km (6 miles) of territory – in some sectors significantly less – on the first day.

side of the town; the first concrete prizes won in the Battle for Berlin. Into the early hours of the morning Katukov's tank units continued to press the attack, sending scores of tanks in to blast away at the German positions, which continued to offer stubborn and deadly resistance, destroying a huge number of those tanks with point-blank Panzerfaust, 88mm, and 155mm artillery fire. As dawn approached, the forward Soviet strike forces had gained something like 5-10km (3-6 miles).

Still wanting the breakthrough which would shatter German resistance on the Heights, Zhukov ordered a fresh assault, beginning with another 30-40 minute bombardment, to commence in the morning. His armies were to use the intervening nighttime hours to regroup, resupply, and redeploy from the day's fighting, which had left them badly disorganised and scattered. At the same time, to deny the Germans any respite during this regrouping, and to soften the defences which had obviously suffered little during the first massive bombardment, Zhukov called in 800 Petlyakov Pe-2 bombers from the Red Army's Long-Range Aviation force to pound the German strong-points. At 0900 hours sharp, the First Belorussian loosed a 30-minute artillery barrage, with still more aerial bombardment. And again, even before the barrage was ended, wave after wave of Soviet infantry and armour swarmed up the slopes toward Seelow. Soviet commanders were surprised and amused to notice that the tank crews had concocted an ingenious defence against the deadly *Panzerfäuste*: they had scavenged mattresses of bare bedspring coils from German houses and attached them in bunches to the fronts of their T-34s, so that the Panzerfaust shells literally bounced off before they could detonate. After several hours of vicious combat, towards 1100 hours, the 11th Guards Tank Corps and 8th Guards Mechanised Corps reached the north-south railway line which ran along the edge of the Heights, capturing both Friedersdorf and Dolgelin, south of Seelow. At the same time, the 11th Tank Corps together with the 35th Guards Rifle Division of Fourth Guards Corps had punched their way into Seelow from the north against severe resistance. Elsewhere, Third and Fifth Shock Armies with Ninth Guards Tank Corps succeeded in forcing the Alte Oder and began to chip away at the German strong-point at Kunersdorf. By the end of the day, Chuikov's Eighth Guards and Babadzhanyan's 11th Guards Tank Corps finally captured Seelow, through which the Reichsstraße 1 ran directly west to Berlin.

The First Belorussian Front now stood poised, literally, on the road to Berlin. But the battle for the Heights was far from over. Despite the day's gains, Zhukov was frustrated and worried. The flanks continued to offer dogged resistance to Third Shock and

Above: Despite high morale and a will to fight, the German defenders were taking a beating. South of Küstrin, Konev's First Ukrainian Front was making quick progress against Schörner's Army Group Centre.

47th Armies, and the hindmost line of the Germans' Forward Defence Zone remained largely intact. Zhukov's forces were a full day behind the schedule worked out with the Stavka, and he had learned that Konev's First Ukrainian Front had been enjoying much more impressive success than the First Belorussian, and might beat it into Berlin, reaping the glory of raising the Soviet Hammer and Sickle over the Reichstag. Zhukov's two radio-telephone conversations with Stalin during the previous day had not been pleasant. His first report, in the afternoon, had informed the Soviet leader that they were encountering unexpectedly heavy resistance in securing the Seelow Heights, but that the enemy's lines had been breeched. Stalin casually replied that Konev had managed to cross the Neisse 'without difficulty' and was advancing rapidly towards his primary targets. Ordered to reinforce his artillery and bomber support of the tank armies and report back again before the end of the day, Zhukov had dutifully called back, though as late as possible, hoping to have some success to report. Upon hearing of the continued lack of progress, Stalin became downright surly, chiding Zhukov for sending in the First Guards Tank Army against the original plan and demanding to know whether he could assure the capture of the Heights by the end of the next day, 17 April. He added again, in an undisguised attempt to provoke some jealous competition, that he had been in touch with Konev, who was already in a position to turn part of his forces towards Berlin, and that the Stavka was considering permitting him to do so. Zhukov knew well that there was a real danger that a prolongued assault on the centre of the German forward defences could consume his armies before they ever get to the main target, a loss which could spell catastrophe, even for the 'help' which was being offered from the acceleration of Konev's and Rokossovsky's flanking operations.

Konev, meanwhile, although he had somewhat fewer forces at his disposal than Zhukov, and more targets (including the sizeable cities of Cottbus and Dresden), had no intention of merely providing support to Zhukov's conquest of Berlin. Pressing the gains his troops had made on the first day, he too had ordered a fresh assault on the morning of 17 April, but in this case the attack was directed against new objectives. During the first day of the operation, the First Ukrainian's Third Guards, Fifth Guards and 13th Armies had advanced within a 10km (17 mile) wide corridor to a depth of 14km (almost 9 miles), over halfway to the River Spree and Cottbus. Similarly, the 52nd Army and Polish Second Army had succeeded in advancing nearly 10km (6 miles) towards Dresden. The advance had been so rapid that it left the smouldering woods littered with the shattered remains of German and Soviet tanks, guns, and soldiers, and Busse had been forced to commit his operational as well as his tactical reserves in those sectors. At 0800 hours on 17 April, preceded by a short but heavy artillery barrage, Konev's main strike-force pressed the assault on towards the Spree. With Konev in attendance, the tanks of the Third Guards Tank Army sped to the Spree, reaching it by midday, and without waiting for the construction of any kind of bridges, plunged into the 0.9m (3ft) deep water and roared across the river, which was over 46m (150ft) wide. Although they were too late to cut off the German retreat across the river, the irregular light-arms fire which pinged harmlessly off their T-34s indicated an as yet German unorganised defence. By that afternoon, Konev's armies had driven past Cottbus and were forcing their way to Lübben, the point at which the operational boundary between his and Zhukov's forces had been erased by Stalin.

Pleased with his men's successes, and confident of his ability to press the advantage, Konev placed a call to Stalin. Learning of First Ukrainian's successes, Stalin mentioned Zhukov's difficulties. A period of silence followed, then Stalin cagily asked Konev if it were possible to redeploy Zhukov's mobile tank units and send them through the corridor recently opened by Konev's operations, and on to Berlin from there. Accustomed to Stalin's habit of playing subordinates off against each other, Konev replied smoothly: 'Comrade Stalin, this will take too much time and will add considerable confusion ... The situation on our front is developing favourably. We have adequate forces and we can turn both tank armies towards Berlin.' After listening to Konev's proposal, which included advancing through the headquarters of the German General Staff at Zossen, Stalin agreed. 'Turn your tank armies on Berlin.'

Later that day, in what was without doubt a most unpleasant conversation for Zhukov, the commander of First Belorussian learned from Stalin of the new

Below: Zhukov and Konev's forces acted as a pincer movement on Berlin. Stalin's boundary line between the two ended at Lübben, encouraging Konev to race Zhukov for the ultimate prize of Berlin.

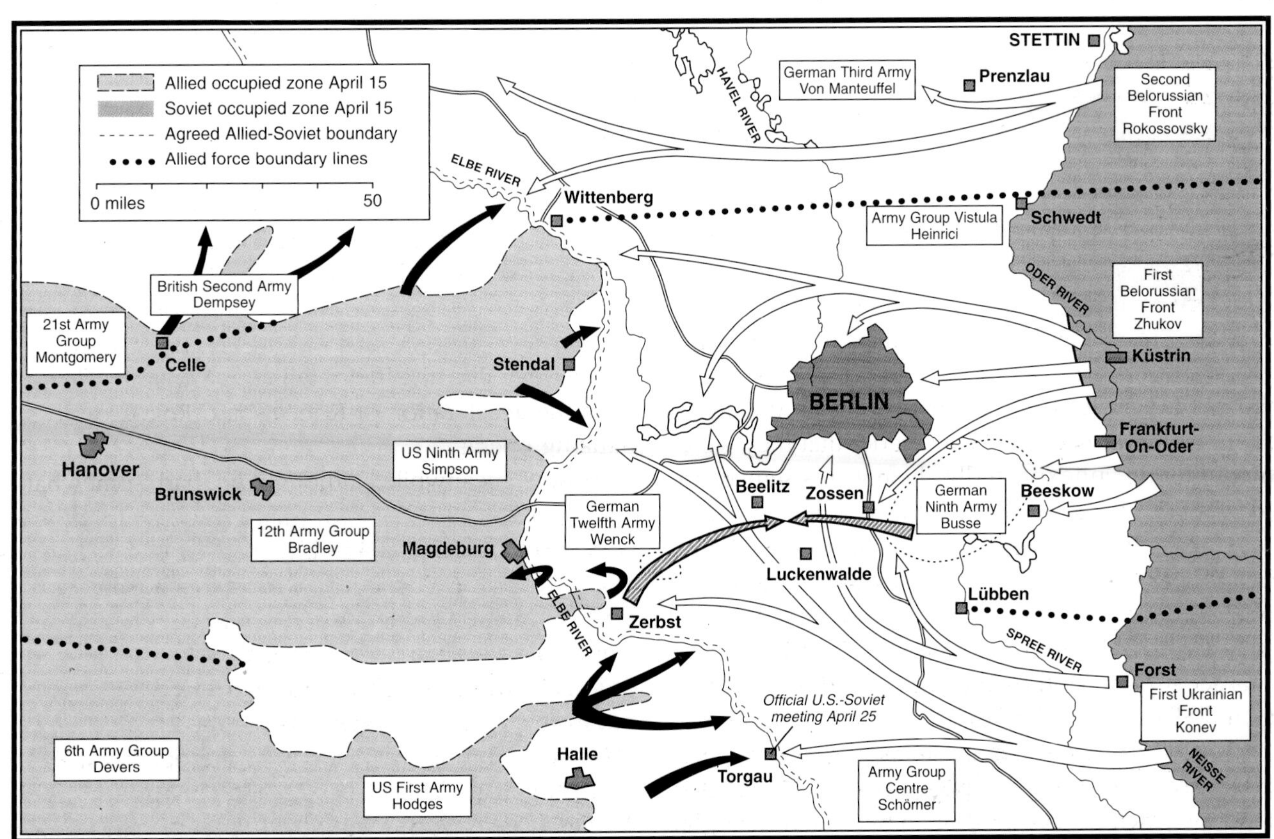

operational boundaries issued by Stavka. The reprimand stung him. A correspondent for the military paper Red Star, Lieutenant Colonel Pavel Troyanovskii, was present when Zhukov received the call from Moscow, and recalled later that 'Zhukov, a man with all the marks of an iron will about his face and a man who did not like to share his glory with anyone, was extremely worked up.' Determined to speed up his advance, whatever the cost, Zhukov now took his own commanders to task. Orders were sent down on 18 April to all army commanders that the pace of the attack must be increased, and that every piece of artillery was to be moved up to the first echelons and positioned no more than a few thousand yards from the forward edge of the front. Further, realising that the biggest cause of his failure so far was a deficient knowledge of the German defences, and thus a wasteful use of artillery and air power, Zhukov ordered all commanders from army down to brigade level to go in person to the forward echelons, inspect their troops' deployment and supplies, and determine the precise locations and strengths of the opposing German forces. They had until 1200 hours on 19 April to complete their reports, redeploy and resupply their units, and issue operational orders for a renewed offensive. In order to avoid the kind of traffic problems which had plagued Chuikov's earlier advance, the commanders of Eighth Guards and Fifth Shock Armies would be responsible for co-ordinating the movements of infantry and armour, exchanging officers with the tank brigades of First and Second Guards Tank Armies. All transport vehicles would be taken off the road, and the soldiers from mechanised infantry units would move on foot. Finally, Zhukov's orders warned, any officer who proved to be 'incapable of carrying out assignments' or showed 'lack of resolution' would be immediately dismissed. They would succeed, or they would be sacked.

Meanwhile, the attack continued. Both sides battled furiously over the final line on the Seelow position. By now the German trenches and foxholes had been pulverised into a barren, pockmarked moonscape reminiscent of the Somme battlefield in World War I. But still the Germans offered determined resistance. Hampered by lack of manoeuvring space, the Soviet attackers found their attempted thrusts repeatedly stalled or beaten back by vigorous German counter-attacks. Major General I.I. Yushchuk's 11th Tank Corps, supporting the Fourth Guards Rifle

Below: German propaganda and prejudices created an almost hysterical fear of the advancing Soviets. Rape, torture, murder, and enslavement were all expected to occur. This graffiti reads, 'Victory or Siberia'.

Corps on the right flank of the Eighth Guards' main attack axis, succeeded in making some progress, grinding their way slowly but determinedly towards Müncheberg. But on Chuikov's other flank, 69th Army had been stonewalled by the German defence, making no appreciable gains for the past 72 hours. It was clear to Chuikov that the German plan was to channel the main force of the attack southwards, away from Berlin. So rather than report the danger to his exposed left flank, which would have meant diverting some of his own troops to assist 69th Army, Chuikov decided to ignore the problem and continue to drive his men towards Berlin. By the evening of the 18th, however, he had dispatched two divisions from his 28th Corps to reinforce that flank. At the same time, north-west of Seelow, Third Shock Army had run into a hornet's nest at Batzlow. As the Soviet troops attempted to battle their way into the village, heavy mortar and artillery fire poured down on them from the surrounding high ground, covering every road and approach, and bringing the drive to a halt. It was decided that only a night attack could succeed in taking the village. So at 2200 hours, after a 30-minute artillery barrage of their own, the Soviet troops moved in, supported by tanks and self-propelled guns. The attack succeeded, but it wasn't until dawn, after some very heavy fighting, that the Germans were driven out and Batzlow was finally taken. From that point, Fifth Shock Army took over to open up and exploit the breach.

By this time, three days of the massive Soviet assault were beginning to tell on the German defenders. On the whole, morale remained remarkably high, but the losses had been heavy. Everywhere shortages, the inexperience of some troops, and sheer exhaustion were taking their toll. Everything from weapons and ammunition to fuel was in critically short supply; in some sectors the troops could only mill about and hope that the Soviets wouldn't reach them before their fuel did. Communications were beginning to break down. In the most crucial sectors, the eastern approach to Berlin from Küstrin, the Germans had already given up almost 30km (18 miles); some command posts had been forced to relocate so often that the troops had no idea where they were or how to contact them. It was not uncommon for reinforcements or officers sent to take over beleaguered units to arrive and discover there was nothing to reinforce or command; the outfits were already captured or wiped

Above: Falling into Soviet hands was the worst fear of any German soldier. Expecting torture or execution, they much preferred capture by the Americans or British. Some chose suicide over surrender to the Soviets.

out or, in a few cases, had abandoned their positions. Adding to the confusion, throngs of civilian refugees clogged the roads, seriously hampering the defenders' mobility.

To the south, Busse's forces were holding steady. But squeezed between Zhukov's relentless assault from the east and Konev's surge upwards, which had already halfway encircled them, this front too started to crumble. Only in the north had the Oder front held intact. General Hasso von Manteuffel's Third Panzer Army, positioned north from Eberswalde to the Oder Bay facing Rokossovky's Second Belorussian Front, had so far been spared the fury of the Soviets' assault. But cruising above the enemy positions on the other side of the Oder in his Storch reconnaissance plane, Von Manteuffel knew it would not be long; with brazen disregard for the German plane, the Soviet troops were busily preparing for a huge offensive. He knew, too, that when Rokossovky's offensive did start, he would be unable to do much to halt it. The Third Panzer Army had very few Panzers left: a large number of them had been reassigned by Heinrici to bolster the Ninth Army's defence of Berlin. He had little faith in the reinforcements he had received in compensation. SS General Felix Steiner, commander of Third SS Corps holding Von Manteuffel's southern flank, reported to his superior with undisguised scorn: 'I have just received 5000 Luftwaffe pilots, each with his little Iron Cross hanging around his neck. Tell me, what am I supposed to do with them?' 'I have no doubt,' Von Manteuffel groused to his staff, 'that on Hitler's maps there is a little flag saying Seventh Panzer Division, even though it got here without a single tank, truck, piece of artillery or even a machine gun. We have an army of ghosts.'

But by far the most threatening and chaotic situation was the one in the centre. Busse's Ninth Army, even as it put up a spirited and ferocious defence, was falling apart. The Red Army had succeeded in smashing open two breaches in the defences before Berlin, and with the breakdown in communications, Busse had a difficult time keeping apprised of the position of the Soviets and his own troops capabilities to counterattack. The desperate plight of the 56th Panzer Corps illustrates this. Positioned on the Seelow Heights, this unit had borne the brunt of Chuikov's main assault. They had held for two days, and had inflicted enormous punishment on the Soviets, but only at the cost of tremendous casualties of their own. One of the units which had suffered the most was the Luftwaffe 9th Parachute Division, which Göring had offered Heinrici with such bravado during the Führer conference on 6 April. After having already been subjected to the full impact of the first assault, as the Soviet tanks now roared up and over the Heights and began slamming into their new lines, the paratroopers panicked and, in the words of 56th's artillery commander Colonel Hans Oskar Wöhlermann, began 'running away like madmen'. Even when Wöhlermann drew his pistol, he could not stop the flight.

Above: The Reichschancellery garden. On the left is the entrance to the Führerbunker, in the centre its observation tower. On 16 January Hitler descended into the bunker, and remained there until his suicide.

The badly mauled 56th Panzer Corps desperately needed reinforcements, and its commander, General Karl Weidling, had been told that the heavily armed 18th Panzer Division, with a full complement of tanks, and the SS Nordland Division would be arriving immediately to buttress their embattled position. But on 18 April, only the Nordland's commander arrived at Weidling's command post north of Müncheberg to announce nonchalantly that his

Left: Some of the many civilian refugees passing through Berlin. Most had either been evacuated or lost their homes in the east, but were given permission to remain no longer than 48 hours in the city.

division was still miles away, and out of fuel. Unsure when it could arrive, he didn't appear to be in any hurry to join the 56th Panzer Corps; the SS disliked having to subordinate themselves to the 'ordinary' Wehrmacht. It was soon too late to rescue the situation at Seelow. The 18th Panzer Division finally arrived just in time to join the retreat. Hard on the heels of that evacuation, in a reminder of both the kind of regime he was fighting to defend and the state of the country's defences, Weidling received a visit from the head of the *Hitlerjugend*, Artur Axmann, who grandiosely announced that his boys were ready to fight for the Fatherland and were taking up positions on the road to protect 56th's rear. Incredulous and disgusted, Weidling made clear to the youth leader, in 'extremely coarse language', as Wöhlermann remembered, that schoolboys would not be thrown into a battle that the Wehrmacht could not master and the SS would not join. After two relocations of his own headquarters in the course of the afternoon, Weidling was by the end of the day ensconced in a makeshift command post in the cellar of a house in Waldsieversdorf, just north-west of the key German strong-point of Müncheberg.

At midday on 19 April, Müncheberg itself became the scene of heavy fighting. Two heavily reinforced corps from Chuikov's Eighth Guards (4th and 29th Guards) concentrated an all-out assault on the city after a 30-minute artillery bombardment. The punishing barrage was creating dangerous cracks in the German defences, but outflanked both to the south and to the north-west by two more tank corps (11th and 11th Guards), there was little room for manoeuvre. Hitler had forbidden any kind of retreat. At about 2000 hours, 82nd Guards Rifle Division stormed into the city; within hours all German resistance had been broken. The fall of Müncheberg, 30km (18 miles) due east of Berlin on the Küstrin-Berlin highway, gave the Soviets the perfect launching point for the next phase of the battle, and a platform from which their artillery could now reach directly into Berlin. At roughly the same time, during the afternoon and evening of 19 April, Zhukov's northern forces succeeded in capturing Wriezen on the Alte Oder, and Rokossovsky reported to Stalin that the Second Belorussian Front was ready to begin its offensive.

Below: Berliners carve up a horse killed in a bombing raid. As the social and economic infrastructure of the city crumbled under the Allied onslaught, civilians relied on their wits, and luck, to survive.

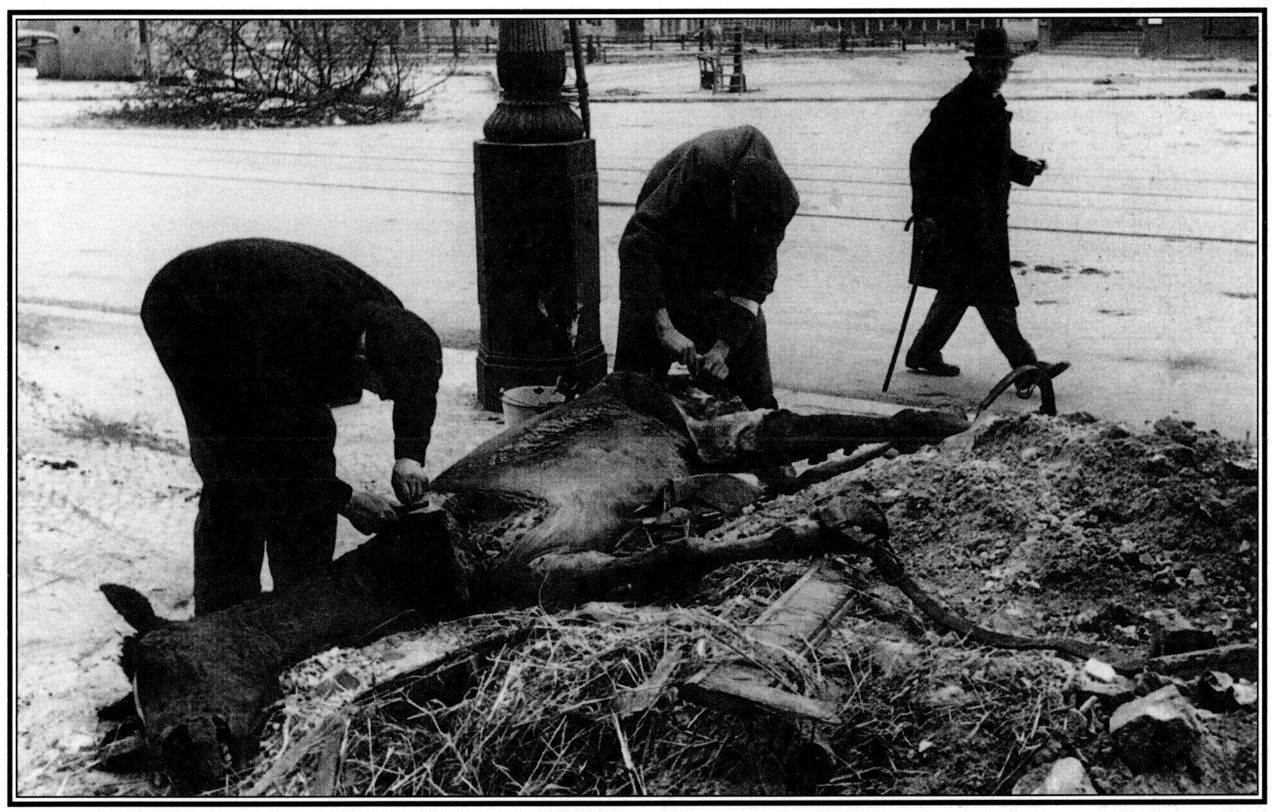

CHAPTER SIX

Berlin Breached

For Berliners, the time had come for them to prepare for the worst. The Red Army was on the threshold of the Nazi capital, and there was now no chance that the city would escape whatever retribution the Russians chose to take either on Berlin itself or its occupants now waiting for the war's end.

'A new and heavy trial, perhaps the heaviest of all, is before us,' droned the front page of the *Völkischer Beobachter*, the official Nazi Party newspaper, on 18 April. In a gloomy mixture of warning, encouragement, and threat, the paper reported the Soviets' surge across the Oder and imminent arrival at the edges of Berlin. 'The word for the day is: Clench your teeth! Fight like the devil! Don't give up one metre of soil easily! The hour of decision demands the last, the greatest, effort!' Berliners were lashed even more insistently with hysterical tales of what could be expected from the Soviet troops: rape, torture, indiscriminate killing and, for those who survived, deportation to the Gulags as slave labour. Throughout the city, the final defences were readied. Barricades were closed on all the major highways and thoroughfares. General Helmuth Reymann, the commandant of Berlin's defences, received orders to dispatch all of his military forces, including the *Volkssturm*, to the city's perimeters to take up second-line positions. Ten *Volkssturm* battalions and an anti-aircraft regiment were duly sent east to reinforce the Ninth Army's attempt to slow the Soviet advance. This departure left the city of Berlin itself, with its three million civilian inhabitants, as Reymann reported to Berlin's *Gauleiter*, Goebbels, essentially defenceless.

Left: A Red Army soldier carrying the ubiquitous PPSh-41 submachine gun crouches for cover during street fighting inside Berlin. The urban environment was ideal for defence, as the Soviets knew themselves, after Stalingrad.

Left: A Soviet T-34 tank rumbles past the burning wreck of a German military car. The T-34 was an excellent tank, capable of matching all but the heaviest of its German opponents.

The entire previous week had been one of increasingly disastrous news: on 13 April, the Soviets had captured Vienna; on 16 April – the same day the Soviets launched their offensive on the Oder – the Americans had taken Nuremburg, the Nazis' show-piece city and the home of their huge rallies during the 1930s; Prague, Linz, and Munich were all in immediate danger of capture; and the Americans and Soviets were only days away from a meeting in central Germany which would sever the country in two. The Frankfurt fortress was still holding out, successfully repelling several Soviet assaults, but with Wriezen and Müncheberg now taken, the Ninth Army was essentially in retreat. A sergeant with the 90th Panzergrenadier Regiment, which had been fighting near Müncheberg, reported how by the end of the day on 19 April, 'the Russians were no longer meeting any resistance, our enormous supply columns being in full flight without any thought of putting up any resistance'. During that night on most of the immediate approaches to Berlin, the survivors of the German units attempting to stop the Soviets were forced to pull back from most of their positions. The Second Battalion of the Kurmark Panzergrenadiers, for example, defended the village of Dolgelin until about midnight, at which point they managed to slip past the Soviets, after destroying almost all of their vehicles, and make their way to the 169th Infantry Division's lines at Carzig. The rest of the Kurmark Division, which was still between Dolgelin and Marxdorf, was ordered to occupy the Berkenbrück-Kersdorf section of the *Autobahn* to cover the

Below: By 19 April, the German defenders were essentially in full retreat. The only units not pulling back steadily toward Berlin's city center were those trapped and isolated by the advancing Soviets.

withdrawal of other units, and then to withdraw to the designated fall-back position along the Dehme and Kersdorfer lakes, adjacent to the river Spree.

Meanwhile, Hitler's insistence that the units on the Ninth Army's southern flank hold their positions on the Oder, from Frankfurt south to just north of Forst, resulted in their being completely cut off from the battle for Berlin by the advances of the First Guards Tank Corps on Zhukov's southern flank. At the same time, Konev's lightning sweep to Cottbus and his swing up to the north threatened this sizeable body of the Ninth with encirclement, and ruined any hope for flexibility in the Germans' response. The Ninth Army's commander, General Busse, summed up the day: 'The fighting on 19 April brought about a further yawning gap in the army's front. It was impossible to close the gaps. The wrestling by the Army Group and the [Ninth] Army for approval to break off had no success.' The Ninth Army, Germany's last defence before Berlin, had been effectively shattered; already in the first four days of battle Busse had been forced to commit all of his reserves, and after the fighting, some 12,000 of the Ninth's men were dead. There was no longer any real hope that the Germans could hold off the Soviets from Berlin. All they could do was to preserve their remaining armies in order to hand them over to the Western Allies. In the judgement of

Above: Katyusha rocket launchers illuminate the night sky on the outskirts of Berlin. Although the Soviet Union was stretching itself to the limit for the last battle, the Germans were in a far, far worse state.

military historian Tony Le Tissier, 'The decisive battle for Berlin was over.'

Even the most fanatical of the Third Reich's elite could by now read the writing on the wall. The steady migration out of Berlin by these 'Golden Pheasants', as they were called in the irreverent Berlin idiom, now increased to a torrent. One of those who had decided that the time had come to turn his back on the capital and its people and flee for the safety of the south was the Third Reich's second-in-command and head of the Luftwaffe, Hermann Göring. On 20 April, shortly after the early-morning bombing which signalled the beginning of Rokossovsky's offensive, while desperate fighting raged little more than 12km (7.5 miles) away, Göring assembled a convoy of 24 heavy Luftwaffe trucks and scores of elite soldiers at his estate, Karinhall, about 80km (50 miles) north-west of Berlin. After his enormous collection of furniture, silver, paintings and antiques – mostly plundered from conquered territories – had been loaded on the trucks, he had his precious Karinhall demolished. While the front-line units scrambled for enough fuel to make it through the next Soviet assault, Göring's convoy,

Above: Most of the bridges on route to Berlin had been destroyed by the retreating Germans, forcing the Soviets to construct new ones. Here an assault gun crosses a pontoon bridge on the way to Berlin.

with its cargo of precious war-booty, roared off with a motorcycle escort towards Bavaria. Göring himself returned to Berlin one last time for the Führer's 56th birthday ceremonies.

Friday 20 April was supposed to have been the day that Hitler would leave for the *Adlershorst* – the 'Eagle's Nest' – near Berchtesgaden. But his increasingly depressed mood left him vacillating even more than normal. While his lieutenants and advisers urged him to leave the city while it was still possible, Hitler swung between denying that the situation was as grave as his military chiefs made it sound, and proclaiming that he could not now, in this moment of crisis, abandon the capital. On this day he rose much later (1100 hours) than normal, and from about 1200 hours onwards received the birthday congratulations of the Third Reich's inner circle, followed by handshakes and expressions of unending devotion from the Berlin *Gauleiters*, lower staff members, and secretaries. In the afternoon, Hitler and his entourage emerged from the bunker for what would be his last moments above ground, breathing the fresh air of the country which his war was now subjecting to utter ruin and destruction. In the garden of the Reichschancellery, the Führer reviewed the troops of the SS *Frundsberg* Division and a group of Hitler Youth. The beaming leader of the *Hitlerjugend*, Artur Axmann, presented the unit and singled out some of those present as having 'recently distinguished themselves at the front'. Those boy-soldiers were decorated by Hitler, and all received a handshake from Germany's 'saviour'. Though his speech was full of wooden optimism about the Soviets' imminent 'greatest defeat yet', he was clearly physically debilitated. 'Everyone was shocked at the Führer's appearance,' Axmann later remembered. 'He walked with a stoop. His hands trembled. But it was surprising how much will power and determination still radiated from this man.' Newsclips filmed by the Nazi authorities in fact reveal a man who appeared to be on the verge of collapse.

Left: The numerous rivers and lakes around and leading into Berlin kept Soviet engineers busy right up until the end of the conflict erecting pontoon and more conventional wooden bridges.

After completing the ceremonies in the garden, Hitler returned for the last time to his subterranean bunker and convened a conference with his top military staff. General Hans Krebs, the man appointed to be the new OKH Chief of Staff after Guderian's dismissal, briefed the others on the bleakness of a situation with which they were all already too familiar: Busse's Ninth Army faced imminent encirclement and Berlin would within days, perhaps hours, be surrounded with no retreat and no avenue for reinforcement. Even if it were possible to preserve the government and war effort after the loss of Berlin, it would be greatly hampered by Germany's being sliced into two geographic sections by the Western Allies' advance. Rebuffing his generals' pleas for him to immediately evacuate with the entire government, Hitler answered, according to his Luftwaffe adjutant, Colonel Nicolaus von Below, 'that the battle for Berlin presented the only chance to prevent total defeat'. Nevertheless, without yet deciding whether he would stay in Berlin or retreat to the Obersalzberg, Hitler agreed to implement an order, formulated some time ago, for the eventuality of the division of Germany. According to the plan, Admiral Dönitz would assume full military authority for the northern half of the country, while Hitler himself would direct the war in the southern half from his Alpine redoubt. In the event that he decided to remain in Berlin, command in the south would go to Field Marshal Kesselring. Now, without indicating whether he would remain in Berlin or not, Hitler duly conferred command in the north on Dönitz, stating that he might yet confer similar authority on Kesselring in the south. It was impossible to figure out what his intentions were. Indeed, at this point Hitler most probably was – perhaps for the first time in his life – quite at a loss about what to do.

Meanwhile, permission was given for the bulk of the German political and military leadership to evacuate to the south, or in Dönitz's case to the north. In all, over 2000 permits were issued to leave the capital. The Berlin commandant's Chief of Staff, Colonel Hans Refior, remembered with scorn the flight of the 'Golden Pheasants'.

'There was something almost comic about the reasons with which state and party functionaries backed up their requests to leave the city. Even though Goebbels had ordered that no man capable of carrying arms is to leave Berlin, we put no difficulties in the way of these 'home fighters' who wanted passes. Why should we hold up these contemptible characters? They all believed that flight would save their precious lives. The majority of the population remained behind. Flight for them was beyond their means anyway because of the transport shortage.'

Those who tried, without permission, were often summarily executed, hung from the lampposts as gruesome warnings of the risk of 'desertion'.

As the Nazi elite fled and the Red Army advanced, the people of Berlin waited. The city, which had stubbornly continued with 'lunatic normalcy'

Below: The delay in achieving his objectives, together with a high casualty rate, convinced Zhukov to revise his original plan, and send some of his second-echelon tank units sweeping around to the north.

through so many dark days, finally began to come to a halt. Factories were closed or abandoned; the subway and streetcars stopped running; mail was no longer delivered; trash no longer picked up; electricity failed in parts of the city; the police, who were needed at the rapidly shrinking front, no longer patrolled the streets. But thanks in part to Speer's earlier interventions, orders to destroy the entire infrastructure of the city should it appear to be about to fall to the Soviets were in most cases ignored. And in another stroke of good fortune – perhaps in celebration of the Führer's birthday, perhaps in an understanding of the apocalypse approaching – the people of Berlin were allocated an extra ration of food: a pound of bacon or sausage; a half pound of rice or oatmeal; 250 dried lentils, peas or beans; one can of vegetables; two pounds of sugar; an ounce of real coffee; a small package of coffee substitute; and some fat. The extra rations, meant to last eight days, were quickly dubbed *Himmelfahrtsrationen* (Ascension Day rations) by the acerbic Berliners: with those rations in their stomachs, they imagined, they would ascend to heaven, courtesy of the Red Army.

The Soviets' success to this point had been costly. At least 33,000 men, according to official Red Army statistics, or more than twice what the Germans had lost, had been killed so far in the operation. In addition, 743 tanks and SPGs had been destroyed; the equivalent of an entire tank army, and 25 per cent of the Soviets' available armoured forces. In view of these losses and his Front's two-day delay in accomplishing Stavka's battle plan goals, and in view, too, of the fact that Konev's First Ukrainian Front could yet reap the laurels for the conquest of Berlin, Zhukov made some revisions to his original plan. The First Guards Tank Army and Eighth Guards Army would continue to operate together as the main, frontal strike-force, driving into Berlin along Reichsstraße 1. But Second Guards Tank Army, which had been operating in the second echelon since leaving Küstrin, would now be divided into its three main constituent corps. The Ninth Tank Corps would join 47th Army and Seventh Guards Cavalry Corps to sweep around Berlin on the north, and then come down on the far side to the Havel and block off any western approach to, or escape from, the city. Meanwhile the First Mechanised Corps and the 12th Guards Tank Corps would push into the northeastern suburbs, opening up a route for the infantry of the Third and Fifth Shock Armies. With the northern, western, and eastern suburbs cut off and occupied, and the south busy with Konev's forces, 69th and 33rd Armies, with the reserve Third Army, would

Below: On the afternoon of 20 April, his birthday, Adolf Hitler emerged from his bunker to review an SS detachment and a Hitler Youth unit with its leader, Artur Axmann, in the Reichschancellery garden.

drive in and destroy what remained of the German Ninth Army. The primary target was designated as the Reichstag.

With little respite, the attack was pressed. On the morning of 20 April, as Hitler was preparing to greet his birthday guests, Allied bombers delivered as their gift a final aerial bombardment. At the same time, the long-range artillery of the Third Shock Army's 79th Rifle Corps began the first ground bombardment of Berlin. Even as the city received this concrete announcement of the Soviets' imminent arrival, ground troops advanced to its outskirts. The 125th Rifle Corps of the 47th Army succeeded in taking Bernau (about 15km (9 miles) to the north-east), while Third Shock and Second Guards Tank Army managed to break free of the deadly morass of the Germans' third defensive line. Once in open country, the armour sprinted ahead of the infantry, to the north-eastern edges of the city at Ladenburg and Zepernick. Meanwhile, Fifth Shock Army, with 12th Guards Tank Corps and elements of 11th Tank Corps, finished up the neutralisation of the third defensive line, and prepared to take Strausberg.

Around 2000 hours on the evening of the 20th, Zhukov issued a radiogram order to the commander of First Guards Tank Army, Marshal M.E. Katukov:

'Katukov, Popiel. [Katukov's Chief of Staff] First Guards Tank has been assigned a historic mission: to

Above: Hitler is introduced to several youngsters who had 'recently distinguished themselves at the front'. These received a special decoration; everyone present received a handshake from the Führer.

Below: All present at the ceremony remarked later how shrunken, ill, and depressed Hitler had seemed. The 20 July 1944 attempt on his life and recent setbacks had taken a serious toll on his physical and mental health.

Above: Fearful of falling victim to a German sniper or machine-gun nest, the advancing Soviet units used armour and artillery to completely pulverise any building which offered a vantage point.

be the first to break into Berlin and hoist the Victory Banner. Personally charge you with organising and execution. From each corps send up to one of the best brigades into Berlin and issue following orders: no later than 0400 hours morning 21 April at any cost to break into the outskirts of Berlin and report at once for transmission to Comrade Stalin and press announcement. Zhukov.'

Zhukov's concern that Stalin be informed as soon as possible after the entry of Soviet troops into Berlin is understandable. His concern that the press also be notified the moment that his soldiers entered the German capital is indicative of the psychological importance of this battle to the weary Soviet soldiers, as well, perhaps, as of the atmosphere of competition pervading the race to Berlin.

Naturally Zhukov wasn't the only one thinking along these kinds of lines. Even before the commander of First Belorussian had issued his order, his rival in the First Ukrainian had radioed orders of his own to the commanders of his Third and Fourth Guards Tank Armies: 'Personal to Comrades Rybalko and Lelyushenko. Order you categorically to break into Berlin tonight. Report execution. 1940 hours, 20.4.45. Konev.' Almost recklessly, Konev pressed his tank commanders on towards Berlin, urging them to abandon the normal concern for maintaining protected flanks. Years later, Konev mused that his generals must have thought he had lost all sense. 'At that moment I knew what my tank commanders must be thinking: "Here you are throwing us into this manhole, forcing us to move without strength on our flanks – won't the Germans cut our communications, hit us from the rear?"' But it worked. Within no more than 24 hours, Rybalko and Lelyushenko had raced 61 and 45km (38 and 28 miles) respectively; by nightfall Third Guards Tank Army was fighting in Zossen, only 40km (25 miles) from Berlin.

Zossen was the location of the supreme headquarters for both the OKH and OKW, though these had hastily evacuated just before the Soviets arrived. One of the OKH's convoys, heading south to Bavaria, had been mistaken for a Soviet column, and was bombed and destroyed by the Luftwaffe. The German defence was by now almost completely on the run. General Heinrici felt that there was really only one last hope to avoid total annihilation by the Soviets. He had to ensure that the battle for Berlin remained outside the city. House-to-house street fighting, he knew, would be a catastrophe: the outmanned Germans' tanks and artillery would be rendered useless, and the slaughter of civilians would be horrific. The only way to ensure fighting outside the city was to pull back the remains of Busse's Ninth Army immediately, before it could be encircled by the First Ukrainian. But Hitler had ordered that the Ninth was to hold its position on the Oder. Heinrici attempted, in the most convincing way he knew how, to get the order remanded. In utter frustration he told Krebs to convey to Hitler that if his request was not met, then 'since this order endangers your [Hitler's] well-being, has no chance of success and cannot be carried out, I request you to relieve me of my command and give it to somebody else. Then I could do my duty as a Volkssturm man and fight the enemy.' The incredulous Krebs told him he would pass the demand along; a short time later he phoned back that the Ninth was to maintain its position, and all available forces were to move into the gap between Busse's army and Schörner's Army Group Centre.

It was clear at this point to Heinrici that the battle for Berlin was lost. Touring the front-lines that night, he noted an air of collapse affecting the forces. Everywhere he went he found troops – individuals and ragged units – in obvious retreat. 'I didn't find one soldier who didn't claim to have orders to get munitions, fuel or something else from the rear.' The area around Eberswalde, north-east of Berlin, was in particular disorder. Heinrici found whole units – even SS – resting in the woods or retreating with the civilian refugees; it was only with some effort that he managed to reorganise and deploy these soldiers. Meanwhile, the Führer conference broke up around 0300 hours on a note of almost comic desperation. Hitler railed that all of 'his' problems were caused by the treason of the Fourth Army, the unit which had been mauled so badly by Konev's forces on the first day of the attack. When Walter Hewel, Von Ribbentrop's representative from the Foreign Ministry, gingerly suggested that any diplomatic initiatives would have to begin immediately, Hitler turned and 'with tired and flagging gait', according to one of his officers, muttered, 'Politics. I have nothing to do with politics any more. That just disgusts me.' In a hint of what he was beginning to contemplate, he turned back to the assembled men and added: 'When I am dead you will have to busy yourself plenty with politics.'

The next day, 21 April, at 1130 hours the central shopping district in Hermannplatz came under direct artillery fire, blowing shoppers and passers-by to bits. Soon after that, shell after shell began pounding the very heart of the Nazi empire: the Reichstag was hit, the huge cupola crashing down into the building and over the street; the Brandenburg Gate had one cornice blown off; the Charlottenburg Palace went up in flames. A foreign correspondent who witnessed the barrage reported that at least one shell was falling every five seconds in the central government district in Wilhelmstrasse. Everywhere the city was strewn with rubble, burning vehicles, and the dead and injured.

Below: The swiftness of First Ukrainian Front's advance guaranteed that Germany would be cut into two halves within days. On 25 April, near Torgau, units of the Red Army made contact with the Americans.

Above: A German motorcycle with sidecar drives past a wrecked Soviet tank outside Berlin. During the first days of the battle, the Soviets had already lost 743 tanks and guns – the equivalent of an entire army.

Earlier that morning, the first elements of Zhukov's forces had entered the north-eastern outskirts of Berlin. Kuznetsov's Third Shock Army with First Mechanised Corps had fought their way into Weissensee and opened up a route into the city. In the course of the day, Fifth Shock Army, supported by 12th Guards Tank Corps, also broke into the city's northern suburbs at Hohenschönhausen and Marzahn. In Bernau, Captain Sergei Golbov watched the surviving German soldiers emerge in surrender from their defences: 'grey-faced, dusty, bodies sagging with fatigue', they seemed to him a sorry lot. Golbov and the other Red Army officers were astonished to see one German officer stagger towards them, waving his blood-spurting arms, and shouting in Polish that they must leave his wife alone. Bandaging the wrists where the German had slashed them, Golbov replied that he had far more important things to do than harass the man's wife, and sent him back to the medics. At least a few Germans in Neuenhagen-Hoppegarten, 19km (12 miles) east of Berlin, were overjoyed to see the arrival of the Soviets. A few secret Communists had burned their *Volkssturm* armbands and turned out with a white banner and huge smiles to watch the Red Army enter. And the behaviour of these units gave them reassurance that their dreams of the Communist society were true, and Goebbel's stories of the depredations of the Soviet soldier only propaganda.

Not all was good news for the Soviets, however. Chuikov's Eighth Guards Tanks, which had been spearheading the assault until Katukov's army took over this role, was struggling against strong resistance in their drive from the east, around Fürstenwalde, Erkner, and Petershagen. The newly christened spearhead unit, First Guards Tank Army, likewise found its advance stymied by counterattacks and minefields on Berlin's eastern approach. On the southern approaches, First Ukrainian Front finally succeeded in severing the right flank of Ninth Army and completely cutting it and the remainder of Army Group Vistula off from Army Group Centre. Third and Fourth Guards Tank Armies continued to race north towards the city with such speed that the infantry unit following it in order to exploit the breach opened by the armour – General A.A. Luchinskii's 28th Army – trailed behind 95km (60 miles) or more.

At Zossen, Third Guards Tank Army's Sixth Tank Corps captured the German High Command's

Right: Soviet gun crews in action. Although there was no longer any real doubt about the outcome of the battle, both sides continued to fight with no diminishing of intensity.

headquarters completely intact with hardly a fight. The majority of the staff and their equipment had already been evacuated, but the amazed Red Army soldiers found a vast complex, strewn with papers, in which telephones were still ringing and the teletype machines still clicking. Large signs had been placed on many of the consoles, pleading in schoolbook Russian: 'Soldiers! Do not damage this apparatus.' One of the Soviet soldiers picked up a phone which was ringing incessantly. In response to a German voice, with immense glee, the soldier replied in Russian: 'Ivan is here. You can **** !' Along with the facility itself, the Soviets had captured its chief engineer, Hans Beltow, and four severely intoxicated Wehrmacht soldiers, one of whom was so helplessly drunk that he had to be stretchered out.

Konev didn't allow his tankers to tarry too long at Zossen. Before the day was out they continued their race towards Berlin, one arm heading north-west, towards Potsdam, the other pushing due north towards the Teltow canal and the Tempelhof district of Berlin. Meanwhile, to the south, Third and Fifth Guards (infantry) Armies, with 13th Army, completed their envelopment of the 'Frankfurt-Guben' group of Busse's Ninth Army, and proceeded to neutralise the remaining German forces in Cottbus. Konev's main concern now was that the two lead tank armies, Third and Fourth Guards, were racing so far ahead of their supporting infantry units that a potentially dangerous gap was opening up between them. The 61st Rifle Division from Luchinkskii's 28th Army was hastily loaded onto every available truck and rushed forward with all possible speed. By the

Below: By 21 April, the central districts of Berlin were coming under artillery fire, causing a great many civilian casualties. Here bodies, horses, vehicles, and possessions lie strewn across a residential street.

evening of 21 April, they had reached Rybalko's tanks and deployed between them and Lelyushenko's Fourth Guards Tanks. Before the day was out, Lelyushenko's men had succeeded in capturing Calau, Luckau, and Babelsberg. In Babelsberg, just outside Potsdam, the tank army's forward detachment, 63rd Guards Tank Brigade, discovered and liberated a concentration camp, still holding its multi-national contingent of prisoners, among them the former French Prime Minister, Edouard Herriot, and his wife. At the end of the day, Rybalko's Third Guards Tank Army was also positioned just before Berlin, poised for assault. Konev now decided to reinforce this unit – his hope for beating Zhukov to the prize of the Reichstag – with breakthrough artillery support – a corps and a division – as well as an anti-aircraft artillery division. He also placed the Second Fighter Corps under Rybalko's sole operational command.

Meanwhile, in the Führerbunker, Hitler believed he had found a way to rescue Berlin's beleaguered situation. Poring over the situation map, he suddenly jabbed it with his finger and announced, 'Steiner!' The SS troops under SS General Obergruppenführer Steiner, positioned near Eberswalde and flanking Von Manteuffel's Third Panzer Army, Hitler believed, could strike south, cutting off Chuikov's drive east, and relinking the embattled Ninth Army with Third Panzer. A little flag bearing the name 'Group Steiner' promptly appeared on the map, and Hitler ordered that every available man, tank, airplane, and gun be diverted to the 'Steiner Attack'. As with so much of German planning at this point in the war, however, the Steiner plan was feasible only in theory. In reality, a 'Group Steiner' barely existed. Steiner had a handful of completely inexperienced troops at his disposal; hardly the necessary strength for an attack of the magnitude and daring Hitler had planned. Steiner recalled the telephone conversation with Hitler as the latter informed him of the new plan.

'As I remember the call, it reached me between 8:30 and 9 p.m. Hitler's exact words were: 'Steiner, are you aware that the *Reichsmarschall* [Göring] has a private army at Karinhall? This is to be disbanded at once and sent into battle.' While I was trying to figure out what that was supposed to mean, he continued, 'Every available man between Berlin and the Baltic Sea up to Stettin and Hamburg is to be drawn into this attack I have ordered.' When I protested, saying that the troops at my disposal were inexperienced, and when I asked precisely where the attack was to take place, the Führer gave me no answer. He simply hung up. I had no idea where or when or with what I was to attack.'

Later, as Steiner was complaining to OKH Chief of Staff Krebs about the impossibility of a 'Steiner

Below: While Hitler and some his generals still hoped for relief from General Wenck's 12th Army, west of the city, facing the Americans at the Elbe, in fact Berlin was almost completely cut off.

Attack', Hitler cut in and 'gave me a long lecture and closed with these words, "You will see, Steiner. You will see. The Russians will suffer their greatest defeat before the gates of Berlin." I told him that I thought the Berlin situation was hopeless. I was completely ignored.' Shortly thereafter, Steiner received his official order to attack. It concluded with the following warning:

'It is expressly forbidden to fall back to the west. Officers who do not comply unconditionally with this order are to be arrested and shot immediately. You, Steiner, are liable with your head for the execution of this order. The fate of the Reich Capital depends on the success of your mission.

Adolf Hitler'

Hitler gave the same warning to the Luftwaffe's Chief of Staff, General Karl Koller, in issuing his instructions to divert all planes and airmen in the north to join the attack. These threats of execution were sober evidence of the extent to which Hitler was aware that he was losing control. Koller, dumbfounded by the order, desperately tried to discover where and when this 'Steiner Attack' was supposed to take place, so that he could send his men there.

The commander of Army Group Vistula, General Heinrici, who was not in any way consulted, or even informed, about the Steiner attack, blew up when he finally heard about it. 'I reject the order!' he told Krebs. Apparently unaware that the Ninth Army had now been completely cut off, he went on insisting that it be immediately withdrawn, and demanded a conference with Hitler. Krebs peremptorily rejected the demand. 'It's just not possible. The Führer is overworked.'

Above: Soviet soldiers move cautiously from house to house, warily looking up into the windows and into the basements for hiding German soldiers and weapon stores.

A little later, Heinrici received two pieces of news which confirmed his fears that he was becoming irrelevant as a military commander, and being circumvented by the sycophantic Nazi clique around Hitler. Firstly, Krebs told him that his Chief of Staff, General Kinzel, was to be replaced by Major General von Trotha, an airy-headed, ardent disciple of Hitler. Secondly, he was told that General Reymann, Berlin Commandant, was being replaced, initially by an upstart Nazi party careerist, Colonel Käther, but by the end of the day by the Führer himself. Both moves were hard blows to Heinrici's efforts to fight the battle as he believed it should be fought. The previous day, despite his objections, the responsibility for Berlin had been placed with Army Group Vistula. When first informed of this, he ordered Reymann to ensure that no bridges or other installations necessary to the survival of Berlin's people were destroyed. That would now be much more difficult.

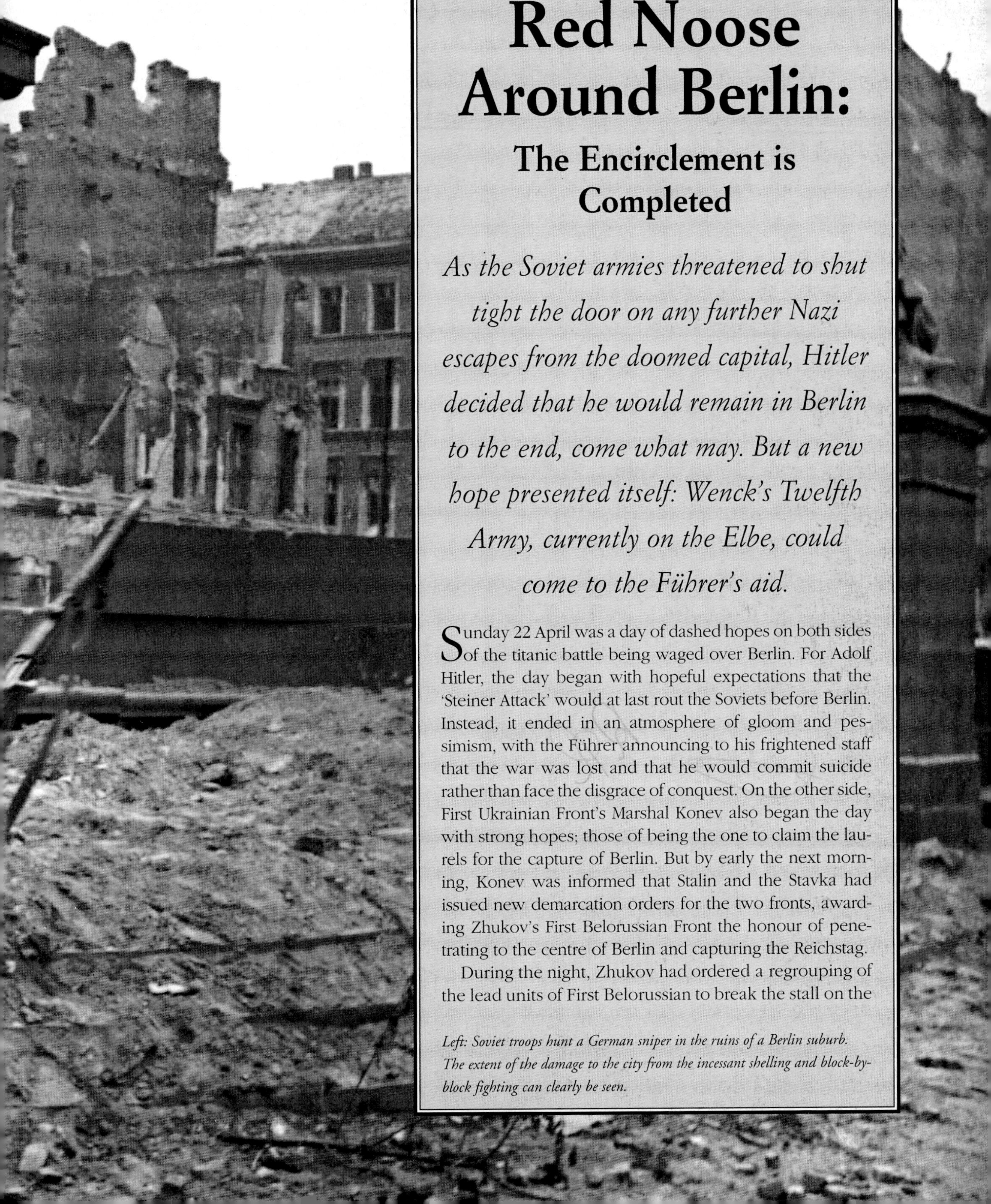

CHAPTER SEVEN

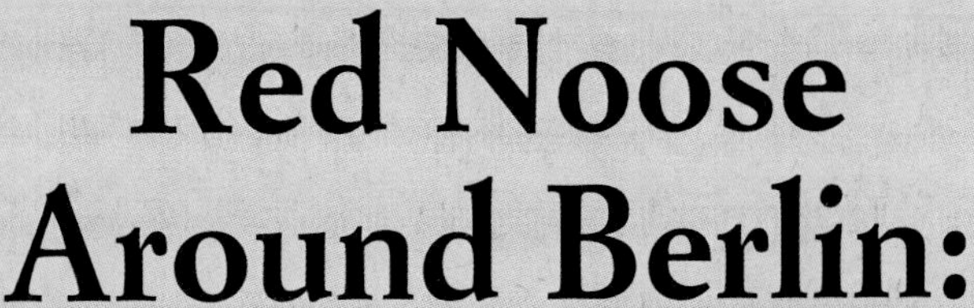

Red Noose Around Berlin:

The Encirclement is Completed

As the Soviet armies threatened to shut tight the door on any further Nazi escapes from the doomed capital, Hitler decided that he would remain in Berlin to the end, come what may. But a new hope presented itself: Wenck's Twelfth Army, currently on the Elbe, could come to the Führer's aid.

Sunday 22 April was a day of dashed hopes on both sides of the titanic battle being waged over Berlin. For Adolf Hitler, the day began with hopeful expectations that the 'Steiner Attack' would at last rout the Soviets before Berlin. Instead, it ended in an atmosphere of gloom and pessimism, with the Führer announcing to his frightened staff that the war was lost and that he would commit suicide rather than face the disgrace of conquest. On the other side, First Ukrainian Front's Marshal Konev also began the day with strong hopes; those of being the one to claim the laurels for the capture of Berlin. But by early the next morning, Konev was informed that Stalin and the Stavka had issued new demarcation orders for the two fronts, awarding Zhukov's First Belorussian Front the honour of penetrating to the centre of Berlin and capturing the Reichstag.

During the night, Zhukov had ordered a regrouping of the lead units of First Belorussian to break the stall on the

Left: Soviet troops hunt a German sniper in the ruins of a Berlin suburb. The extent of the damage to the city from the incessant shelling and block-by-block fighting can clearly be seen.

left flank. Third Shock Army, in the north, was ordered to direct its attack away from the northern suburbs and into the centre of Berlin, in the hopes that it would take some of the pressure off the eastern approaches where Chuikov and Katukov were having so much difficulty. Colonel General Kuznetsov, Third Shock's commander, accordingly redeployed three of his rifle corps into assault groups and assault squads for urban combat and advanced into northern Berlin. Rather than fight for individual buildings, however, the Soviets first subjected the sector to a punishing artillery barrage, with Katyusha rocket launchers firing salvoes of phosphorous rockets into suspected strong-points. Then the tanks moved in, with orders to obliterate everything that could harbour a sniper. With the urban landscape disintegrating under flames and exploding concrete, the Red Army infantrymen moved methodically from rubble heap to rubble heap, clearing out the cellars with flame-throwers, anti-tank rifles, and explosives. The terrified civilians who had taken refuge below now found themselves in the thick of the fighting. Those who fled or were dragged out on to the streets became targets for the Soviet fighter planes swarming overhead.

Above: Wehrmacht units receive a last-minute pep talk from Admiral Dönitz, who would succeed Hitler after the latter's suicide. For most, the war by now no longer had anything to do with Nazi ideology.

By 1000 hours, Kuznetsov's assault groups were pressing their attack into Weissensee. A few squads from the 11th SS Motorised Division and small groups of poorly equipped Volkssturm units were about the only resistance, although the anti-aircraft guns with barrels depressed to ground level did create some problems. The neighbourhood, once a bastion of German Communist sympathy, surrendered quickly. The Red Army soldiers rapidly and professionally secured the sector, rounded up the surviving Germans and put them through a hasty screening process. Some of the men spoke excellent German, but most of the interrogations were conducted by women from the interpreter units which accompanied the first echelon troops. Most of the captured women and those men who could provide convincing anti-Nazi credentials were put to work cleaning up the devastation, while the rest were sent to the rear as prisoners. The soldiers of Third Shock Army pushed on into Berlin.

Above: By Sunday, 22 April, the Soviets had four tank armies and five rifle armies engaged inside the city. However, Stalin issued new demarcation orders which precluded Konev's tank units from taking the Reichstag.

To the east, Chuikov's Eighth Guards and Katukov's First Guards Tank Armies continued to encounter heavy resistance at Erkner and Petershagen, but by the afternoon they had managed to reach the River Dahme, with the Spree only a short distance ahead. An assault crossing was planned for the next day, which would finally bring the units designated to take the Reichstag into Berlin proper. On Chuikov's and Katukov's right flank, Fifth Shock Army, supported by 12th Guards and 11th Tank Corps, also managed to bite deeply into Berlin's eastern defences, driving into Kaulsdorf, Biesdorf, and Karlshorst. On this side of the battle, too, large numbers of prisoners were taken, though General Katukov found himself saddled with one group of prisoners for which he had not been prepared. During the attack on Erkner, he had received a bizarre call from one of his commanders informing him that he had just taken prisoner a number of Japanese. His tanks had happened upon a diplomatic mission of the Japanese Empire, with which the Soviet Union was not yet officially at war. Katukov grimaced, knowing this would be an annoying diplomatic flap, and ordered the Japanese to be brought immediately to his headquarters.

Below: A Volkssturmer *peers around a pile of rubble to aim his Panzerfaust. Though they each carried only one shot, the personal anti-tank weapons proved to be devastatingly effective in close, urban combat.*

At about the same time that Zhukov's forces were wresting these gains in the east and north, the daily Führer conference was getting under way in the bunker beneath the Reichschancellery. Earlier conferences, despite all the setbacks and crises which had been plaguing the German war effort since Stalingrad, had all tended to be marked by the manic, insistent optimism of Hitler and his clique of true believers. On this day, however, none of that optimism was in evidence. The Oder front had crumbled entirely; Busse's Ninth Army was destroyed or encircled, unable to come to the aid of Berlin; the 56th Panzer Corps had gone lost, its commander, General Karl Weidling ordered arrested and executed on suspicion of desertion; the Red Army was heading toward an encirclement of the city; and, to Hitler's absolute fury, the 'Steiner Attack' had never materialised. All through the morning, the Führerbunker had been demanding to know by phone when the attack had been launched. Himmler and the SS repeatedly assured him that it would take place and succeed. At one point, Himmler is said to have told Hitler that it had already happened, only to be contradicted by Luftwaffe reports. Shortly after 1500 hours it was confirmed that no attack had occurred, and no orders issued by Steiner. To make matters worse, the dutiful withdrawal of troops in the north to support Steiner had left those sectors dangerously weak and, in fact, the Soviets had broken into Berlin itself.

Above: Two Red Army infantrymen pose proudly in front of the parliament building in Vienna. The capital of Austria had been taken by the Soviets on 13 April. Three days later, Nuremberg fell.

At first Hitler lapsed into one of his characteristic, apoplectic screaming fits, hurling verbal abuse at Steiner, the SS, his generals, even the German people: everyone had betrayed him, he shrieked, he was surrounded by nothing but lies, treason, corruption, and cowardice. But then the Führer seemed to visibly shrink, his energy and self-certainty collapsing in upon itself. All was lost, he mumbled, the end had come. Ignoring the protests of those in attendance,

Below: Gleefully carrying the 'Tricolore', liberated French PoWs join German refugees and freed female political prisoners from all over Europe on their migration westward past a Soviet tank column.

Hitler announced calmly that the Third Reich had been a failure, and had deserved to fail. This frightened the generals and his staff even more than the violent outbursts to which they had become accustomed. To several of those present, the Führer seemed to have suffered a complete breakdown. In a grotesque reversal of the type of scene which usually took place in the staff room, the generals hurried to assure Hitler that there was yet hope for a reversal of their situation. All present attempted to convince him that Germany still needed his leadership and that he must leave Berlin and carry on the fight from the south. But Hitler would not listen; he appeared to be as single-minded and determined in his despair as he had been in his expectations of triumph. To everyone's horror, he calmly announced that he would remain in Berlin until the end, and would then shoot himself.

Chief of Staff of the OKW, Field Marshal Wilhelm Keitel, tried to steer him back to reality, urging that there were only two options: an immediate offer of capitulation before Berlin was utterly destroyed, or an immediate flight to Berchtesgaden where Hitler could attempt negotiations from a stronger position. But, according to Keitel, Hitler 'did not let me get beyond these words. He interrupted and said, "I have made this decision already. I shall not leave Berlin. I shall defend the city to the end. Either I win this battle for the Reich's capital or I shall fall as a symbol of the Reich." ' Hitler ordered Keitel and the rest of the general staff to evacuate to Bavaria, but insisted that he would remain and die with his dream for a new Germany. Keitel was outraged. 'In seven years, I have never refused to carry out an order from you, but this one I shall not carry out. You can't leave the Wehrmacht in the lurch!'

Finally, OKW Chief of Operations, Colonel General Alfred Jodl, offered a suggestion which seemed to pique Hitler's interest. Convinced that the Americans were not going to advance any further east, Jodl suggested that Wenck's 12th Army, which had been facing them off on the Elbe, could march immediately to Berlin, link up with the Ninth, and at least prevent the complete encirclement of the city. Hitler agreed and dispatched Keitel to the western front. There, just past 0100 hours, with much bluster and waiving of his field marshal's baton, Keitel ordered Wenck to leave his position on the Elbe and push with all speed towards Potsdam.

Still Hitler's apocalyptic mood remained. When some of the generals objected that their men would not fight for Göring, to whom Hitler planned to turn

Below: A female Red Army soldier of the Second Ukrainian Front directs traffic after the conquest of eastern Austria. The sign in Russian points the way to Vienna.

over supreme command of the Third Reich after his death, he responded, 'What do you mean, fight? There's not much fighting left to be done, and when it comes to negotiating, the *Reichsmarschall* can do that better than I.' Hitler then spent the next several hours going through documents and selecting hundreds to be taken out into the garden and burned. This done, he summoned the Goebbels family to come live in the bunker until the end, when they would all die together. Josef and Magda Goebbels, among the truest and most fanatical of Hitler's disciples, both agreed that the only honourable course of action in this darkest hour of the new Germany was to fall in battle or commit suicide. The day before, Goebbels had summoned his staff and railed that,

'The German people have failed. In the east they are running away, in the west they are receiving the enemy with white flags. The German people themselves chose their destiny. I forced no one to be my co-worker. Why did you work with me? Now your little throats are going to be cut! But believe me, when we take our leave, the earth will tremble.'

While this drama was unfolding in the bunker deep beneath the city, the Soviets continued their relentless drive towards its heart, with five rifle and four tank armies now committed inside Berlin. In the south, First Ukrainian Front's Third Guards Army, reinforced by three rifle divisions from the 28th Army, continued to strike due north towards Tempelhof, while Lelyushenko's Fourth Guards Tank Army also swept around the city's south-western edge. For the first time since the Berlin assault began, units of First Belorussian and First Ukrainian Fronts were in a position to co-ordinate their efforts. Lieutenant General F.I. Perkhorovich's 47th Army of the First Belorussian drove off to the west, and then back to the south-east into Berlin, while Ninth Guards Tank Corps, also from the First Belorussian, was designated to strike along the north-western edge, and then south-west towards Potsdam to link up with Konev's forces. By 1900 hours on 22 April, the Ninth Guards tanks and the infantry of 125th Rifle Corps had succeeded in fighting their way across the Havel and had established a bridgehead east of Hennigsdorf.

Farther to the south, the main force of Konev's First Ukrainian continued its thrust west from the Neisse. Near Treuenbrietzen, the Fifth Guards Mechanised Corps discovered another concentration camp, this one holding large numbers of Allied PoWs. The camp was still manned by its SS guards, and a fire-fight ensued between the Soviet

Below: General Walther Wenck (left) confers with Marshal Antonescu and General (later Field Marshal) Schörner in 1944. Wenck's hurriedly organised 12th Army was Hitler's last hope for the relief of Berlin.

Above: A Red Army corporal enjoys a cigarette next to his field gun during a break in the combat. The Soviet military was made up of conscripts from all over the multi-national Soviet Union.

reconnaissance group and the guards. The squad's leader, Lieutenant Zharchinski, was fatally wounded in the exchange, but before he died he shot down the camp's commandant, and the defence crumbled. Among the liberated prisoners was Major General Otto Ruge, the commander of the Norwegian army. From Treuenbrietzen, the Fifth Guards Mechanised Corps charged on to Jüterbog and the Luftwaffe base located there. So rapid was their advance that the Soviet tanks roared onto a parade ground where a Luftwaffe division was just forming up. The appearance of the Red Army sent most of the German men and machines scattering, but virtually all of the weapons and airplanes (144 damaged planes, 362 aircraft engines, and 3000 bombs) became the possessions of the Soviets' Ninth Guards Fighter Division.

Konev's main hope to penetrate the Reichstag, Rybalko's Third Guards Tank Army, with the Ninth Mechanised Corps in the lead, battled their way up from the Spremberg area, crossed the Nuthe canal, and continued to surge towards the Berlin ring-road. By that evening, they had struck into the southern suburbs of Marienfelde and Lankwitz, and reached the Teltow canal, only to be brought up by withering fire from the other bank. The Germans had already destroyed the bridges, and the massive, reinforced concrete walls of the factories lining the canal created an almost impregnable rampart ideally suited for defence. Konev ordered Rybalko to prepare an assault crossing with massed artillery (3000 guns, SPGs, and mortars) focused on a single sector.

During the course of the same day, Third Guards Army also completed its conquest of Cottbus and put the final touch on the bottling up of the remnants of the German Ninth Army's 'Frankfurt-Guben' group. Since the collapse of the last defensive line at Müncheberg on 19 April, Busse had been fighting desperately to protect his diminished army's northern flank, even as it and the Frankfurt garrison, as per Hitler's orders, tried to retain their forward positions in the face of the pounding Soviet assaults toward Fürstenwalde. Under Stavka orders to have the Ninth Army surrounded by 24 April, on 21 April Konev had sent scouts from Rybalko's Third Guards Tank Army north to Königs Wusterhausen, bringing them right up to Chuikov's troops.

The noose was almost closed, but the Soviet encirclement was stretched thinly enough for the Germans to hope to maintain escape routes west to the Elbe, and north-west across the Spree towards

Right: Exhaust smoke from diesel engines rises into the air as Soviet armour moves through forests on the outskirts of Berlin, aiming to encircle the city and prevent any senior Nazi figures escaping.

Above: Berlin civilians and firemen push the hulk of a streetcar destroyed by bombing out of the road. Until the last few days of the war, Berlin's streets were kept clear for military use.

Berlin. Busse had at his disposal three infantry divisions to protect these routes: the 156th, at Lietzen; and the remnants of the Kurmark and SS *Nederland* Panzergrenadier Divisions. In addition, part of the 32nd SS *30 Januar* Grenadier Division had been redeployed to shield the route along the Spree River and Oder-Spree Canal, from Fürstenwalde to the Müggelsee.

The situation inside the noose was becoming quite desperate. Huddling with the Wehrmacht troops in the Spreewald were tens of thousands of refugees from the east and residents hiding from the fighting in the surrounding areas. Food was plentiful enough, but a hotch-potch intermixing of civilians and soldiers greatly exacerbated internal communications problems. In addition, fuel and ammunition were in critically short supply, and the helpless Germans in the pocket were being subjected to round-the-clock bombing and fighter harassment from the Red Army's Second, 16th, and 18th Air Armies.

On 21 April, the trapped defenders ran out of artillery shells. As soon as he was informed of this, Heinrici advised Busse to ignore the orders from the supreme headquarters, find a way to disengage from the enemy, and abandon the positions on the Oder. The next day he telephoned Krebs and insisted that if the Ninth Army were not allowed to retreat immediately, it would be trapped and split in two by the end of the day. Krebs phoned back several hours later, with permission only for the Frankfurt garrison to abandon its position and join the Ninth Army in its existing location.

Right: Wehrmacht soldiers build a wooden fortification to hold off the Soviets. Ordered to remain on the Oder rather than retreat to Berlin, part of Busse's Ninth Army had become almost entirely cut off.

It took the Frankfurt defenders three more days, until 25 April, to effect their breakout. By that time Konev had sent in the balance of the 28th Army to finish sealing off of the pocket, while Fifth and 13th Guards Armies, assisted by Fourth Guards Tank Corps, blocked any potential escape to the Elbe. On 24 April, First Belorussian's Third Army linked up with First Ukrainian's 28th Army at Teupnitz, thereby completing the encirclement of the Ninth Army. Busse decided to heed Heinrici's advice and began preparing for a break-out, planned for 28 April.

Rybalko's men were now no more than about 11km (7 miles) from Chuikov's Eighth Guards Tank Army, and Lelyushenko's Fourth Guards tanks only 32km (20 miles) from Perkhorovich's men. The encirclement now almost complete, there was a real possibility that the Berlin garrison could be cut in two by the Red Army's pincer movement. This would put Rybalko's men in an excellent position to reach the Reichstag. At about 0100 hours, however, Konev received Stavka Directive No. 11074. Classified secret, it informed the commanders of First Belorussian and First Ukrainian Fronts that henceforth the demarcation line between their respective zones of operation would run from Lübben to Teupnitz, Mittenwalde, and Mariendorf, terminating at the Anhalter Station in Berlin. The order placed the Reichstag building, the prize target, securely within Zhukov's area of operations; the new line ran approximately 137m (150yds) to the west of the Reichstag, leaving Konev's Front on the wrong side.

The commander of First Ukrainian wasted no time on anger, however. The orders were clear, and his men were still going to play a crucial role in the conquest of Berlin. Indeed, the soldiers of the Third Guards Tank Army were already poised to strike into the heart of the city. Across the Teltow Canal they could clearly see the German trenches, pillboxes, and dug-in Panzers. Konev planned a massive artillery assault to precede the canal crossing. Surpassing what he and Zhukov had inflicted on the Germans at the beginning of the Berlin attack a week ago, Konev ordered 55 minutes of massed fire by 1420 guns – a concentration of 650 guns per front-kilometre – timed to begin at 0620 hours on 24 April, an unusual time which, it was hoped, would catch the defenders off guard. The concentration of artillery was so intense, and the targets so plentiful, that 400 of the guns were designated for open-sight firing, blasting away indiscriminately, with aimed fire saved for certain buildings and street crossings. After the barrage was over, three corps from Rybalko's

Below: Barricades, like this one across a street near the centre of Berlin, were ultimately of scarce value. The Soviets' artillery allowed them to simply neutralise the sectors beyond the barricades by blasting them.

army would be committed to the assault crossing. The right flank, Ninth Mechanised Corps, had orders to advance towards Buckow, make contact with Katukov's First Guards Tank Army from the First Belorussian, and assist it in crossing the Dahme. Liaison officers from each tank army had already been in contact, and Rybalko instructed the Ninth's 70th and 71st Mechanised Brigades to drive up to Marienfelde and secure the necessary street crossings for First Guards Tank Army.

Lelyushenko's Fourth Guards Tank Army, meanwhile, received orders to continue its drive on Potsdam and meet up with the First Belorussian's 47th Army to complete the encirclement of Berlin. By the end of the day, the gap was only 24km (15 miles). Sixth Guards Mechanised Corps set its sights on Brandenburg, some 30km (18 miles) west of Potsdam, managing to cover nearly 24km (15 miles) that day, and tearing apart the Germans' Friedrich Ludwig Jahn Division in the process.

Zhukov also began immediately implementing Stavka's new orders. He directed 47th Army to push with all speed towards Spandau and send one division with a brigade from Ninth Guards Mechanised Corps to link up with Lelyushenko's tank army at Potsdam. He also flatly ordered Chuikov and Katyukov to force a crossing of the Spree and break into the Templehof, Steglitz, and Marienfelde areas no later than 24 April. Bogdanov's Second Guards were ordered to launch a simultaneous attack against Charlottenburg, in the city's western districts. The commanders of First Belorussian were told to organise their units into assault squads for street fighting, and to commence round-the-clock operations, day and night, with combined infantry and tanks. To this end, Zhukov had redeployed several tank corps and brigades to the primary assault units: Third Shock Army, Fifth Shock Army, and Eighth Guards Army. After being subjected to some of the worst fighting in the Berlin campaign, the First Belorussian Front at last began making some real progress. Kuznetsov's Third Shock, reinforced by Ninth Tank Corps and joined by First Mechanised and 12th Guards Tank Corps, blasted its way to the Wittenau-Lichtenberg railway line deep in the northern and north-eastern suburbs, and cleared out a number of large apartment blocks. Berzarin's Fifth Shock, with 11th Tank Corps adding to its strength, reached the Spree near Karlshorst and managed to gain a tenuous bridgehead on its far side, ready for a full-scale assault crossing. Chuikov's Eighth Guards smashed its way up to the Spree and Dahme rivers. On reaching the eastern bank of the Spree, they discovered a number of abandoned barges, motorboats, and other watercraft, which they quickly pressed into service. The Dnieper Flotilla had also made its way up the rivers and assisted all of the units in their crossings. Chuikov's soldiers and tanks quickly destroyed the

Below: As the noose tightened around Berlin, Marshal Rokossovsky's Second Belorussian Front was subduing the North German Baltic coast. After fierce fighting, his armies took Stettin on 25 April.

Right: As the military situation disintegrated, many SS officers took it upon themselves to patrol the battle areas looking for deserters or shirkers, who were usually promptly executed.

German resistance in this sector, took Wuhlheide, then Adlershof, and by the evening of the 23rd were fighting in Alt-Glieicke and Bohnsdorf, in an ideal position for the link-up with Rybalko.

That night, guns fired celebratory salvoes in Moscow. The greatest battle of the war was reaching its climax. Berlin was surrounded on three sides, with only three roads out to the west. With Zhukov's successes, the final trap would be sprung within days, even hours. But it had cost the Red Army heavily. Losses were staggering, with many companies down to as few as 20-30 men. Regimental commanders were forced to regroup their men into two battalions, rather than the usual three. The forests, roadsides, and gardens of eastern Germany, from the Oder to Berlin, were filled with tens of thousands of hastily buried dead Red Army soldiers. But they were littered, as well, with the corpses of German soldiers, civilians, and entire towns.

At the same time as the people of Moscow were celebrating their armies' victories, however, Konev found himself faced with a major battle on his rear. During the night of the 22nd, a large German force of two infantry divisions and 100 tanks from the Fourth Panzer Army attacked north-west from the area around Bautzen, on First Ukrainian's left flank, some 40km (25 miles) north-east of Dresden and 25km (15 miles) west of Görlitz. Driving towards Spremberg, the German armour sliced into First Ukrainian's side, exploiting the weak seam between 52nd Army and the Second Polish Army. The Polish divisions, which were protecting the left flank of Zhadov's Fifth Guards Army, were thrown into chaos as the Germans ripped into them and blasted their supply and communications lines. For two days the 'Görlitz Group' hacked its way north, towards Spremberg, and appeared to be on the verge of cracking the Soviet ring around the trapped Ninth Army. If it could succeed, there was a reasonable hope that the pressure on Berlin's south side could be lifted, and the city perhaps saved long enough for a negotiation with the West.

Konev recognised the threat to his position (and his hopes for playing a major role in the city's capture), and responded quickly. First Ukrainian's Chief-of-Staff, General I.E. Petrov, was dispatched to the embattled lines to re-group and re-order the chaotic situation. After making his review and issuing his orders, Petrov left Major General V.I. Kostylëv behind to co-ordinate the defensive effort. Kostylëv, First Ukrainian's Chief of Operations Administration, performed his job brilliantly, immediately re-establishing contact with the cut-off Second Polish Army, and mounting a counter-attack with 52nd and Fifth Guards Armies. By the

Right: Another Wehrmacht deserter executed by the SS. Despatch riders and messengers were especially at risk from the roving death squads, even if they had signed orders authorising their absence from the front.

evening of the 24th, the German thrust had been brought to a halt.

Above: A Soviet assault gun rumbles past defiant graffiti which vows that 'Berlin will remain German'. By 23 April, Berlin had been surrounded on three sides, with large sections already under Red Army control.

The German Supreme Command's last real hope of salvaging the situation rested now with General Wenck's 12th Army, which was positioned south-west of the city, facing off the Americans and British across the Elbe. At just after 0100 hours on 23 April, Field Marshal Keitel had arrived at Wenck's headquarters in Wiesenburg forest with the General Staff's orders to turn and race for Berlin. With rare directness, the OKW Chief of Staff told Wenck about Hitler's breakdown, and pleaded, 'It is your duty to attack and save the Führer's life.' The two commanders agreed on a plan that would bring the 12th Army into Berlin via Nauen and Spandau. Wenck thought he could mount the attack in about two days. 'We can't wait two days,' stated Keitel. After Keitel had left, Wenck consulted with his commanders and decided to get as close to Berlin as possible, without giving up their positions on the Elbe. It wasn't so much a question of remaining there to stop the Western Allies, as it was preserving an evacuation route to them. 'With our flanks on the river we keep open a channel of escape to the West,' Wenck said. 'It would be nonsense to drive toward Berlin only to be encircled by the Russians. We will try for a link-up with the Ninth Army, and then let's get out every soldier and civilian who can make it to the west.'

At the same time, the missing 56th Panzer Corps, whose commander, Karl Weidling, had been ordered arrested and shot for suspicion of desertion, was roaring south through the city's eastern suburbs, trying to rejoin the bottled-up Ninth Army. In the previous day's fighting, the 56th had been pushed to the very outskirts of the city by the Soviets and, in a muddle of conflicting orders, had become completely lost and cut off. The confusion had almost certainly been the result of action by the infamous 'Seydlitz Troops', German soldiers who had been captured on the eastern front and won over to, or blackmailed to join, the Soviet cause. They were named after General Walther von Seydlitz-Kurzbach, a German prisoner after Stalingrad in 1943, who had agreed with several others in September of that year to join the *Bund Deutscher Offiziere* (BDO: League of German Officers). These men worked with the German Communist 'National Committee for a Free Germany' in exchange for assurances that Germany's 1938 borders would be respected and that the Soviet Union would adopt a 'reasonable' Germany policy in the event of a Wehrmacht rising against Hitler. After training in the Soviet Union, they were sent behind German lines to try to stir up resentment against the war and against Germany's leaders and, most destructively, to sow disinformation, false orders, and general confusion. During this crucial phase of the battle for Berlin, there were numerous reports of German officers or paratroopers roaring up on a motorcycle to a unit with verbal 'orders' to move to a different location. Not all such orders were

Right: Some of the most ferocious fighting in the Berlin campaign occurred as Third Guards Tank Army, from Konev's First Ukrainian Front, attempted to gain a crossing of the Teltow canal.

followed, but enough were to cause no small amount of problems to the German defensive effort.

After becoming separated from his parent unit and wandering around for nearly a day with his tanks, Weidling finally went to a public phone, called headquarters in Berlin, and was from there patched through by radio to Busse's Ninth Army. He was immediately given instructions to drive south about 24km (15 miles) to the vicinity of Königs Wusterhausen and Klein Kienitz, and there break through the ring of surrounding Soviets to rejoin the Ninth. After issuing orders to his men, Weidling himself went back into the city to confront Krebs and Hitler about his death sentence. A relieved but, according to Weidling's recollections, broken Führer received him happily and cancelled the arrest order. To Weidling's alarm, however, he was told that his orders to attack south and rejoin the Ninth had been superceded; the 56th Panzer Corps was now to wheel around and return to Berlin, where Weidling would be taking over as Commandant of the city.

Earlier that day, just after dawn on the 23rd, three German soldiers stole across the Elbe river and surrendered themselves to US 30th Infantry Division at Magdeburg. These were no run-of-the-mill desertions, however. Leading the small group was Lieutenant General Kurt Dittmar, known on both sides of the battle-lines as 'the voice of the German High Command'. Dittmar's radio broadcasts were considered by Germans and enemies alike as among the most reliable and accurate in the country. With him were his

Below: Central Berlin in 1945, showing the position of the Führerbunker. The East-West Axis was converted into a rudimentary airstrip after the other Berlin airfields were captured by the Soviets.

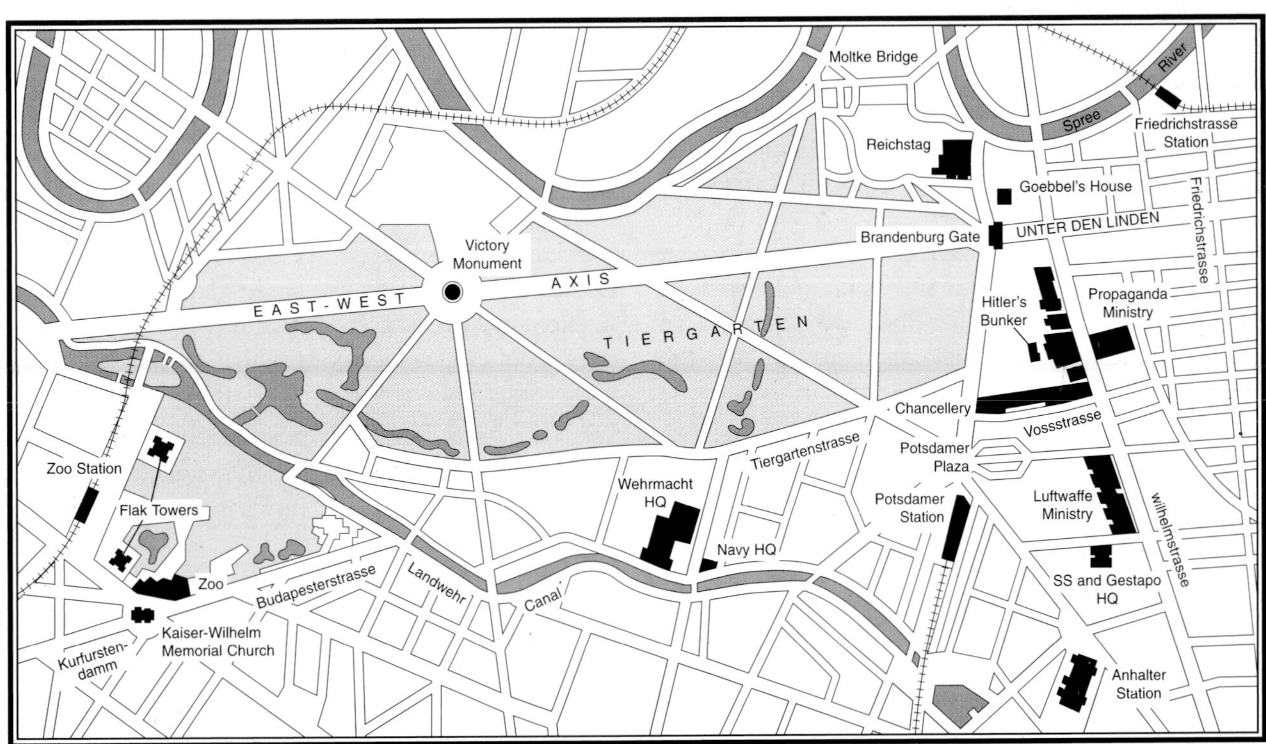

Above: Racing past a dead German soldier, Soviet infantrymen storm a position. Once the penetration of the city had finally been achieved, the Soviets made rapid progress, although the costs were enormous.

16-year-old son, Eberhard, and Major Werner Pluskat, a veteran of the German resistance to the Normandy invasion and the commander of the 'Magdeburg Guns', which were partly responsible for the US Ninth Army's stall at the Elbe. The trio was immediately taken to the 30th Infantry Division's headquarters and interrogated. One piece of intelligence in particular was seized on: Dittmar insisted that the Führer was in Berlin. For the past few days, Allied intelligence had been unsure of Hitler's whereabouts, but it was generally assumed that he had left Berlin for the 'National Redoubt' before the Soviets attacked. An Allied spy living in Berlin, Carl Johann Wiberg, had sent a message to London on 18 April: street gossip said that Hitler was still in the city, but there had not been time to check and circulate the report. Now Dittmar was telling the American intelligence officers that the much-feared Redoubt was a myth, a romantic dream or a colossal propaganda ploy. Hitler was still in Berlin. 'Hitler will either be killed there,' Dittmar stated matter of factly, 'or commit suicide.'

The mood in the Third Reich's leadership circles continued to be one of confusion and despair. Luftwaffe Chief of Staff General Karl Koller had deliberately stayed away from the meeting in the Führerbunker on 22 April, fearing that it would consist of little but Hitler's abuse of his generals. That evening, his liaison officer, General Eckard Christian, had phoned him, highly agitated, and told him that the Führer had broken down completely, had decided to die in Berlin, and was at that moment burning his papers. Christian, a devout National Socialist, became so incoherent that Koller decided to go over to the new OKW headquarters, in Krampnitz between Berlin and Potsdam, to find out what was happening. There General Jodl confirmed Christian's report, adding what Hitler had said about Göring taking over negotiations with the Allies. The two men agreed that this meant the Führer had authorised Göring to begin negotiations with the West which would end the war, and perhaps yet save Berlin. Feeling that there was no time to lose, Koller hurtled off to Munich in a fighter plane at 0330 hours on the morning of the 23rd to speak with Göring.

Arriving at the Adlershorst around noon, Koller filled Göring in on the recent events in Berlin. It is fair to say that Göring had been looking forward with barely concealed anticipation to the moment when he would succeed Hitler as Germany's Führer. However, under the current circumstances, he was worried. Any impetuous action on his part could be used against him by his arch-rival, head of the Party Chancellery, and Hitler's secretary, Martin Bormann. 'If I act now, I may be stamped as a traitor,' he said to his staff; 'if I don't act, I'll be accused of having failed to do something in the hour of disaster.' After consulting with legal advisors and carefully studying Hitler's decree of 29 June 1941, which proclaimed him successor to the Führer in the event of the latter's death or incapacitation, Göring decided to move cautiously ahead. Believing that Hitler's decision to remain in Berlin to die, and his isolation from Germany's political and military command as Berlin was sealed off by the Soviets were tantamount to his inability to govern, Göring drafted the following telegram to Berlin.

'My Führer!

In view of your decision to remain in the fortress of Berlin, do you agree that I take over at once the total leadership of the Reich, with full freedom of action at home and abroad as your deputy, in accordance with your decree of 29 June 1941? If no reply is received by 2200 tonight, I shall take it for granted that you have lost your freedom of action, and shall consider the conditions of your decree as fulfilled, and shall act for the best interests of our country and our people. You know what I feel for you in this gravest hour of my life. Words fail me to express myself. May God protect you, and speed you quickly here in spite of all.

Your loyal

Hermann Göring'

At precisely the same time that these actions were taking place in the Bavarian Alps, a rather different kind of meeting – though one with a similar goal – was taking place in Lübeck, on the German Baltic coast. *Reichsführer* SS Heinrich Himmler, one of those who had been present at the 22 April Führer-conference, had secretly summoned SS General Walther Schellenberg to meet with him and Swedish Red Cross representative Count Folke Bernadotte in the Swedish consulate in Lübeck. At the meeting, '*der treue* Heinrich' (the loyal Heinrich), as Hitler often fondly referred to Himmler, announced with grave pathos that 'the Führer's great life is drawing to a close'. Indeed, Himmler said, Hitler might already be dead, and it was incumbent upon them to do whatever was necessary to save the Reich from ravishment by the Soviets. Asserting for himself the powers of the Führer, Himmler proposed to contact the Western Allies with an offer of surrender, while continuing the war in the east until the Americans and British could arrive to take up their positions against the Soviets. Schellenberg had for months

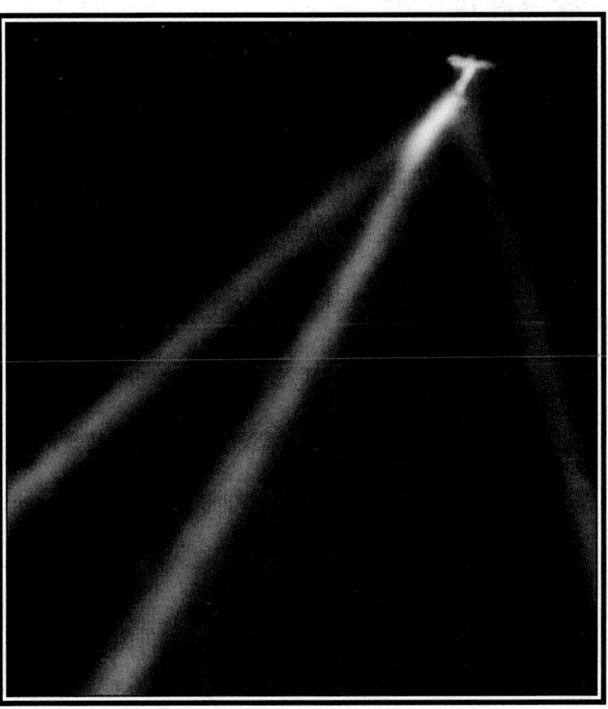

Right: German anti-aircraft searchlights target a Soviet bomber. In the final days, Soviet aircraft were flying very few ground support missions: the smoke, artillery shells, and Katyusha rockets made it too dangerous.

Below: Two German soldiers prepare to launch Wurfkörper rockets from a half-track. Known as a 'Foot Stuka', these unstabilised rockets were very inaccurate, but deadly if on target.

Above: Another salvo of Katyusha rockets being fired at German positions in early April. Row upon row of launchers have been set up, capable of launching immense destructive power on the enemy.

been working on Himmler, trying to convince him to break with Hitler and exert his power to end the disastrous war, and he readily agreed, as did Bernadotte. A letter was drafted and, at Bernadotte's insistence, Himmler signed it.

On the same dramatic evening of 23 April, still another meeting was taking place which aimed at the abrogation of Hitler's power and authority. Hitler's chief architect and Armaments Minister, Albert Speer, had been in Hamburg where he had been conspiring with his friend Karl Kaufmann, Gauleiter of Hamburg. The two had agreed upon plans to stifle Hitler's 'Götterdämmerung' order and preserve the city's bridges and infrastructure. Then Speer secretly recorded a speech at the city's radio studios, in which he announced to the German people that the war was lost, ordered all resistance to cease, and called on the German people to hand over to the Allies intact all resources, factories, and prison camps, with their inmates. He instructed Kaufmann to broadcast the speech in the event of Hitler's death, or if anything were to happen to Speer himself, expecting, as he was, his arrest and execution at any time. On the night of the 23rd, the speech recorded and his efforts to save Germany's material infrastructure as complete as they could be, Speer heard about Hitler's breakdown and decision to die in Berlin. Unconcerned about his own safety, he decided to return to Berlin and confront his one-time friend and mentor, Hitler, with his activities of the past weeks, and accept his end. He left Hamburg immediately, driving as far as roads would permit to Rechlin. From there he flew into Gatow, Berlin's western-most airfield, and then on to the bunker at the Reichschancellery in a tiny Fiesler Storch, landing directly before the Brandenburg Gate on the East-West Axis thoroughfare. Ushered in immediately to see Hitler, Speer quickly confessed that a 'conflict between personal loyalty and public duty' had led him to sabotage the Führer's scorched-earth orders. Fully expecting to be arrested and probably immediately shot, Speer was surprised when Hitler displayed no anger or resentment at all.

Speer remained in the bunker some eight hours, speaking with Hitler, Eva Braun, and the others of that inner circle. He joined the others' efforts to dissuade Hitler from remaining in Berlin and ending his life. But Hitler was strangely serene and resolute. He elaborated for Speer the manner in which he would choose his death: he would not personally fight on the barricades, lest he be wounded and captured, but would remain in the bunker directing the battle until the last moment when he would shoot himself and have his corpse burned

Right: A 152mm (6in) howitzer sits in a Berlin street waiting for its next target to be allocated. Huge guns like this one were fired point blank at fortified German positions, blowing them out of the way.

so that the Soviets would be unable to use it for propaganda purposes.

While these discussions were going on the telegram arrived from Göring. It was handed first of all to Bormann, who saw in it the opportunity to remove once and for all the man who stood in the way of his hopes for the succession as Führer, although by this point, there was little left to lead. After some delay, Bormann brought the telegram to Hitler, describing it breathlessly as an 'ultimatum'. Pointing out the 2200 hours deadline for action, Bormann reminded Hitler, ever suspicious of his subordinates, that six months earlier, Göring had been suspected of attempting negotiations with the Allies. Bormann warned him that Göring was obviously aiming to 'usurp' the Führer's power in order to reopen such negotiations and capitulate before the enemy. 'Hitler,' Speer recalled, 'was highly enraged. He said that he had known for some time that Göring had failed, that he was corrupt and a drug addict.' Egged on by Bormann, Hitler sent Göring a reply telegram informing him that he had committed high treason, the penalty for which was death, but that in view of his long service to the party and state his life would be spared, provided that he immediately resigned his positions. The telegram required an immediate yes or no. On his own authority, Bormann issued instructions in the Führer's name to the SS headquarters in Berchtesgaden which placed Göring and his staff in SS custody, under arrest, by the morning of the next day.

Tuesday 24 April brought an unpleasant shock to Marshal Zhukov as well. He had received reports from Eighth Guards Tank Army that Konev's forces had already broken into Berlin. The Stavka's new directive had guaranteed to First Belorussian Front the honour of capturing the Reichstag and bearing the distinction of being the 'Conquerors of Berlin'. But if Konev's First Ukrainian beat them to the city centre, there would be precious little anyone could

Below: A Soviet gun crew reloads their field gun while supporting regular infantry engaged in clearing barricades. By this stage the Germans possessed very few working tanks or armoured vehicles.

Above: More devastation caused by artillery or bomb damage. The damage done to Berlin's housing, and transportation network during the battle required years to heal.

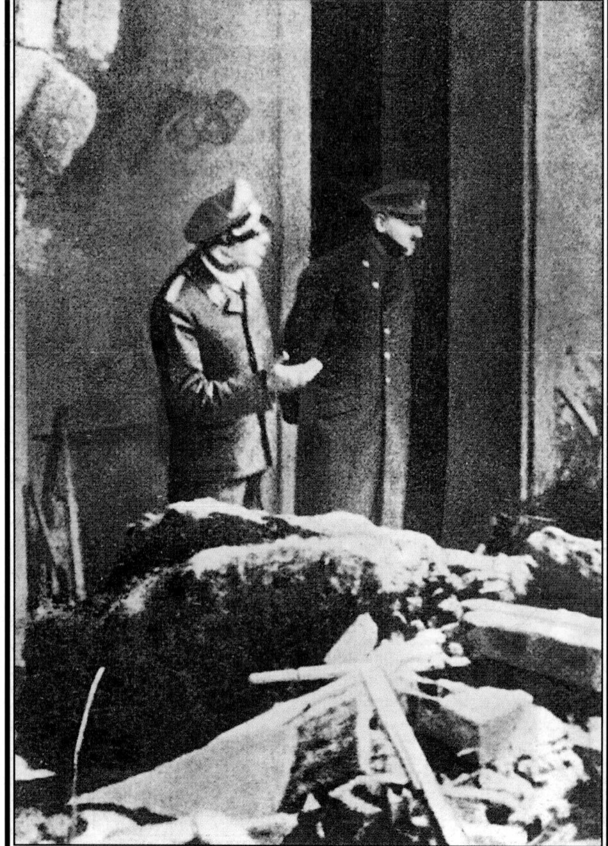

do, plan or no plan, to prevent them from moving forward and claiming those laurels. That evening Zhukov telephoned Chuikov, demanding to know the source of the reports: Were they true? Where were they? How did he know? Chuikov was taken aback by his commander's irritability, and answered that at about 0600 hours, units on 28th Rifle Corps' left flank had made contact with Rybalko's Third Guards tanks near Śchonefeld airfield and that the commander of the 28th, General Ryzhov, confirmed the reports. But Zhukov remained worried and sceptical. He ordered Chuikov to send 'reliable staff officers' out to discover which units of the First Ukrainian were in the city, and what their orders were. Chuikov complied, but before the officers could report back, Rybalko himself turned up at Chuikov's command post and telephoned Zhukov.

Left: The last known photograph of Hitler alive. Taken by a guard outside the bunker exit, it shows him inspecting the latest bomb and artillery damage to the Reichschancellery.

The combined forces of First Belorussian and First Ukrainian had by the end of the day fully invested the southern districts of Britz, Buckow, Rudow, Johannisthal, and the airfield at Adlershof. Lelyushenko's Fourth Guards Tank Army raced from Potsdam towards Ketzin in the north-west to complete the encirclement. Towards 1200 hours on 25 April, the noose finally closed around Berlin, when Sixth Guards Mechanised Corps from the First Ukrainian, and the 328th Rifle Division of the 77th Rifle Corps (47th Army) and 65th Guards Tank Brigade (Second Guards Tank Army) from the First Belorussian Front met in Ketzin. The ring around Berlin consisted of no fewer than nine armies: the 47th, 3rd and 5th Shock, 8th Guards, 1st, 2nd, 3rd and 4th Guards Tank Armies, and elements of the 28th Army. Another five armies – the 3rd, 69th, 33rd, 3rd Guards, and the rest of the 28th – bottled up the 'Frankfurt-Guben group' of the Germans' Ninth Army.

Below: Advance units of the US First Army and the Fifth Guards Army of the Soviet Army make their historic meeting at the village of Torgau on the River Elbe, 25 April 1945.

Also on 25 April, the armies of the Soviet Union and the United States made their historic rendezvous at Torgau on the Elbe, completing Germany's division into two separate halves. Konev reported to Moscow that at 1330 hours, units of 58th Guards Rifle Division from Fifth Guards Army had made contact with a reconnaissance group from the 69th Infantry Division of the US First Army, outside Strehla, near a riverbank strewn with the bodies of dead civilians. At roughly the same time, the Second Battalion from the 173rd Guards Rifle Regiment (58th Division) came upon a US patrol from the 69th Division near Torgau; the American and Soviet troops, upon whose enmity towards each other the Germans were still desperately counting, greeted each other with respect and formal salutes. Later in the day, at 1640 hours, an 'official' meeting was arranged at Torgau. Lieutenant William Robertson of the United States 69th Infantry Division, and Lieutenant Alexander Sylvashko of the Red Army's 58th Guards Rifle Division embraced each other. The next day, the photo was printed all over the world.

CHAPTER EIGHT

Hammer and Sickle over the Reichstag

The Soviet grip on the Reich capital was tightening minute by minute, and every soldier under Zhukov's command was keen to be the first to raise the Red Banner over the Reichstag. Only a few hundred metres away, Hitler was preparing to end his life with a pistol and a cyanide capsule.

The Third Reich's capital city was burning. By 25 April, Berlin was cut off from the rest of Germany and shelled continually; any semblance of a normal city routine had completely disappeared. In virtually all parts of the city, water and gas service had ceased; in many parts of the city, there was no electricity. Many streets were completely impassable due to rubble; in any event, there was almost no gasoline left for transportation. Newspapers ceased their operations. On 22 April, the last plane had left Tempelhof airport, with nine passengers bound for Stockholm. And on the same day, the telegraph office shut down for the first time in its 100-year history. The last message received read: 'Good luck to you all.' It had come from Tokyo.

Petty crime skyrocketed as the inhabitants of Berlin turned to looting as a survival strategy. One of the looters' targets was the huge Karstadt department store on

Left: Soldiers of the 756th Rifle Regiment of 150th Division, Third Shock Army, move towards the heavily damaged Reichstag building under a white flag, hoping to negotiate a quick surrender from the defenders inside.

Above: Soviet troops march past a knocked-out German 'Panther' tank turret used as a strongpoint. Stalin had ordered all Berlin taken by 1 May, but the Soviets did manage to capture the Reichstag on time.

Hermannplatz. Thousands of people crammed into Karstadt, grabbing everything in sight but especially food and warm clothing. The store supervisors eventually let them get away with whatever food they could find, though they tried to prevent them taking anything else. Later, after driving the remaining civilians out, the SS, rumoured to have had 29 million marks' worth of supplies in the basement, dynamited the store to prevent the Russians from appropriating its contents.

There no longer seemed to be a coherent German defence plan. Though the German forces fought on stubbornly and occasionally with brutal success, it was uncoordinated and sporadic. There were many signs of a general breakdown of the will to resist. At the telephone exchange in the Schöneberg district, the employees were instructed to take off their uniforms and burn their party books and badges.

Konev was now particularly worried about Wenck's 12th Army and the increasing pressure on the south-west sector, Treuenbrietzen. On 24 April, the same day that the 'Görlitz Group' was successfully beaten back on the southern flank, Panzers from 12th Army's 41st and 48th Panzer Corps smashed into the thinly stretched left flank of Lelyushenko's Fourth Guards Tank Army. Simultaneously, units of the German 20th Army Corps launched an infantry attack, covered by artillery bombardment, aimed at taking back Treuenbrietzen, 35km (21 miles) south of Potsdam. The attack continued throughout the day and was repeated at night. The Soviets managed to hold their lines, however. Fighting with fierce determination, the 10th Guards Mechanised Brigade holding the town allowed the German troops to advance very close, and then opened up with heavy machine-guns, mowing the Germans down, while hidden tanks roared out of their ambushes and crushed the foot-soldiers underneath their treads. Responding to the armoured attack on Fourth Guards Tank's flank, meanwhile, Yermakov's Fifth Guards Mechanised Corps established a mobile anti-tank reserve unit from 51st Guards Tank Regiment and set up a number of fixed anti-tank positions and tank or artillery ambush sites. Yermakov also mobilised the Soviet PoWs just liberated from German concentration camps, issuing them with captured Panzerfausts and organising them into teams of 10–25 men in anti-tank strong-points.

The next morning, two German divisions supported by the 243rd Assault Gun Regiment again attacked the 10th Mechanised Brigade's positions in Treuenbrietzen, while a separate attack was launched against the nearby Beelitz-Buchholz sector.

Again, the Germans were held off, this time with the support of First Guards Ground-Attack Air Corps, which streaked out at low altitude and dumped anti-tank bombs on the Germans. With the arrival of 147th Rifle Division from the 102nd Rifle Corps (13th Army) and the 15th Rifle Regiment, the semi-encirclement of Treuenbrietzen was broken and the Soviets' lines secured.

The Soviets' problems didn't end there. During the night of 25/26 April, the German formations of the trapped 'Frankfurt-Guben Group' began final preparations for a massive break-out effort. There were some 200,000 men and 2000 guns from the Ninth Army, with about 300 tanks from the Fourth Panzer Army in the encircled position. Fuel and ammunition were in critically short supply; the Luftwaffe had attempted a few supply drops, but their planes were at this point too few, and most of the drops missed their target. The Germans siphoned all the fuel they could from wrecked vehicles, and planned to use up most of their heavy ammunition in the opening artillery barrage which, it was hoped, would shock the Soviet lines enough to allow the infantry units to smash through and link up with Wenck's 12th Army. At 0800 hours on the morning of the 26th, an ad hoc battle group formed from units of the 21st Panzer, Kurmark Motorised and 712th Infantry Division launched their attack, striking at the point in the surrounding Soviet lines where Third Guards met 28th Army, near Halbe. At the same time, a supporting attack was launched by Fifth Army Corps from the west towards Halbe and Baruth, while Fifth Jäger and 11th SS Panzer Corps struck from the north and south-east. The Soviets fought back fiercely; in many sectors it came to hand-to-hand combat. But by 1000 hours the attack towards Baruth had made substantial

Below: By the 25th, the Germans could no longer rely on any coherent defence plan. Many military commanders began to see their primary task as protecting civilians and providing them with escort to the west.

Above: An attempt to seek shelter in a German armoured vehicle has cost this young woman her life. The Soviet artillery and rocket barrages became more concentrated as the ring tightened around the bunker.

progress, cutting the Soviet's main supply line along the Barth-Zossen road. The Soviet 395th Rifle Division managed to hang on to Baruth, and gradually the 50th and 96th Rifle Divisions pushed the German units away from the city and into the woods. The split in Third Guards Army's lines near Halbe was hastily patched up, and the German forces from the 'Frankfurt Guben Group' once more bottled up. At the same time, Wenck's drive towards Berlin slackened.

By this time Rokossovksy's long-expected assault with Second Belorussian Front had been launched, although in view of Zhukov's successes on Berlin's north side, its mission to outflank the city from the north had been cancelled and replaced by Stavka's original instructions from 6 April to drive west to take Stettin, smashing von Manteuffel's Third Panzer Army, the last substantial unit left in Heinrici's Army Group Vistula. With Second Shock Army assigned to cut down the Stettin defence, Rokossovsky pushed the rest of his Front to the west, and by 25 April they had reached the Randow river and battered open Third Panzer Army's front lines. Von Manteuffel and Heinrici knew precisely what Rokossovksy would try to do: envelop the army from the south and south-west, cutting it off from Berlin and from an escape to the west. And indeed, General Batov's First Don Guards Corps was advancing to the Stettin-Neubrandenburg-Rostock line and threatening to totally cut off the Germans. Von Manteuffel reckoned he could last another day at most. Heinrici, fed up with the directives from the Führerbunker and alarmed by the breakdown in command and control, against the express orders of Hitler ordered von Manteuffel to begin withdrawal and to give up the Stettin fortress as well. Keitel, making a sudden visit to the northern front, was astonished to find not the strong and resolute defence he had expected, but instead a full-scale, organised retreat. Furious, he sought a meeting with Heinrici and von Manteuffel in which he demanded to know why a retreat was in progress and ordered them to hold their positions. When the two explained that holding the positions was no longer possible and that they could not in good conscience comply with the orders, Keitel 'went into such a tantrum', as von Manteuffel remembered, 'that neither Heinrici nor myself could understand what he was saying'. After a short argument, Keitel suddenly threatened Heinrici with his Field Marshal's baton and said, 'Colonel General Heinrici, as of this moment you are relieved as commander of the Army Group Vistula. You will return to your headquarters and await your successor.' He then turned on his heels, stalked back to his car, and left.

Berlin's situation was now nearly beyond hope. In the north, Army Group Vistula had been almost completely routed. In the west, Wenck had slowed his drive to the city, leery of losing his foothold on the Elbe, and to the Allies. In the south, the remains of the Ninth Army were still bottled up and Konev's armies were wreaking utter devastation inside the southern districts. And in the east, Zhukov's forces were finally beginning to make substantial gains. Altogether, eight Soviet armies were strangling and stabbing at the city. On 26 April, First Belorussian and First Ukrainian Fronts launched a co-ordinated final assault, aimed at penetrating to the central districts and taking the Reichstag along with the Third Reich's main governmental buildings. With 12,700 guns and mortars, 21,000 Katyusha rocket launchers, and 1500 tanks and self-propelled guns, 464,000 Soviet troops were massed for the effort. As artillery pounded the city mercilessly, reducing whole neighbourhoods to smoldering ruins and piles of wreckage, the 16th and 18th Soviet Air armies flew hundreds of bombing sorties over the ruined, burning city. The final push into the city's central districts began on several sides simultaneously.

On the south-east, Rybalko's Third Guards Tank Army, supported by infantry from Luchinsky's 28th

Above: Hundreds of German helmets collected by the Soviets. During the final campaign from the Oder to the Reichstag, the Germans had sacrificed the equivalent of 93 full divisions, as well as some 100,000 civilians.

Below: The Spree River, which winds through Berlin from the south-east to northwest, was an important objective. On average, Soviet assault squads were assigned no fewer than three or four artillery guns.

Above: Two gaunt, weary, and clearly frightened SS soldiers surrender. A Red Army political officer examines their documents. All of the Soviet advance units had soldiers available who spoke excellent German.

Army, prepared to force the Teltow canal. The massed artillery had smashed a path through the dense, fortified structures on the other side, and the infantrymen and tanks – including the Red Army's newest and heaviest 'Josef Stalins' – began swarming across. On one side, the German defenders remained strong enough to knock Ninth Mechanised Corps back to the southern bank, but elsewhere Rybalko's troops succeeded in gaining footholds on the northern side. Within hours, the assault engineers had erected two pontoon bridges, and the tanks poured across. To Rybalko's west, Lelyushenko's Fourth Guards Tank Army was still struggling to make a crossing, prompting instructions from Konev to turn to the east and use Rybalko's bridges. The fighting was extremely brutal and desperate, exactly the kind of terrifying, close-quarters urban combat both sides had hoped to avoid. After artillery and air support had reduced the most likely bunkers and fortified positions to heaps of concrete, wood and glass, the Soviet infantrymen cautiously but efficiently scurried from ruin to ruin, flinging open doors, clearing cellars and buildings with machine-guns, grenades and flamethrowers, while the tanks blasted anything large enough to harbour a sniper or machine-gun nest, and roared over the bodies of those too wounded or slow to dodge them.

Once across the Teltow, Third Guards Tank Army's forces pushed on towards Schmargendorf, Steglitz, Grunewald, and Pichelsdorf. Their goal was to link up with Bogdanov's units driving down from the north-west, and cut off those German forces still holding Potsdam and Wannsee. Within a few hours, Seventh Tank Corps had made it, pushing all the way through to the Havel, within 1830m (2000yds) of Bogdanov's tanks. Further east, Chuikov's Eighth Guards had also gained a crossing over the Teltow and were driving towards Tempelhof airfield. The Soviet commander was determined that if Hitler were still in the city, he would not be allowed to escape. A single airplane out of Tempelhof to Bavaria seemed the most likely scenario for the Führer's attempted flight, so the capture of the airfield was given a top priority. Although no such plans existed by this time, the airfield was heavily

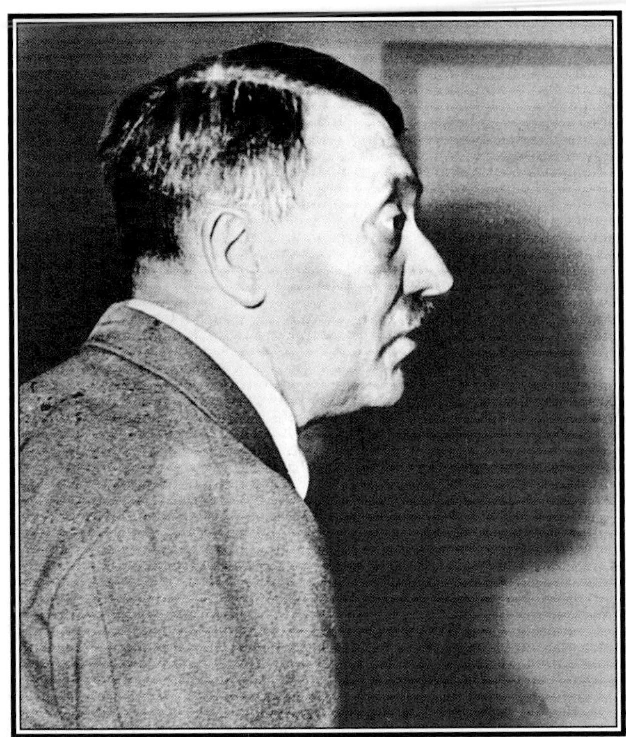

Above: The face of Adolf Hitler clearly shows the effects of Germany's defeats in this undated photograph. On 22 April, Hitler had already made up his mind to remain in Berlin and take his own life.

Below: By 27 April, the twin pincers of the Soviet assault were squeezing Berlin in two. The Germans were left only controlling a narrow, but heavily defended, strip of the city's central district.

defended. Dug-in tanks, SS troops, and anti-aircraft batteries ringed the field with its underground hangars which, according to the accounts of captured German soldiers, held a number of aircraft with a relatively large supply of fuel. Chuikov sent two rifle divisions to outflank the airfield from the west and east, then sent the bulk of his army up from the southern perimeter. The Soviet tanks raced onto the runways, raking the area all around with machine-gun fire and tank guns, and spun around to block the entrances to the hangars. By noon, Tempelhof was under Red Army control. While a few German planes still attempted to fly into the city via Gatow to the East-West axis, by this time the Soviets were making very few sorties for ground-support. The dense smoke rising in hundreds of columns all over the city, reducing visibility to a few hundred yards, made flight extremely hazardous.

Meanwhile, further east, the 39th Guards Rifle Division had advanced to the Spree and, using the shattered remains of a bridge, gained a foothold on the western bank. House-to-house fighting ensued, with the Soviet troops often dynamiting 'tunnels' through the buildings to pass from street to street. Under intense pressure to accelerate the liquidation of each sector and get to the 'main prize', both Zhukov and Konev made heavy use of artillery to obliterate an area before the troops moved in. The

Above: One of the most heavily defended parts of Berlin, and the scene of some of the fiercest fighting, was in the vast park known as the Tiergarten, adjacent to the government district and Brandenburg Gate.

average assault squad was supported by no fewer than three or four field guns. Forced to divert his drive to the city's west side to deal with the Wannsee garrison – some 20,000 German troops – Lelyushenko incurred the wrath of Konev, who impatiently demanded that Fourth Guards Tank Army use 10th Mechanised Corps to take Wannsee – no later than 28 April – and send Sixth Mechanised Corps on to Brandenburg. In First Belorussian's sector, Third Shock Army was ordered to strike towards the Tiergarten (zoo), which lay hard on the west side of the central government district, and make contact with Chuikov's Eighth Guards, who had succeeded in gaining the Landwehr canal. By the end of the following day, 27 April, German control of Berlin, the capital of the Thousand-Year Reich, was a narrow strip no more than 5.5km (3.5 miles) at its widest, running roughly 16km (10 miles) east to west.

Conditions in the city were apocalyptic. Everywhere was destruction and death. Civilians huddled in cellars and bunkers and, as often as not, were killed there when the ceilings and walls crashed in on them. If they survived the initial pounding by the Soviet artillery, they were shortly thereafter rousted out of their hiding places by Red Army soldiers and herded into makeshift interrogation centres or, sometimes, burned alive by flamethrowers. In those districts where the Soviets had not yet arrived, zealous SS units searched for deserters and promptly strung them up from the nearest lamppost, or simply shot them.

The Berliners, particularly the women, were terrified of the Russians, expecting the worst. For much of the battle, though, the Red Army's behaviour was not what they had been led to believe. Pia van Höven, a housewife in Schöneberg, described to Cornelius Ryan how she and several neighbour women had been taken by surprise by a number of Soviet soldiers while attempting to prepare a meal for the people hiding in the cellar of her apartment: 'Quietly I raised my arms, knife in one hand, potato in the other.' But the heavily armed soldiers only asked, in German: 'Soldiers here? *Volkssturm*? Any guns?' When she and the other women shook their heads, the soldiers simply came in, took their watches, and left, saying, 'Good Germans.' Other Berliners, Jews who had managed in various ways to remain in the city, were even more relieved when the Soviets showed up. Siegmund Weltlinger was one. He and his family had been hiding in a friend's apartment. When the Soviet troops entered the building, their officer called out: 'Russki no barbarian. We good to you.' After discovering several hidden revolvers and some discarded uniforms, however, the Soviets lined up the building's inhabitants to be shot. Siegmund stepped forward and proclaimed that he and his family were Jewish. As Ryan relates the story told him by Weltlinger,

'The young officer smiled, and shook his head, made a motion as though cutting his throat and said, 'No more Jews alive.' Over and over Siegmund repeated that he was a Jew. He looked at the others lined up against the wall. A few weeks earlier, many of these people would have turned him in had they known his whereabouts. Yet Siegmund now said in a clear, loud voice: 'These are good people. All of them have sheltered us in this house. I ask you not to harm them. These weapons were thrown away by the *Volkssturm*.' His statement saved the lives of all the tenants. Germans and Russians began hugging each other. 'We were drunk,' Siegmund said, 'with happiness and joy.' The Soviet officer immediately brought food and drink for the Weltlingers and stood anxiously watching them, and urging them to eat.'

But not all experiences with the conquering Soviets were so joyful. Behind the first assault came motley troops, often former prisoners, without the

Above: The lead Red Army units into Berlin were for most part highly disciplined, motivated, professional soldiers. Those that followed, often prison conscripts and released prisoners of war, were much less so.

discipline and military pride of the advance units. Ignorant and contemptuous of the German language, often drunk and enraged, these Soviet soldiers rampaged through the city, looting, killing, and raping women.

Confusion reigned at virtually all levels of the German defensive effort. Where communications still existed, orders came from a bewildering variety of sources, often contradicting each other. And most of the orders emanating from the Führerbunker had become little more than frantic requests for information: Steiner's location, the position of Wenck's army, how soon they would be able to relieve Berlin. When OKH Assistant Chief of Staff General Erich Dethleffsen went to the bunker on 25 April, he found a situation of 'complete disintegration': an unguarded entrance; no effort to search his briefcase or check him for weapons (the normal routine since the attempt of 20 July 1944); empty bottles littering the cramped rooms; soldiers digging a trench just outside the entrance. Hitler's mood in these last days swung wildly between a maudlin despair and resolution to die, and an almost manic expectation of imminent salvation by Wenck. Hanna Reitsch, a flamboyant female pilot who was one of Hitler's favourites, described how he strode 'about the shelter, waving a road map that was fast disintegrating from the sweat of his hands and planning Wenck's campaign with anyone who happened to be listening'.

But Wenck was making no serious effort to reach Berlin, and certainly not to save Hitler. While doubts about his loyalty began creeping into discussions in the bunker, Himmler, '*der treue* Heinrich', was

Left: A Soviet officer prepares to give the signal to his mortar teams to launch their weapons. The 120mm (4.7in) mortar's indirect fire was of less military use in the close confines of the city's streets.

actively making peace overtures to the Allies. On 25 April, Washington was informed by its ambassador in Sweden that an offer of negotiation from Himmler had been received. The text of the message was cabled to the State Department, and President Truman – only 13 days in office – was summoned to the Pentagon. According to the message, Hitler was ill and would be dead in a few days, if he wasn't already; Himmler was willing to surrender, but only to the Western Allies, not to the Soviets. When he was asked by Bernadotte what he would do if the Allies refused, he had replied: 'Then I shall take command on the eastern front and die in battle.' Speaking by scrambler phone to Churchill, Truman stated flatly: 'We cannot accept it. It would be dishonourable, because we have an agreement with the Russians not to accept a separate peace.' Churchill agreed, and the matter was dropped. When Stalin was informed by the British and Americans of Himmler's peace feeler, and their joint response, he thanked them and promised that the Red Army would 'maintain its pressure on Berlin in the interests of our common cause'.

Below: Delighted with his trophy, a young Red Army soldier carries away the head of Adolf Hitler taken from a statue in some captured government building. The taking of war booty was considered legitimate.

Two days later, 28 April, was a particularly desperate day in the bunker. With advance Soviet units within shooting distance of the Chancellery, Hitler and his inner circle awaited news of the opening of Wenck's relief attack, and even of an attack from Steiner in the north. At 2000 hours, Bormann radioed a series of messages to Admiral Dönitz which give an indication of the growing panic and paranoia taking over the bunker.

'Instead of urging the troops forward to our rescue, the men in authority are silent. Treachery seems to have replaced loyalty! We remain here. The Chancellery is already in ruins ... Schörner, Wenck, and others must prove their loyalty to the Führer by coming to the Führer's aid as soon as possible.'

Regardless of what they wanted to do, neither Wenck nor anyone else was in a position to rescue the situation in the city centre. With the Soviets closing in on all sides, bringing with them total destruction block by block, any kind of real co-ordination of the military elements in the city was practically impossible. Much of the resistance was carried out by desperate *Volkssturm* and Hitler Youth units. Shortages of all manner of supplies were chronic. The new Commandant of the city garrison, General Weidling, pleaded with the Luftwaffe for air-drops, and a few Messerschmitt 109s and Junkers Ju52s parachuted some medical supplies into the dying city, but only small quantities of ammunition were flown in. At one point, the East-West Axis, which was being used as a landing strip, was closed to further flights when a Junkers crashed into a house. Attempting to destroy bridges and other key installations as they withdrew towards the city centre, the Germans were frustrated by the shortage of explosives (as well as by Speer's refusal to supply bridge plans) and had to resort to improvised aerial charges. Casualties in the city mounted horrifically. The hospitals and refugee centres were jammed full, though most of the dead and wounded remained scattered in the streets and piled in cellars or under collapsed buildings. Inside the two massive flak towers located in the central district, thousands of people huddled together while Soviet shells thumped into the concrete walls and steel-shuttered windows, the impressive batteries of anti-aircraft guns on the roof now all but useless.

Amidst reassuring reports from Krebs that the defence was holding and that the Luftwaffe was preparing to airlift reinforcement troops into the city,

Above: Hanna Reitsch, a daredevil pilot and friend of Hitler, was one of the last people to leave the bunker, and Berlin. She had attempted to convince Hitler to let her fly him out of Berlin, but the Führer refused.

Below: A Fieseler Fi-156 'Storch' belonging to OKH Chief of Staff Heinz Guderian, similar to the aircraft piloted by Hanna Reitsch during her daring, eleventh-hour flight into and out of Berlin.

Weidling reported to Hitler at 2200 hours that the garrison had only a two-day supply of ammunition, at best. He outlined the civilian population's catastrophic situation, with food and water unavailable, and the dead and wounded lying untended. The general insisted on an immediate attempt to break-out to the west. He proposed to organise three ranks for the effort: the lead echelon to consist of the Ninth Parachute and 18th Motorised Divisions reinforced by all of the available tanks and self-propelled guns; followed by a second formed from 'Group Mohnke' and a Marine battalion and including the bunker's headquarters staff; and a third from what was left of the *Münchenberg* Panzer Division, the *Bährenfänger* battle group, 11th SS *Nordland* Division, and a rearguard of the Ninth Parachute. It is doubtful whether such an effort could have succeeded in breaking out of the besieged city, particularly in the absence of any accurate information on the position of Wenck's 12th Army. In any event, Hitler refused to consider any kind of 'retreat'.

By this time radio communications with the army had completely broken down; the bunker's only contact with the city outside was the naval radio channel. Later that night, the besieged men radioed a request to patch through some news of what was happening in the outside world. The navy transmitted a Reuter dispatch from the BBC which had been picked up by the Propaganda Ministry's listening post. Its broadcast acted like a bombshell in the

Above: By 28 April, Soviet units were driving from two different directions towards the Tiergarten, and the main governmental quarter. Here a Soviet soldier dashes across Moltke Street, close to the Reichstag.

bunker. The report detailed Himmler's negotiations with the Swedish ambassador and his offer to surrender the German armies in the west to Eisenhower. First Göring, now Himmler. Hanna Reitsch, who was still in the bunker, described the report as 'a death-blow to the entire assembly. Men and women alike screamed with rage, fear and desperation, all mixed into one emotional spasm.' For Hitler, the news was almost unbearable. Himmler had been perhaps the only man in the Third Reich whom he did not suspect of some level of disloyalty; he had trusted him completely. '[Hitler] raged like a madman. His colour rose to a heated red and his face was virtually unrecognisable ... After the lengthy outburst Hitler sank into a stupor and for a time the entire bunker was silent.' It was, Hitler told the assembled people, the single worst act of treachery he had ever known. He ordered Reitsch and General Ritter von Greim, whom he had a few days earlier appointed head of the Luftwaffe in Göring's place, to fly out of Berlin, co-ordinate an all-out Luftwaffe bombing of the Soviet armies ringing the capital, and see to it that Himmler was arrested. 'A traitor must never succeed me as Führer!' he told them. 'You must get out to insure that he will not.' Before Reitsch left, Eva Braun said to her: 'Poor, poor Adolf. Deserted by everyone, betrayed by all. Better that ten thousand others die than that he be lost to Germany.'

A few minutes later the assembly inside the bunker received news that the Red Army was closing on the Potsdamer Platz, a block away. Explosions could already be heard. It was estimated that they would storm the Chancellery by 30 April, only a day away. Hitler made his final decision: this was the signal for his own private 'Götterdämmerung'. Sometime after 0100 hours in the early morning of 29 April, Hitler married Eva Braun. A city councillor who had been fighting in a *Volkssturm* unit a few blocks away had been rounded up to officiate at the brief ceremony. After this 'death wedding', as one of Hitler's secretaries referred to it, a grotesque wedding breakfast was held, complete with champagne. For a while, Hitler was in his natural element again, his old self, holding court and pontificating to the assembled disciples, recounting in lengthy detail his life-story of triumphs and prophesies. But now it had ended, he concluded, and so was the dream of the Third Reich. The wedding party ended in gloom and despair, with several of those present withdrawing in tears.

Hitler then summoned one of his secretaries and began dictating his last will and testament. It was, as was Hitler's wont, long and rambling, replete with self-serving and grandiose reconstructions of history. Parts of them bear repetition here. After a lengthy disquisition on the Jews' 'sole responsibility' for the war and the millions of deaths it had caused – including, fantastically, the deaths of the millions of Jews killed in the concentration camps – Hitler explained his reasons for remaining in Berlin.

'After six years of war, which in spite of all setbacks will one day go down in history as the most glorious and heroic manifestation of the struggle for existence of a nation, I cannot forsake the city that is the capital of this state ... I wish to share my fate with that which millions of others have also taken upon themselves by staying in this town. Further, I shall not fall in the hands of the enemy, who require a new spectacle, presented by the Jews, to divert their hysterical masses.'

'I have therefore decided to remain in Berlin and there to choose death voluntarily at that moment when I believe that the position of the Führer and the Chancellery itself can no longer be maintained. I die with a joyful heart in my knowledge of the immeasurable deeds and achievements of our peasants and workers and of a contribution unique in history of our youth which bears my name.'

Hitler followed that with an exhortation to the German people, bizarrely, 'not to give up the struggle'. While National Socialism might be dead for the moment, he promised, 'the seed has been sown that will grow one day ... to the glorious rebirth of the National Socialist movement of a truly united nation'. He enjoined the country's military leaders 'to strengthen with every possible means the spirit of resistance of our soldiers in the National Socialist belief, with special emphasis on the fact that I myself, as the founder and creator of this movement, prefer death to cowardly resignation or even to capitulation.'

Before concluding the document, Hitler took out his final, formal revenge against his officers and intimates who, he believed, had betrayed him.

'Before my death, I expel former Reich Marshal Hermann Göring from the party and withdraw from him all the rights that were conferred on him by the decree of 20 June 1941 ... Before my death, I expel the former *Reichsführer* of the SS and the Minister of the Interior Heinrich Himmler from the party and from all his state offices. Apart altogether from the disloyalty to me, Göring and Himmler have brought

Below: Even after the Red Banner had been hoisted from the roof of the old German parliament building, it took 300 Soviet troops almost a day to clear out a much larger number of German troops in the basement.

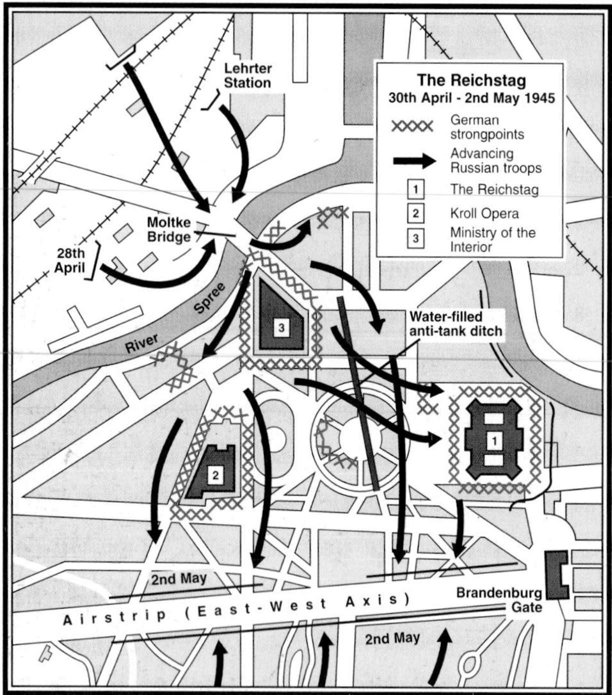

Left: The attack on the Reichstag came across the Moltke bridge. The crossing of the open ground in front of the Reichstag itself was a perilous business for the Soviet infantry tasked with the assault.

irreparable shame on the whole nation by secretly negotiating with the enemy without my knowledge and against my will, and also by illegally attempting to seize control of the state.'

Hitler appointed Admiral Dönitz to be President of the Reich and Supreme Commander of the Armed Forces, while Goebbels was given the post of Chancellor and Bormann that of Party Minister. Given his conviction that the war was lost, it was unclear precisely what these men were expected to do with their newly gained political positions but, in a characteristic lapse in sense of reality, Hitler closed the document thus: 'Above all, I enjoin the government and the people to uphold the racial laws to the limit and to resist mercilessly the poisoner of all nations, international Jewry.' It was now after 0400 hours. Exhausted, Hitler went to bed, for the last time in his life.

On 29 April, the Soviet tanks closed in for the kill. Chuikov's Eighth Guards blasted their way across the Landwehr canal and opened an assault on the Tiergarten. The huge zoological garden housed a number of heavy fortifications and weapons. Smoke and flames issued from all sections of the zoo; terrified animals came under intense machine-gun and artillery fire. Chuikov personally oversaw the operation to break into the Tiergarten. Reconnaissance units reported that it might be possible for small infantry units to break in using the underground railway tunnels. The tanks fought ferociously to take the bridge into the southern edge of the park on Potsdamerstrasse, but the Germans defended it with fierce determination. After several drives had been beaten back, the Soviets loaded up one tank with sandbags soaked in diesel fuel and sent it across the bridge. The fire from the other side promptly ignited the fuel-soaked sandbags, but the tank continued moving, its gun blazing. The apparition so alarmed and confused the SS troops defending the bridge that they scattered. The Soviets took advantage of the chaos to rush more tanks across, finally succeeding in seizing the courtyard on the other side.

Now the Tiergarten could be stormed. The two giant flak towers on the western edge remained impregnable but essentially harmless by this point; they were mostly ignored by the Soviets. Off to the northwest, the 756th Rifle Regiment (150th Division) mounted an assault on the infamous Moabit Prison. Rumours circulated among the Red Army soldiers that Goebbels himself was in command. After taking the prison, the soldiers excitedly searched through the captured Germans, but Goebbels was not there. Nevertheless, some 7000 prisoners, many of them Allied prisoners of war, were released and their places in the cells filled by German soldiers.

Chuikov's Eighth Guards and Rybalko's Third Guards tanks were by the evening of the 28th bearing down on the eastern edge of the Tiergarten, towards the Reichstag, no more than a few hundred yards beyond the north-eastern corner. Rybalko, perhaps unaware of the change in the battle zones ordered by the Stavka, was determined to get his tanks across the Landwehr canal and into the main governmental district. Konev no doubt would have seized whichever opportunity presented itself to realise that wish, without overtly disobeying orders. But as the battle wore on and the combat sectors narrowed, he became concerned that Rybalko's forces were in danger of a collision with Chuikov's, which could seriously disrupt the momentum of the battle and endanger Soviet lives. He therefore ordered Rybalko to turn westwards at the Landwehr canal and make for the Tiergarten's western edge, where he was to link up with the Seventh Guards Tank Corps and 20th Rifle Divison. Rybalko, shocked and infuriated, argued vociferously and on the brink of insubordination, but Konev held firm, and Rybalko's attack was shifted north-west towards Savigny station. Facing a relative weakness after Third Guards Tank Army's turn to the north-west – which left the 57th Tank Brigade alone holding the centre – a number of German battle groups tried to fight their way out to the Havel. Stiffened by tanks and SPGs, they made some progress, but eventually crashed into Perkhorovich's 47th Army as it drove into the city centre from the very direction of their escape.

On the city's south-west side, the Potsdam garrison had fallen to Lelyushenko's tanks on 27 April, and he was now pressing 10th Guards Tank Corps and 350th Rifle Division (from 13th Army) on towards the heavily manned 'Wannsee Island'. The attack continued throughout the day, but without any significant progress. Meanwhile, as Sixth Mechanised Corps followed Lelyushenko's orders to race further west to Brandenburg to cut off the potential escape route, they suddenly slammed into

Above: The battered remains of the once proud Reichstag, a now useless anti-aircraft gun in front of it. The symbolic hoisting of the Red Banner from the roof of the Reichstag meant the end of the Third Reich.

Below: Soviet troops march through the city they have captured, no doubt feeling that the end of the war was finally at hand. The Reichstag can be seen in the background, at the end of the street.

Right: A total of 89 heavy artillery guns and Katyusha rocket launchers were trained on the Reichstag for a thunderous barrage before the infantry stormed it, turning the structure into a ruin.

Wenck's 12th Army. Although Wenck, it seems, was in no rush to push his way too far into the Soviet forces, he quickly launched further attacks into the Treuenbrietzen sector, leaving Lelyushenko's left flank in an extremely difficult position, caught in a reversed front by Wenck's forces to the west and the Ninth in the east.

By the evening of the 28th, Zhukov's lead forces were preparing the final assault on the Reichstag. Chuikov's Eighth Guards advanced from the south, Berzarin's Fifth Shock Army with 11th Tank Corps from the east, and Kuznetsov's Third Shock Army – the unit designated to make the actual seizure – from the north-west. The spearhead unit from Third Shock was General S.N. Perevertkin's 79th Rifle Corps. They had two major obstacles to overcome before they reached the Reichstag building. First, the Moltke Bridge would have to be seized and a crossing of the Spree forced. To this task was assigned 171st Rifle Division. Then, after the corner building on the opposite Kronprinzenufer had been cleared, the 171st would have to join the 150th Division in neutralising the huge complex of the Ministry of the Interior – 'Himmler's House' – which was expected to mount a terrific resistance. Late on the 28th, the Germans attempted to blow the Moltke Bridge, but the explosion left the centre

Below: May Day, 1945. With Hitler dead, and the Reichstag in their hands, exultant Red Army troops ride IS-2 tanks through the Brandenburg Gate on the Soviet holiday.

section hanging precariously in place. The Soviet soldiers tried to force a crossing but were driven back by murderous fire from German pillboxes. Shortly after midnight, however, two Soviet battalions succeeded in blasting their way through the barricades and across the bridge, where they proceeded to clear the surrounding buildings to allow a crossing in force.

At 0700 hours the next morning, Soviet artillery began a 10-minute pounding of 'Himmler's House'. Mortars were also hauled up to the second floor of a next-door building and fired point-blank through the windows. The infantry began the assault, but it was another five hours before they managed to storm into the complex's central courtyard. The fighting was intense and vicious. Close-range combat was pushed from room to room and up and down the stairways. Finally, at 0430 hours on 30 April, the Ministry of the Interior building was secured, and the Red Army troops began taking up their positions for the storming of the Reichstag.

While this battle raged, just a few hundred yards away, the last Führer-conference was getting underway in the bunker. General Weidling reported on the situation, sparing nothing in his description of the city's, and the Third Reich's, plight. There was virtually no ammunition left, all of the dumps being now located in Soviet-occupied sectors of the city; there were few tanks available and no means for repairing those damaged; there were almost no Panzerfausts left; there would be no airdrops; an appalling number of the 'troops' left defending the city were red-eyed youngsters in ill-fitting *Volkssturm* uniforms, or feeble and frightened older men or those who had been earlier deemed unfit for military service. It was inevitable, Weidling told Hitler, that the fighting in Berlin would end soon, probably within a day, with a Soviet victory. Those present reported later that Hitler gave no reaction, appearing resigned to his fate and the fate he had inflicted on the country. Still, when Weidling requested permission for small groups to attempt break-outs, Hitler categorically refused. Instead he glared dully at the situation maps, on which the locations of the various units had been determined by listening in to enemy radio broadcasts. Finally, around 0100 hours, Keitel reported to the Führer that Wenck was pinned down, unable to come to the Chancellery's aid, and that the Ninth was completely bottled up outside the city. It was over. Hitler made his decision to kill himself within the next few hours.

Around noon on the 30th, the regiments of the 150th and 171st Rifle Divisions were in their start positions for the attack on the Reichstag. In a solemn though brief ceremony, several specially prepared Red Victory Banners were distributed to the units of Third Shock Army which, it was thought, stood the best chance of being the first to hoist it over the Reichstag. In 150th Division, one banner was presented to 756th Rifle Regiment's First Battalion, commanded by Captain Neustroyev; another went to Captain Davydov's First Battalion of the 674th Regiment; a third to the 380th's First Battalion, led by Senior Lieutenant Samsonov. Banners were also given to two special assault squads from 79th Rifle Corps, both of them manned by elite volunteer Communist Party and Komsomol (Young Communist League) members.

At 1300 hours, a thundering barrage from 152mm and 203mm howitzers, tank guns, SPGs, and Katyusha rocket launchers – in all, 89 guns – was loosed against the Reichstag. A number of infantrymen joined in with captured Panzerfausts. Smoke and debris almost completely obscured the

Below: When the Reichstag was finally taken on 30 April, Soviet soldiers swarmed through its elegant hallways to scrawl graffiti recording their presence, and their feelings about the Germans.

Left: The eagle has landed: Soviet soldiers examine a decorative Nazi eagle clutching a wreathed swastika amid the rubble inside the Reichstag after the latter's capture.

bright, sunny day. Captain Neustroyev's battalion was the first to move. Crouching next to the captain, Sergeant Ishchanov requested and was granted permission to be the first to break into the building with his section. Slipping out of a window on the first floor of the Interior Ministry building, Ishchanov's men began crawling across the open, broken ground towards the Reichstag, and rapidly secured entrances at several doorways and holes in the outer wall. Captain Neustroyev took the rest of the forward company, with their Red Banner, and raced across the space, bounding up the central staircase and through the doors and breaches in the wall. The company cleared the first floor easily, but quickly discovered that the massive building's upper floors and extensive underground labyrinth were occupied by a substantial garrison of German soldiers. One floor at a time, they began attempting to reduce the German force. The task uppermost in everyone's mind was to make their way to the top and raise the banner; the soldiers who succeeded in this symbolic act, it had been promised, would be made Heroes of the Soviet Union. Fighting their way up the staircase to the second floor with grenades, Sergeants Yegorov and Kantariya managed to hang their battalion's banner from a second-floor window, but their efforts to take the third floor were repeatedly thrown back. It was 1425 hours.

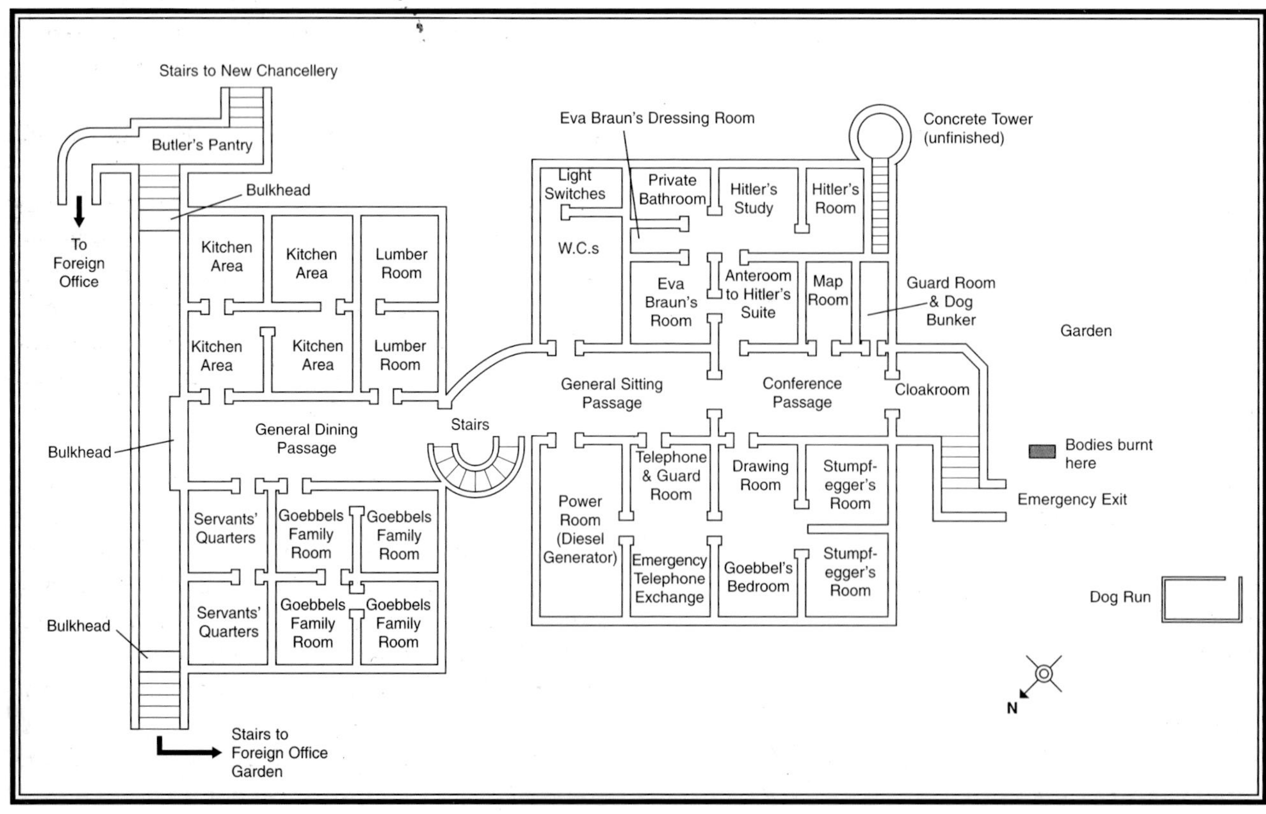

Immediately after the beginning of the attack on the Reichstag, German tanks counter-attacked against the Soviet troops dug in around the Interior Ministry building. The 380th Regiment, which had been attempting to storm the north-western side of the Reichstag, came under withering fire and was forced to back off and call for help from an anti-tank battalion. Meanwhile, on the second floor, Captain Neustroyev radioed a request for a combat group to support his men and ordered them to clean out the German machine-guns still on the second floor. Sergeants Yegorov and Kantariya were entrusted with the banner once again, and the battalion readied for the battle to take the third floor.

At approximately the same time that the Red Army sergeants had hung their Red Victory Banner from the Reichstag's second-floor window, Hitler sat down to his last meal with a couple of secretaries; a lunch of spaghetti with a light sauce. The Hitler newlyweds then bade a formal goodbye to the assembled, tearful staff. To Gertrud Junge, one of the secretaries, Eva Hitler said, 'Give my greetings to Munich and take my fur coat as a memory; I always liked well-dressed people.' After the farewells, Hitler and his wife went into their private quarters and closed the door. After a brief interruption by a completely distraught Magda Goebbels, who wanted to see her Führer one last time, everyone waited tensely. After five minutes, a muted shot was heard, and Bormann entered the room, followed by Colonel Otto Günsche and Hitler's valet. Günsche recalled the scene:

'Hitler was sitting in a chair. Eva was lying on the couch. She had taken off her shoes and placed them neatly together at one end of the couch. Hitler's face was covered with blood. There were two guns. One was a Walther PPK. It was Hitler's. The other was a smaller pistol he always carried in his pocket. Eva wore a blue dress with white collar and cuffs. Her eyes were wide open. There was a strong stench of cyanide. The smell was so strong that I thought my clothes would smell for days – but this may have been my imagination.'

Within an hour, both bodies were wrapped in blankets and carpets and taken up into the garden. There they were placed in a shallow hole, doused with gasoline, and set on fire. The Führer was gone,

Left: A plan of the Führerbunker beneath the Chancellery garden. The spot is shown where the bodies of Hitler, Eva Braun and the Goebbels were burnt after their suicides.

Above: Red Army officers stand amid the devastation inside the Reichstag building. Note the rubble and debris strewn over the floor, testimony to the efforts needed to subdue the German defenders.

like his dream of a Third Reich. But Berlin still writhed in its death throes.

Towards 1800 hours, another strong assault was launched up into the third floor of the Reichstag. This time the Red Army infantrymen succeeded in blasting their way through the German machine-gun positions. Three hundred Soviet soldiers now occupied the German parliament building but a much larger number of heavily armed German soldiers remained in the basement levels. However, the Soviets enjoyed the better position and after a number of tense hours, in the early morning hours of 1 May – the Soviet workers' holiday, and the target date for their conquest of Berlin – they finally cleared the remaining Germans from the building. Even before all German opposition had been wiped out, at 2250 hours, two Red Army infantrymen climbed out onto the Reichstag's decimated roof and hoisted the Red Victory Banner. Berlin was under the control of the armies of the Soviet Union.

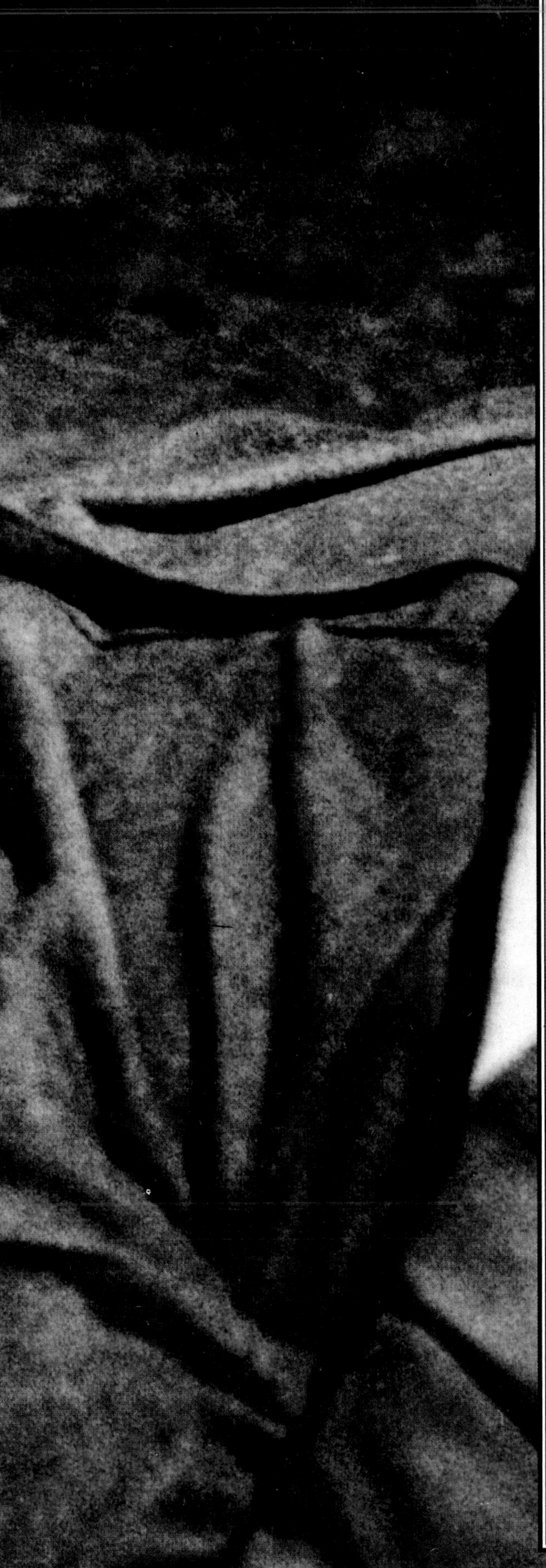

CHAPTER NINE

The End Comes

Although Hitler was dead, his fanatical supporters fought on. It was not until 2 May 1945 that the Soviets were able to obtain a ceasefire and general surrender of all the remaining forces in the capital. Although victory was theirs, the immediate task for the victors was to re-establish vital services to the city.

The battle for the Reichstag was over, but the battle for Berlin continued. No one any longer doubted the outcome. Fierce fighting continued in the Tiergarten, where some 5000 German troops stubbornly held on in an area reduced now to only a few thousand yards. Perkhorovich's 47th Army held a line running from Spandau to Potsdam, including the western bank of the Havel. Rybalko's tanks continued pushing north-west, clearing out the Wilmersdorf district with tanks and infantry. Seventh Guards Tank Corps was sent racing up from Zossen to help reduce the stubborn resistance in Westend; by the end of the day, the Germans still held a 457m (500yd) breach between Rybalko's tanks and the Second Guards Tank Army. Throughout the city centre, fighting continued, with small assault squads of Germans and Soviets hunting each other through smoke and rubble. German resistance was in many cases still desperately fierce. But the reality of the situation, and the shortages of supplies – both for combat and sheer survival – began to take their toll on morale. Despite the gangs of SS vigilantes stalking the streets, desertions increased dramatically. German soldiers and civilians alike were demoralised and traumatised. All over the city, hundreds,

Left: The body of Heinrich Himmler, Reichsführer SS and head of the Gestapo, after his suicide on 23 May 1945. In April he had begun negotiations with a Swedish diplomat to send peace feelers to the Western Allies.

perhaps thousands of Germans followed their Führer and took their own lives. In the Pankow district alone, 215 suicides were recorded during the last weeks of the war. Most suicides in these final days were by women, terrified of falling into the hands of the Red Army. Indeed, the Soviet soldiers, their lust for blood and revenge inflamed by huge caches of alcohol found in German governmental and military offices, began to rampage through the city in a horrifying manner. Gang rapes were commonplace, as were looting and torture. Certainly not all participated in such behaviour but a sizeable minority probably did. The occasional executions by conscientious officers whose men were found violating regulations against this kind of criminal behaviour did little to slow the reign of terror.

General Weidling was agonising over his next course of action. In the late afternoon of 30 April, his armies still maintained a tenuous line from Alexanderplatz to the Spittalmarkt, running diagonally through the central district, north-east to south-west. But within hours that line would be cut in two. Should he order a breakout, or try to hold the line? Before he could make a decision, he was summoned to the Führerbunker, where he received news that changed everything. In the presence of Goebbels, Bormann, and Krebs, Weidling was told of Hitler's death, and their plans to attempt to begin negotiations with the Soviets. For the time being, the Führer's death was to be kept secret; only the Soviet commanders would be informed of it and of the new government. Krebs would cross the lines with proposals for a German capitulation.

Above: Josef Goebbels with Field Marshal Ferdinand Schörner. By May, Schörner's Army Group Centre (near Prague) was virtually the only German formation offering effective resistance to the Allies.

At 2330 hours on 30 April, Lieutenant Colonel Seifert, commander of sector Z in Berlin, appeared at the juncture of Fifth Shock and Eight Guards Armies with a request to speak to their commander. The commander of the 102nd Guards Rifle Regiment took the papers Seifert bore and passed them up the Soviet chain of command from 35th Guards Rifle Division to Fourth Guards Rifle Corps. The Soviet command agreed to a meeting with Krebs, Colonel von Dufving (Weidling's Chief of Staff), an interpreter, and a single soldier. The Soviet troops had been instructed to hold their fire as the men made their way, one by one, from the bunker through the specified sector to General Chuikov's command post. At 0350 hours on 1 May, the German delegation reached Chuikov, who was with his political staff and a trio of well-known Soviet war correspondents. The German officers entered with all of the dignity and formal military bearing for which they had been trained. When some Red Army soldiers attempted to remove their sidearms, Krebs objected strenuously, arguing that the rules of honourable warfare

Left: General Krebs (right, back to the camera) outside Chuikov's command post in Berlin during the negotiations for the surrender of Berlin on the morning of 1 May 1945. He later committed suicide.

demanded respect for one's opponent in defeat. The Soviets relented.

The discussions began immediately, with Chuikov in telephone contact with Marshal Zhukov, conducting a three-way conversation. Krebs informed the Soviets of Hitler's suicide (about which Chuikov claimed he already knew), the new government's desire to end the war, and a request for a cease-fire during the negotiations. Zhukov immediately put in a call to Stalin, who wanted to know the whereabouts of Hitler's body, and insisted that talks would only be held after an unconditional German surrender to all three Allied Powers. Krebs replied that he was empowered at this point only to offer talks, and could not offer an immediate surrender without consulting the new government.

The talks went back and forth, with Krebs seeking formal Soviet recognition of a new government as a basis for talks, and the Soviets insisting on a full capitulation first. Suddenly, around 0430 hours, Krebs surprised those present by saying, in very good Russian, that the Germans were aware of the extent of the Soviets' power as much as the Soviets were. Chuikov then demanded to know, in light of this, what the point of further fighting was. 'We will fight to the very end,' Krebs replied. When Chuikov demanded again a general surrender, Krebs refused, arguing that such a capitulation would invalidate their existence as a government and hence their ability to negotiate on their nation's behalf.

For hours the exchange went on, the two generals quibbling over the ability of the Germans to continue any form of resistance, the possibility of a rival government being formed by Himmler, and whether or not the end of Berlin was in fact the end of Germany. As the wrangling dragged on into the morning, with more Soviet generals and political officers arriving, Krebs attempted to appeal to the Soviets' Communist ideology. If they did not recognise this new government, he warned, the Western Allies could make a deal with a Himmler government and fasten a strengthened Anglo–French 'capitalist order' on a weakened Germany which, he continued, could not be in the Soviet Union's interests. It did not impress them. Finally, at 1015 hours, Moscow cut short the talks with an ultimatum: if a

Below: The remnants of the German armed forces faced a bleak future. Former Wehrmacht officers are here treated by Red Cross volunteers before being sent east to prisoner of war camps.

Left: General Karl Weidling after surrendering the city to the Red Army, 2 May 1945. Weidling, the former commander of the 56th Panzer Corps, had been appointed Berlin's new commandant on 23 April.

full capitulation were not agreed to immediately, full-scale military operations would recommence. But so that Krebs could agree to it gracefully, General Sokolovsky, Zhukov's Deputy Commander, suggested an act of surrender and the simultaneous announcement of the formation of a new government, with the Soviets providing a radio transmitter in Berlin to broadcast the message to all of Germany and to the Western Allies.

There was no direct cable between Chuikov's command post and the bunker, so von Dufving and the interpreter were sent back on the hazardous journey to deliver the offer to Goebbels. As soon as he arrived at the bunker, von Dufving was taken into custody by the SS and ushered in to Goebbels. The terms Krebs reported contained several points: the surrender of Berlin; all those surrendering to give up their arms; officers and men alike to be spared their lives; the wounded to receive medical care; the possibility of talks with the Allies to be secured by radio. To these terms Chuikov had added his own note:

'Your government will be given the possibility of announcing that Hitler is dead, that Himmler is a traitor and to treat with the three governments – USSR, USA and England – on complete capitulation. Thus we are acceding partly to your request. Will we help you establish a government? Absolutely not! But we will give you the right to furnish a list of those persons whom you do not wish to see regarded as prisoners of war. We give you the right after capitulation to present a statement to the United

Below: A Soviet T-34 rolls across a bridge into the heart of Dresden on the last day of the war in Europe. The effects of the Allied bombing campaign on the city's buildings can clearly be seen.

Above: The inner courtyard entrance into the Reichschancellery. Designed by Albert Speer and built during 1938, its huge offices and galleries boasted extensive marble and ebony panelling.

Nations. The ultimate fate of your government will depend on them.'

Apparently Chuikov had little faith in the outcome of these proposals, or perhaps he merely wished to re-emphasise to the Germans their plight. Picking up a phone after von Dufving had left, he barked orders to re-open military operations. 'Pour on the fausts, and the shells. And no more talks. Storm the place!' Soviet artillery shells and Katyusha rockets began again slamming into the Reichstag, the Chancellery, and the elegant government buildings of the central district. The Soviet tanks and infantry continued their ruthless drive to wipe out all pockets of armed German presence from the Tiergarten to Charlottenburg. At 1600 hours an SS colonel arrived with the bunker's response at the same junction where Seifert had first made contact. Signed by Bormann and Krebs, and authorised by Goebbels, it flatly rejected the Soviet terms and announced the resumption of battle. The SS officer was returned to his own lines, and the telephone lines which had been maintained with portions of the German lines were hastily cut. At 1830 hours the Soviets responded in full force. Every gun they had, every rocket launcher and mortar poured fire on the suffering city. Destroyed buildings erupted in flames, smoke, and flying rubble. Third Shock, Eighth Guards and Second Guards Tank Armies prepared for a last push to clear the remaining part of the Tiergarten, while Lelyushenko's tanks finally completed the destruction of the German garrison in Wannsee, and Rybalko's Third Guards tanks cleared out Wilmersdorf and Halensee.

At 0215 hours on 2 May, Chuikov was brought a transmission received by 79th Guards Rifle Division. It was timed 0040 hours: 'Hello, hello. 56th Panzer Corps speaking. We request a cease-fire. At 1250 hours Berlin time will send emissaries to the Potsdam Bridge. Recognition sign – white flag. We await reply.' The signal had been sent five times, in Russian. The 79th Guards had sent the reply, 'Understand you. Understand you. Am forwarding your request to higher authority.' Several other Soviet units also picked up the transmission. Although wary of another round of fruitless talks, Chuikov sensed a difference in this feeler. He instructed 47th Rifle Division to let the Germans through when they showed up at the bridge.

At the appointed time and place, Colonel von Dufving, accompanied by two majors from Weidling's 56th Panzer Corps, informed the commander of 47th Division, Colonel Semchenko, that Weidling had decided to capitulate. He carried a statement signed by Weidling certifying what he said. Von Dufving told Semchenko that a surrender would take a minimum of three to four hours to effect, but that speed was of the essence to ensure its completion before dawn and to circumvent Goebbels' order that anyone attempting to surrender be shot in the back. With Chuikov's permission, Semchenko sent the delegation back to their own lines with an acceptance of their request. The general surrender of 56th Corps was ordered for 0700 hours, while Weidling and his staff would be allowed across the Soviet lines at 0600 hours to be taken as the first prisoners.

At about the same time, however, Chuikov received another report of a German delegation, supposed to have come from Goebbels, which wanted to negotiate terms. Irritated, and somewhat confused, Chuikov nevertheless permitted it to be brought to his command post. In fact, the four-man delegation had been dispatched by Goebbels' deputy, Hans Fritzsche, and came bearing a letter signed by the latter and addressed to Zhukov: 'Dr. Goebbels is no longer among the living. I, as one of those remaining alive, beg you to take Berlin under your protection. My name is well known. Signed, Director of the Propaganda Ministry, Dr Fritzsche.'

When the Reichschancellery came under intense shelling after the breakdown in Krebs' first attempt at negotiation, the 500–600 people left in the bunker were confronted with the stark reality of their situation. There was nothing to be done from there anymore; no battle to direct or country to lead. Some chose to attempt a breakout from the bunker in small groups. They planned to make their way through the labyrinthine tunnels underneath the Chancellery building and into the subway system. Arriving at the Friedrichstrasse station, they would then emerge above ground, well past the cordon of Soviet troops ringing the central district. From there the hope was to join up with any German battle group that could be found, and head north. During the night of 1/2 May, four separate break-out efforts took place in various parts of the city. The largest was led by Major General Sydow of the First Flak Division and Major General Mummert of the Müncheberg Panzer Division. From the Tiergarten bunker a large number of soldiers and civilians made their way through subway tunnels to the Olympic Stadium, and on to Spandau, where they emerged unhindered. An attempt at daybreak to force the two bridges remaining over the Havel and escape to the west turned into a bloodbath, however, as Soviet artillery, mortars, aircraft, and infantry fire blocked their route. It's impossible to say how many Germans succeeded in making it to the American and British lines. The exodus was enormous.

Below: US troops move into Berchtesgaden, site of Hitler's mountain home in the Bavarian Alps, in the south of Germany. Once feared as the 'National Redoubt', the south proved relatively easy to capture.

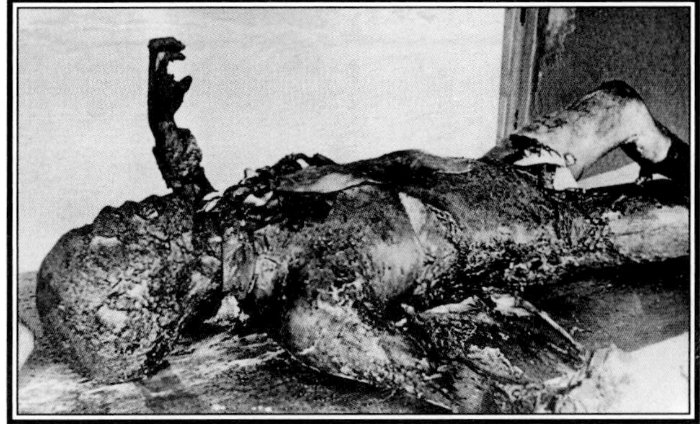

Left: The charred body of Josef Goebbels, discovered by the Soviets on 2 May. Goebbels and his wife Magda had killed themselves the night before, after administering poison to their five children.

Although many made it, many others were quickly killed or captured by the Soviets.

A number of others in the bunker, believing that there was nothing left on either side of the immediate frontlines, decided to follow Hitler into death. For days now, Josef and Magda Goebbels had been planning their suicides. At about 1830 hours on the evening of 1 May, they decided that the time had come. After administering poison to each of their five children, the devout Nazi couple went to their own room, bit down on cyanide capsules, and shot themselves. In accordance with the instructions he left, their bodies were taken out into the garden, and like those of Adolf and Eva Hitler a day and a half earlier, doused with gasoline and burned. Krebs, Hitler's adjutant General Burgdorf, and captain of the SS bunker guards, Franz Schedle, also committed suicide.

So Hans Fritzsche took it upon himself to try to end the carnage which the leaders had left behind. Chuikov quickly interrogated the delegation he sent, receiving their assurances that the German troops would obey any instructions from Fritzsche. After conferring with Zhukov, Chuikov issued an acceptance of their offer.

'Marshal Zhukov accepts the surrender of Berlin and is issuing orders for the cessation of military operations – that is the first thing. Second: inform all soldiers, officers and civilians that all military property, buildings and communal valuables must be intact. And no demolitions! Especially of military installations! Third: you will proceed with one of your officers to Herr Fritzsche, he can then make his broadcast and then be brought back here.

Below: Soldiers of the 150th Red Army Rifle Regiment point to the shallow trench where earlier they had uncovered several badly burned human corpses. In front of the hole are several empty petrol cans.

Above: Soviet counter-intelligence officers comb through the garden of the Reichschancellery building, next to the entrance to the bunker. The Allies were extremely concerned to verify the Führer's fate.

Fourth: I affirm – we guarantee the lives of soldiers, officers and generals, medical aid to the wounded. Fifth: see that there is no provocative shooting and other sabotage.'

Meanwhile, Weidling's surrender delegation had arrived at the appointed place and formally surrendered the 56th Panzer Corps. Perhaps wanting a back-up for Fritzsche's claim of control over the military, Chuikov and Sokolovsky urged Weidling to order a general surrender. Weidling at first declined, saying that he had no authority over the SS troops, who were planning on a breakout to the north, and that the lack of communications made it impossible to issue orders to every group of German soldiers out there capable of offering continued resistance. But finally the Soviet commanders prevailed, and Weidling wrote out the following order:

'On 30 April 1945 the Führer took his own life and thus it is that we who remain – having sworn him an oath of loyalty – are left alone. According to the Führer's order, you, German soldiers, were to fight on for Berlin, in spite of the fact that ammunition has run out and in spite of the general situation, which makes further resistance on our part senseless. My orders are: to cease resistance forthwith. Signed, Weidling, General of Artillery, former Commandant of the Berlin defence zone.'

By this time, the Soviet troops had completed their conquest of the Reichstag; the remaining German soldiers holed up in the basement finally surrendered around 0500 hours. The 150th Rifle Regiment of the 301st Rifle Division (Fifth Shock Army) had captured the Reichschancellery building and in it discovered a tremendous cache of trophies, including

Left: An American intelligence officer looks around the living quarters of the Führerbunker. Bedding had been removed from beds to wrap up the corpses of Hitler, Eva Braun, and the Goebbels.

the huge bronze eagle which had adorned the Nazi 'parliament', the Adolf Hitler standard, and Field Marshal Erwin Rommel's baton. And behind it, in the garden, after searching for several hours for the entrance to the bunker, the troops stumbled upon a grisly discovery: the charred remains of Goebbels and his wife. The overpowering stench discouraged them from any immediate further investigation, but the 301st's commander, Major General Antonov, put the entire area under special guard.

Shortly after midday, radio broadcasts and loudspeakers all over the city carried the news of Hitler's suicide and Weidling's surrender of the city. The text of his order calling an end to all resistance was read repeatedly. At approximately 1500 hours on 2 May, the Soviet guns fell silent in Berlin. Sporadic, isolated fighting would continue for several days, but the Battle for Berlin was over. It had been a titanic struggle, and a costly one. The Soviet command estimated that throughout the entire campaign from the Oder to Berlin, the Elbe and the Baltic, they had wiped out some 70 German infantry divisions, 12 Panzer divisions, and 11 motorised divisions. Approximately 480,000 German soldiers and officers were reported captured, as well as 1500 tanks and SP guns, 10,000 field guns and mortars, and an undetermined number of aircraft. On 2 May alone, in Berlin, Zhukov took 100,000 prisoners, and Konev another 34,000. The city of Berlin lost an estimated 100,000 civilians killed. The Soviet losses were no less staggering: the three Soviet Fronts together reported 304,887 men and women killed, wounded or missing; and 2156 tanks and SP guns, 1220 field guns and mortars, and 527 combat aircraft destroyed. Another 56,480 Polish and Soviet soldiers from other formations also fell in the Berlin effort. The total loss in human life was thus on the order of a half a million.

While the clean-up and organisation of the military occupation administration was proceeding, a SMERSH (Soviet counter-intelligence) team had been joined by an expert in forensic medicine from Moscow for a task regarded as 'highly important'. Their mission was to determine, conclusively, what had happened to Hitler, and to locate and positively identify his body. While the team was interrogating the German officers who had identified the bodies of Goebbels and his wife, word came that several more bodies had been found in the bunker area, one of them thought to be Hitler's. Soldiers and SMERSH officers had discovered two badly burned bodies under a thin layer of earth and partially sticking out of a bomb crater in the garden. Another uniformed body was discovered close by, in an emergency water tank; it had Hitler's features. The Soviet soldiers were tremendously excited by this last discovery, sure that they had the Führer's corpse, and hastily reburied the other bodies. When it was noticed that the body was dressed in darned socks, however, doubts began to grow; the Führer of the Third Reich would hardly have been so poor or modest as to wear patched clothing. When German prisoners were brought in to identify the body, either they could not recognise Hitler, or they refused to say so.

Below: The wooden box in which the Soviets placed the remains of Eva Braun. Hitler's long-time companion and mistress, she finally married him on the night of 29 April, just hours before their suicide.

Left: Berliners watch as Allied forces take control of the city. Berlin, like Germany as a whole, came under the control of the four occupying powers: France, Great Britain, the Soviet Union, and the United States.

On 5 May, Lieutenant Colonel Ivan Klimenko, the commander of the SMERSH unit for 79th Rifle Corps (Third Shock Army), who had been first on the scene after discovery of the bodies in the bunker garden, ordered the bodies in the crater to be dug back up. But this time, four bodies were found – two dogs and a man and woman – wrapped in blankets. The back of the head of one of the human corpses had been shattered by a bullet. The remains were transported under guard to Third Shock Army's headquarters at Buch, on the north-eastern side of the city. A German prisoner, SS soldier Mengershausen, said he had witnessed the cremation of Hitler, and could confirm his burial spot. On 8 May, an autopsy was begun. Two technicians who had worked in the offices of Hitler's dentist, Fritz Echtmann and Käthe Heusermann, were asked to draw a diagram of Hitler's teeth. When compared to the teeth of the corpse with the shattered skull, they seemed to match. When the entire lower jaw and dental bridges were shown to the technicians, they positively identified them as Hitler's.

The end of the battle for Berlin did not immediately mean an end to the war, although it could continue afterwards only in a disorganised, obviously futile manner. For most of the German units maintaining some form of military discipline and cohesion, their only thought was to get to the Elbe and surrender to the Americans or British. This was the case for the last formations to survive the battle for Berlin; Busse's Ninth Army and Wenck's 12th. For days, the Ninth had been fighting desperately to reach Wenck to the south-west of Berlin, and so gain an avenue to the Elbe. The First Ukrainian Front's main concern was to take Berlin's central district, rather than block the Ninth's escape, but the fighting was still difficult, and made more so by the Ninth's precarious supply situation; there was

Below: Soviet troops hand out bread rations to German women in the Potsdam district of Berlin. The Allies found themselves responsible for ensuring the feeding, housing, and overall welfare of the city's population.

almost no ammunition left, and few weapons, and hundreds of civilian refugees had joined their columns. On 1 May, down to their last tank, Busse's men were pushing forward with all they had, when they heard firing coming from behind the Soviets, who started breaking. Lieutenant General Wolf Hagemann leapt out of his tank with the only weapon available, a shotgun, and began pumping shells at the Soviets. Within minutes, the Ninth Army made contact with the 12th Army; of their original 200,000 men, 40,000 had survived. Generals Busse and Wenck, exhausted and filthy, walked silently up to each other and shook hands. By 7 May, both armies had made it to the Elbe and surrendered to the Allies.

The largest body of German forces remained, ironically, not in Germany but in Czechoslovakia. Army Group Centre, now under the command of Field Marshal Ferdinand Schörner, still held Prague and most of Bohemia and Moravia with more than

Right: A GI poses for a snapshot on top of an 88mm (3.45in) gun in front of the Reichstag. The extent of the destruction of the city from the ceaseless air-raids and the battle itself is clearly visible.

Above: The Soviet Military Administration in Germany was from the outset plagued by corruption and unruly behaviour by the occupying Soviet soldiers. Next to rape, theft was one of the greatest problems.

600,000 men. It would take another week of bitter fighting by nearly three million Soviet, Polish, and American forces before Prague was finally taken by the Soviets on 9 May – General Patton's US Third Army having halted in Pilsen (now Plzen) – and

Above: Removed from their house while Soviet soldiers demolish unsafe buildings in the capital, this old man and his wife sit obstinately in the street near Schlesischer Bahnhof.

Below: A few days after Soviet and British troops linked up on the Elbe, Field Marshal Montgomery reviews a detachment of Cossack Guards at the headquarters of Marshal Rokossovsky.

another two days after that before the last resistance from Army Group Centre had been liquidated.

On 4 May, all German forces remaining in northwestern Germany were surrendered by the High Command to General Montgomery. On 5 May, Army Group G, in southern Germany, surrendered to the Americans. And on that same day, the new commander of the German Navy, Admiral Hans von Friedeburg, arrived at Eisenhower's headquarters in Rheims to negotiate a general surrender. Friedeburg had hoped to establish some conciliatory terms for the new government, and above all to delay negotiations long enough to allow those who could to make their way from the Soviet-occupied parts of Germany to the west. But Eisenhower was adamant. 'I told General Smith,' he remembered, 'to inform Jodl that unless they instantly ceased all pretence and delay I would close the entire Allied front and would, by force, prevent any more German refugees from entering our lines. I would brook no further delay.' Informed of Eisenhower's demand, Admiral Dönitz, who had been named by Hitler as his successor, radioed General Jodl at 0130 hours on 7 May and authorised him to sign the documents of surrender without any further delay or negotiation. At 0241 hours, in SCAF headquarters in Rheims, Germany surrendered unconditionally to the armies of the United Nations, and the Third Reich ceased to exist.

Above: The accused during the International Military Tribunal, held in Nuremberg from November 1945 to August 1946. From left to right are Göring (arm on box), Hess, Ribbentrop and Keitel.

The Battle for Berlin was emblematic not only for the end of the war, but also for the type of war which World War II had become, and what it meant for the next half-century. First and foremost, it was a grim symbol of the terrific costs and total devastation which characterised the war, particularly in the east. Military formations were wiped out, and cities and civilian lives sacrificed in a manner and in numbers never seen before. Vanquished and victorious alike had had vast parts of their countries utterly destroyed, and their economies severely damaged. The war in the east was as close to 'Total War' as humanity has ever come.

Second, while it might be true that with the political will, the Western Allies could have made it to Berlin ahead of the Soviets, the Soviets' conquest of Berlin nonetheless exemplifies the Red Army's importance in the success of the war against Germany. While General Eisenhower has been celebrated, and won election to the US presidency as 'the man who defeated Hitler', there are few historians, even in the West, who doubt that if that honour belongs to one man, it belongs more properly to Zhukov, or perhaps Stalin. The Soviet Union bore an appallingly disproportionate amount of the fighting and losses in the war; from December 1941 to November 1942, as Jonathan House and David Glantz have recently pointed out, some nine million Soviet and German troops battled on the eastern front, while perhaps a few hundred thousand British engaged the Germans and Italians in relatively small actions in North Africa. The battle of Kursk alone involved two million soldiers. Even after the second front was opened with the Normandy invasion in June 1944, some 2.1 million German troops – nearly 62 per cent of Germany's total strength – were facing six million Soviet troops in the east. The majority of German losses came also in the east: 10.76 million of the German armed forces' total casualties of 13.48 million (nearly 80 per cent) came on the eastern front. And to the United States' and Britain's losses of roughly 400,000 and 430,000 respectively, the Soviet Union suffered military losses of nearly 29 million with another 15 million or so civilian casualties. But it was not merely that the Soviets suffered more. As important for the conclusion of the war were the military talent, bravery, and sheer perseverance of the Soviet armed forces.

The importance of the war to the Soviet Union and the astronomical costs it inflicted on the country, however, also helped deepen the rift between the Soviets and the Western Allies, a rift which would eventually become the Cold War. Here too, Berlin was a symbol. From the beginning, the governments and armed forces of the three Allied nations bickered over the right to take Berlin. Suspicions and mistrust between the Soviets and the West were abundant. Even apart from those larger, geo-political concerns, the Soviet leadership was adamant after the horrors of the Germans' 'Operation Barbarossa' that never again must an invasion of Russian territory be allowed to occur. The German attack and the heavy load of the fighting forced on the Soviet Union strengthened traditional Russian paranoia and isolationism, and convinced the Soviets that the bulwark must be constructed in Germany and Eastern Europe. In May 1945, the people of Berlin, in desperate fear of the Red Army, and sure that the United States and Britain were different kinds of enemies than the Soviets, established a pattern of fleeing to the west. It would become an enduring symbol of a divided Europe for the next 50 years.

Soviet Order of Battle (16 April 1945)

2ND BELORUSSIAN FRONT (*Rokossovsky*)
2nd Shock Army
108th, 116th Rifle Corps
65th Army
18th, 46th, 105th Rifle Corps
70th Army
47th, 96th, 114th Rifle Corps
49th Army
70th, 121st Rifle Corps
191st, 200th, 330th Rifle Divs
19th Army
40th Gds, 132nd, 134th Rifle Corps
5th Gds Tk Army
29th Tk Corps, 1st Tk, 47th Mech Bdes
Air Forces
4th Air Army 4th Air Aslt, 5th Air Bomber, 8th Air Fighter Corps

1ST BELORUSSIAN FRONT (*Zhukov*)
61st Army
9th Gds Rifle Corps
12th, 75th Gds, 415th Rifle Divs
80th Rifle Corps
212th, 234th, 356th Rifle Divs
89th Rifle Corps
23rd, 311th, 397th Rifle Divs, 312th Gds, 1811th, 1899th SP Aslt Arty Regts

1st Polish Army
1st Pol Inf Div 'Tadiuscz Kosciuszko', 2nd, 3rd, 4th, 6th Pol Inf Divs, 1st Pol Cav Bde, 4th Pol Hy Tk Regt, 13th Pol SP Aslt Arty Regt, 7th Pol SP Aslt Arty Bn

47th Army
77th Rifle Corps
185th, 260th, 328th Rifle Divs
125th Rifle Corps
60th, 76th, 175th Rifle Divs
129th Rifle Corps
82nd, 132nd, 143rd Rifle Divs
70th Gds Ind Tk Regt, 334th, 1204th, 1416th, 1825th, 1892nd SP Aslt Arty Regts

3rd Shock Army
7th Rifle Corps
146th, 265th, 364th Rifle Divs
12th Gds Rifle Corps
23rd, 52nd Gds, 33rd Rifle Divs
79th Rifle Corps
150th, 171st, 207th Rifle Divs
9th Tank Corps
23rd, 95th, 108th Tk Bdes, 8th Mot Rifle Regt, 1455th, 1508th SP Aslt Arty Regts

5th Shock Army
9th Rifle Corps
230th, 248th, 301st Rifle Divs
26th Gds Corps
89th, 94th Gds, 266th Rifle Divs, 199th Gds Arty Regt
32nd Rifle Corps
60th Gds, 295th, 416th Rifle Divs, 1054th Arty Regt, 11th, 67th Gds, and 220th Tk Bdes, 92nd Ind Tk Regt, 396th Gds and 1504th SP Aslt Arty Regts

8th Gds Army
4th Gds Rifle Corps
35th, 47th, 57th Gds Rifle Divs
28th Gds Rifle Corps
39th, 79th, 88th Gds Rifle Divs
29th Gds Rifle Corps
27th, 74th, 82nd Gds Rifle Divs, 7th Gds Tk Bde, 84th Gds, 65th, 259th Ind Tk Regts, 371st, 374th Gds, 694th, 1026th, 1061st, 1087th and 1200th SP Aslt Arty Regts

69th Army
25th Rifle Corps
77th Gds, 4th Rifle Divs
61st Rifle Corps
134th, 246th, 247th Rifle Divs
91st Rifle Corps
41st, 312th, 370th Rifle Divs
117th, 283rd Rifle Divs, 68th Tk Bde, 12th SP Aslt Arty Bde, 344th Gds, 1205th, 1206th, 1221st SP Aslt Arty Regts

33rd Army
16th Rifle Corps
323rd, 339th, 383rd Rifle Divs
38th Rifle Corps
64th, 89th, 169th Rifle Divs
62nd Rifle Corps
49th, 222nd, 362nd Rifle Divs
2nd Gds Cav Corps
3rd, 4th, 17th Gds Cav Divs
1459th SP Aslt Arty Regt, 95th Rifle Div, 257th Ind Tk Regt, 360th, 361st SP Aslt Arty Regts

Air Forces
16th Air Army
3rd Air Bomber Corps
241st, 301st Air Bomber Divs
6th Air Bomber Corps
326th, 339th Air Bomber Divs
6th Air Aslt Corps
197th, 198th Air Aslt Divs
9th Air Aslt Corps
3rd Gds, 300th Air Aslt Divs
1st Gds Air Fighter Corps
3rd, 4th Gds Air Fighter Divs
3rd Air Fighter Corps
265th, 278th Air Fighter Divs
6th Air Fighter Corps
234th, 273rd Air Fighter Divs
13th Air Fighter Corps
193rd, 283rd Air Fighter Divs
1st Gds, 240th, 282nd, 286th Air Fighter Divs, 2nd, 11th Gds Air Aslt Divs, 113th, 183rd, 188th, 221st Air Bomber Divs, 9th Gds, 242nd Air Night Bomber Divs, 16th, 72nd Air Recce Regts, 93rd, 98th Air Observation Regts, 176th Gds Air Fighter Regt, 226th Air Tpt Regt

18th Air Army
1st Gds Air Bomber Corps
11th, 16th Gds, 36th, 48th Air Bomber Divs
2nd Gds Air Bomber Corps
2nd, 7th, 13th, 18th Gds Air Bomber Divs
3rd Gds Air Bomber Corps
22nd Gds, 1st, 12th, 50th Air Bomber Divs
4th Gds Air Bomber Corps
14th, 15th Gds, 53rd, 54th Air Bomber Divs, 45th Air Bomber Div, 56th Air Fighter Div, 742nd Air Recce Regt

Mobile Forces
1st Gds Tk Army
8th Gds Mech Corps
19th, 20th, 21st Gds Mech Bdes, 1st Gds Tk Bde, 48th Gds Tk Regt, 353rd, 400th Gds SP Aslt Arty Regts, 8th Gds M/C Bn
11th Gds Tk Corps
40th, 44th, 45th Gds Tk Bdes, 27th Gds Mech Bde, 362nd, 399th Gds and 1454th SP Aslt Arty Regts, 9th Gds M/C Bn
11th Tk Corps
20th, 36th, 65th Tk Bdes, 12th Mot Rifle Bde, 50th Gds Tk Regt, 1461st, 1493rd SP Aslt Arty Regts, 64th Gds Tk Bde, 19th SP Aslt Arty Bde, 11th Gds Ind Tk Regt, 12th Gds M/C Bn

2nd Gds Tk Army
1st Mech Corps
19th, 35th, 37th Mech Bdes, 219th Tk Bde, 347th Gds, 75th, 1822nd SP Aslt Arty Regts, 57th M/C Bn
9th Gds Tk Corps
47th, 50th, 65th Gds Tk Bdes, 33rd Gds Mech Bde, 341st, 369th, 386th Gds SP Aslt Arty Regts, 17th Gds M/C Bn
12th Gds Tk Corps
48th, 49th, 66th Gds Tk Bdes, 34th Gds Mech Bde, 79th Gds Tk Regt, 387th, 393rd Gds SP Aslt Arty Regts, 6th Gds Ind Tk Regt 5th Gds M/C Regt, 16th Gds M/C Bn

Front Reserves
3rd Army
35th Rifle Corps
250th, 290th, 348th Rifle Divs
40th Rifle Corps
5th, 129th Rifle Divs
41st Rifle Corps
120th, 269th Rifle Divs
1812th, 1888th, 1901st Sp Aslt Arty Regts
2nd Gds Cav Corps
3rd, 4th, 17th Gds Cav Divs, 1459th SP Aslt Arty Regt, 10th Gds RL Regt
3rd Gds Cav Corps
5th, 6th, 32nd Gds Cav Divs, 1814th SP Aslt Arty Regt, 3rd Gds RL Regt
7th Gds Cavalry Corps
14th, 15th, 16th Gds Cav Divs, 1816th SP Aslt Arty Regt, 7th Gds RL Regt
3rd Gds Tk Corps
3rd, 18th, 19th Gds Tk Bdes, 2nd Gds Mot Rifle Bde, 375th Gds, 1436th, 1496th SP Aslt Arty Regts, 10th Gds M/C Bn
8th Gds Tk Corps
58th, 59th, 60th Gds Tk Bdes, 28th Gds Mot Rifle Bde, 62nd Gds Ind Tk Regt, 301st Gds and 1817th SP Aslt Arty Regts, 6th Gds M/C Bn, 244th Ind Tk Regt
31st, 39th, 51st, 55th Ind Armd Train Bns
Naval Forces
Dnieper Flotilla
1st, 2nd, 3rd River Boat Bdes

1st UKRAINIAN FRONT (*Konev*)
3rd Gds Army
21st Rifle Corps
58th, 253rd, 329th Rifle Divs
76th Rifle Corps

106th, 287th Rifle Divs
120th Rifle Corps
127th, 149th, 197th Rifle Divs
25th Tk Corps
111th, 162nd, 175th Tk Bdes, 20th Mot Rifle Bde, 262nd Gds and 1451st SP Aslt Arty Regts, 389th Rifle Div, 87th Gds Ind Tk Regt, 938th SP Aslt Arty Regt

13th Army
24th Rifle Corps
121st Gds, 395th Rifle Divs
27th Rifle Corps
6th Gds, 280th, 350th Rifle Divs
102nd Rifle Corps
117th Gds, 147th, 172nd Rifle Divs
88th Ind Tk Regt, 327th, 372nd Gds, 768th, 1228th SP Aslt Arty Regts

5th Gds Army
32nd Gds Rifle Corps 13th, 95th, 97th Gds Rifle Divs
33rd Gds Rifle Corps
9th Gds Airborne, 78th Gds, 118th Rifle Divs
34th Gds Rifle Corps
14th, 15th, 58th Gds Rifle Divs
4th Gds Tk Corps
12th, 13th, 14th Gds Tk Bdes, 3rd Gds Mot Rifle Bde, 29th Gds Tk Regt, 293rd, 298th Gds SP Aslt Arty Regts, 76th M/C Bn

2nd Polish Army
5th, 7th, 8th, 9th, 10th Pol Inf Divs
1st Pol Tk Corps
2nd, 3rd, 4th Pol Tk Bdes, 1st Pol Mot Rifle Bde, 24th, 25th, 26th Pol SP Aslt Arty Regts, 2nd Pol M/C Bn, 16th Pol Tk Bde, 5th Pol Ind Tk Regt, 28th Pol SP Aslt Arty Regt

52nd Army
48th Rifle Corps
116th, 294th Rifle Divs
73rd Rifle Corps
50th, 111th, 254th Rifle Divs
78th Rifle Corps
31st, 214th, 373rd Rifle Divs
7th Gds Mech Corps
24th, 25th, 26th Gds Mech Bdes, 57th Gds Tk Bde, 291st, 355th Gds, 1820th SP Aslt Arty Regts, 5th Gds M/C Bn, 213th Rifle Div, 8th SP Aslt Arty Bde, 124th Ind Tk Regt, 1198th SP Aslt Arty Regt

Air Forces
2nd Air Army
1st Gds Air Aslt Corps
8th, 9th Gds Air Aslt Divs
12th Gds Air Fighter Div
2nd Gds Air Aslt Corps
5th, 6th Gds Air Aslt Divs
11th Gds Air Fighter Div
3rd Air Aslt Corps
307th, 308th Air Aslt Divs
181st Air Fighter Div
4th Air Bomber Corps
202nd, 219th Air Bomber Divs
6th Gds Air Bomber Corps
1st, 8th Gds Air Bomber Divs
2nd Air Fighter Corps
7th Gds, 322nd Air Fighter Divs
5th Air Fighter Corps
8th Gds, 256th Air Fighter Divs
6th Air Fighter Corps
9th, 22nd, 23rd Gds Air Fighter Divs, 208th Air Night Bomber Div, 98th, 193rd Gds Air Recce Regts, 222nd Air Tpt Regt

Mobile Forces
3rd Gds Tk Army
6th Gds Tk Corps
51st, 52nd, 53rd Gds Tk Bdes 22nd Gds Mot Rifle Bde, 385th Gds, 1893rd, 1894th SP Aslt Arty Regts, 3rd Gds M/C Bn
7th Gds Tk Corps
54th, 55th, 56th Gds Tk Bdes, 23rd Gds Mot Rifle Bde, 384th Gds, 702nd, 1977th SP Aslt Arty Regts, 4th Gds M/C Bn
9th Mech Corps
69th, 70th, 71st Mech Bdes 91st Tk Bde, 383rd Gds, 1507th, 1978th SP Aslt Arty Regts, 100th M/C Bn, 16th SP Aslt Arty Bde, 57th Gds, 90th Ind Tk Regts, 50th M/C Regt

4th Gds Tk Army
5th Gds Mech Corps
10th, 11th, 12th Gds Mech Bdes, 24th Gds Tk Bde, 104th, 379th Gds and 1447th SP Aslt Arty Regts, 2nd Gds M/C Bn
6th Gds Mech Corps
16th, 17th, 35th Gds Mech Bdes, 28th, 117th, 118th Gds Tk Regts, 423rd, 424th Gds SP Aslt Arty Regts, 19th Gds M/C Bn
10th Gds Tk Corps
61st, 62nd, 63rd Gds Tk Bdes, 29th Gds Mot Rifle Bde, 72nd Gds Tk Regt, 416th, 425th Gds SP Aslt Arty Regts, 7th Gds M/C Bn, 68th Gds Tk Bde, 70th Gds SP Aslt Arty Bde, 13th, 119th Gds Ind Tk Regts, 7th Gds M/C Regt

Reserves
28th Army
38th Gds Rifle Corps 50th, 54th, 96th Gds Rifle Divs
20th Rifle Corps
48th, 55th Gds, 20th Rifle Divs
128th Rifle Corps
61st, 130th, 152nd Rifle Divs
31st Army
1st Gds Cav Corps
1st, 2nd, 7th Gds Cav Divs
143rd Gds A/Tk Arty Regt, 1224th SP Aslt Arty Regt, 152nd Tk Bde, 98th Ind Tk Regt, 368th Gds, 416th, 1976th SP Aslt Arty Regts, 21st, 45th, 49th, 58th Ind Armd Train Bns

Order of Battle of the Main German Forces (16 April)

ODER-NEISSE FRONT
Army Group Vistula (Heinrici)
3rd Pz Army
'Swinemünde' Corps
402nd Inf Div, 3rd Naval Div
XXXII Corps
'Voigt' Inf Div, 549th VGr Div, Stettin Garrison, 281st Inf Div
'Oder' Corps
610th, 'Klossek' Inf Div
XXXXVI Panzer Corps
547th VGr Div, 1st Naval Div

9th Army
CI Corps
5th Lt Inf Div, 606th, 309th 'Berlin' Inf Divs
Corps Reserve
25th PzGr Div, 5th Pz Bn, 25th Arty Regt, 111th SPG Trg Bde '1001 Nights' Combat Gp
LVI Pz Corps
9th Para Div, 20th PzGr Div
Corps Reserve
'Müncheberg' Pz Div, 920th SPG Trg Bde
XI SS Pz Corps
303rd 'Döberitz', 169th, 712th Inf Divs
Corps Reserve
'Kurmark' PzGr Div, 502nd SS Hy Tk Bn

Frankfurt an der Oder Garrison
V SS Mtn Corps
286th Inf Div, 32nd SS '30. Januar' VolGr Div, 391st Sy Div
Corps Reserve
561st SS Tk-Hunting Bn
Army Troops
156th Inf Div, 541st VGr Div

Army Group Reserve
III SS 'Germanic' Pz Corps 11th SS 'Nordland', 23rd SS 'Nederland' PzGr Divs, 27th SS 'Langemarck', 28th SS 'Wallonien' Gren Divs

OKW RESERVE
18th PzGr Div

Army Group Centre (Schörner)
4th Pz Army
V Corps
35th SS Police Gren Div, 36th SS Gren Div, 275th Inf Div, 342nd Inf Div
Corps Reserve
21st Pz Div, 305th Army Flak Bn

ELBE FRONT
12th Army (*Wenck*)
XX Corps
'Theodor Körner' RAD Div (3rd RAD), 'Ulrich von Hutten', 'Ferdinand von Schill', 'Scharnhorst' Inf Divs
XXXIX Pz Corps
'Clausewitz' Pz Div, 'Schlageter' RAD Div (1st RAD), 84th Inf Div
XXXXI Pz Corps
'von Hake', 199th [1 Regt only], 'V-Weapons' Inf Divs, 1st HJ Tk-Destroyer Bde, 'Hermann Göring' JagdPz Bde
XXXXVIII Pz Corps 14th Flak Div, 'Leipzig' Battle Gp [8 Bns], 'Halle' Battle Gp [8 Bns]
Ungrouped Formations
'Friedrich Ludwig Jahn' RAD Div (2nd RAD), 'Potsdam' Inf Div

Index